The Best of All Possible Worlds? Leibniz's Philosophical Optimism and Its Critics 1710–1755

Brill's Studies in Intellectual History

General Editor

Han van Ruler (*Erasmus University Rotterdam*)

Founded by

Arjo Vanderjagt

Editorial Board

C. S. Celenza (*Georgetown University, Washington DC*)
M. Colish (*Yale University, New Haven*)
J. I. Israel (*Institute for Advanced Study, Princeton*)
A. Koba (*University of Tokyo*)
M. Mugnai (*Scuola Normale Superiore, Pisa*)
W. Otten (*University of Chicago*)

VOLUME 322

The titles published in this series are listed at *brill.com/bsih*

The Best of All Possible Worlds? Leibniz's Philosophical Optimism and Its Critics 1710–1755

By

Hernán D. Caro

BRILL

LEIDEN | BOSTON

Cover illustration: "Vergleichung des Lehrgebäudes des Herrn Pope von der Vollkommenheit der Welt, mit dem System des Herrn von Leibnitz: Nebst einer Untersuchung der Lehre von der besten Welt. Eine Abhandlung, welche den, von der königl, Akademie der Wissenschaften und schönen Künste zu Berlin, aufgesetzten Preis vom Jahre 1755 davon getragen hat." (Translated by Christian August Wichmann), Leipzig: Langenheim, 1757. German translation of Adolf Friedrich Reinhard's French treatise "The System of Mr. Pope Concerning the Perfection of the World, Compared With That of Leibniz, With an Examination of Optimism", winner of the philosophical contest of the Prussian Academy of Sciences in Berlin for the year 1755.

Library of Congress Cataloging-in-Publication Data

Names: Caro, Hernán D., author.
Title: The best of all possible worlds? Leibniz's philosophical optimism
    and its critics 1710–1755 / Hernán D. Caro.
Other titles: Leibniz's philosophical optimism and its critics 1710–1755 |
    Brill's studies in intellectual history ; 322.
Description: Leiden ; Boston : Brill, 2020. | Series: Brill's studies in
    intellectual history, 0920-8607 ; 322 | Includes bibliographical
    references and index.
Identifiers: LCCN 2020032237 (print) | LCCN 2020032238 (ebook) | ISBN
    9789004218468 (hardback) | ISBN 9789004440760 (ebook)
Subjects: LCSH: Leibniz, Gottfried Wilhelm, Freiherr von, 1646–1716. Essais
    de théodicée. | Leibniz, Gottfried Wilhelm, Freiherr von,
    1646–1716—Influence. | Optimism. | Theodicy. | Good and evil. |
    Philosophy, Modern—18th century.
Classification: LCC B2590.Z7 C37 2021 B2599.O7 (print) | LCC B2590.Z7
    B2599.O7 (ebook) | DDC 149/.5—dc23
LC record available at https://lccn.loc.gov/2020032237
LC ebook record available at https://lccn.loc.gov/2020032238

Typeface for the Latin, Greek, and Cyrillic scripts: "Brill". See and download: brill.com/brill-typeface.

ISSN 0920-8607
ISBN 978-90-04-21846-8 (hardback)
ISBN 978-90-04-44076-0 (e-book)

Copyright 2020 by Koninklijke Brill NV, Leiden, The Netherlands.
Koninklijke Brill NV incorporates the imprints Brill, Brill Hes & De Graaf, Brill Nijhoff, Brill Rodopi, Brill Sense, Hotei Publishing, mentis Verlag, Verlag Ferdinand Schöningh and Wilhelm Fink Verlag.
All rights reserved. No part of this publication may be reproduced, translated, stored in a retrieval system, or transmitted in any form or by any means, electronic, mechanical, photocopying, recording or otherwise, without prior written permission from the publisher. Requests for re-use and/or translations must be addressed to Koninklijke Brill NV via brill.com or copyright.com.

This book is printed on acid-free paper and produced in a sustainable manner.

Contents

Acknowledgments IX

Introduction 1

1 The *Theodicy* and Leibniz's Philosophical Optimism 5
   1 Philosophical Optimism: The System of the Best and the Meaning of Evil 9
      1.1 *The Best of All Possible Worlds* 9
      1.2 *Evil and Evils in the Best of All Possible Worlds* 14
   2 The Foundations of Philosophical Optimism 27
      2.1 *The Theoretical Genealogy of Optimism* 28
      2.2 *Leibniz's God* 30
      2.3 *The Principles of (Divine) Reason* 36
   3 The Problem of Freedom and Leibniz's Theory of Hypothetical Necessity 46
      3.1 *Is Leibniz's God Really Free?* 46
      3.2 *Moral or Hypothetical Necessity* 50

2 Eternal Truths, the Choice of the Best, and the Almighty Reality of Sin: Budde and Knoerr's *Doctrinae orthodoxae de origine mali* (1712) 55
   1 Two Conceptual Hazards: Metaphysical Evil and Uncreated Eternal Truths 57
      1.1 *Metaphysical Evil or the Necessity of the Bad* 57
      1.2 *Eternal Questions on Eternal Truths* 59
   2 "God Did Not Identify Several Worlds, but Immediately the Best": Against the Divine Choice of the Best 70
   3 Not a Wonderful World – The Best of All Possible Worlds after Sin 75
   4 Final Comments and Open Questions 84
      4.1 *On Useful Misunderstandings and the Two Gods* 84
      4.2 *On Dogmatic Assumptions and Theoretical Effectiveness* 88

3 A Jesuit Attacks: Louis-Bertrand Castel's Review of the *Theodicy* in the *Journal de Trévoux* (1737) 90
   1 The Happy Rationalist 94
      1.1 *"Nothing More than a Physicist": Leibnizian Optimism as Hyperbolic Rationalism* 95
      1.2 *"Everything Is Good, Everything Is Better, Everything Is Very Good"* 100
   2 God's Freedom and Evil in the Best of All Worlds: Some New Names for Usual Criticisms of Optimism 104
      2.1 *"Nothing More than a Spiritual Spinozism": Optimism, Necessitarianism, and the Problem of Divine Freedom* 105
      2.2 *Against the Best World* 109
   3 Final Comments and Open Questions 112
      3.1 *The Theoretical Consistence of Optimism and the Faith in Reason* 112
      3.2 *Is Everything Good?* 116

4 Banning the Best World, God's (Supposed) Freedom, and the Principle of Sufficient Reason: Christian August Crusius's Criticism of Optimism (1745) 122
   1 Conceptual Flaws and the Moral Danger of Optimism 125
      1.1 *Against the Best of All Possible Worlds* 125
      1.2 *The Fallacy of Optimism* 127
      1.3 *Optimism, the End of Freedom, and Crusius's Voluntarist Response* 131
   2 On the Use and Limits of the Principle of Sufficient Reason 133
   3 Final Comments and Open Questions 140
      3.1 *The Perfection of the Best of All Possible Worlds* 141
      3.2 *The Arguments Against the Principle of Sufficient/Determinant Reason* 143

5 The Prize-Contest on Optimism of the Prussian Academy of Sciences: Adolf Friedrich Reinhard's *Examen de l'optimisme* (1755) 146
   1 Reinhard's Picture of Optimism 150
   2 Against Optimism 156
      2.1 *Is the Most Perfect of All Possible Worlds Possible?* 157
      2.2 *Once Again: Theological Voluntarism* 162
   3 Final Comments and Open Questions 165
      3.1 *The Paradoxes of Unlimited Freedom* 165
      3.2 *The Relevance of Reinhard's Examen at the Beginning of the End of Optimism* 168

6 Early Counter-optimism: Main Arguments and the Nature of
   the Conflict   172
   1   Counter-optimism: An Inventory of Arguments   172
       1.1   *The Best of All Possible Worlds*   172
       1.2   *The Foundations of Optimism*   175
       1.3   *Leibniz's Theory of Uncreated Eternal Truths*   176
       1.4   *The Principle of Sufficient Reason*   177
       1.5   *Hypothetical Necessity and Freedom*   178
       1.6   *Counter-optimism and Voluntarism*   180
   2   Classifying Counter-optimism: The Intellectualism-Voluntarism
       Schema   183
   3   Some Comments on the Feasibility of Intellectualism
       and Voluntarism   187

Conclusions   194

Bibliography   201
Index   222

Acknowledgments

Several foundations provided crucial support for the development of this work. The Carl und Max Schneider-Stiftung of the Humboldt University in Berlin granted me a "Prodoc-Stipendium" for the year 2009. The Rolf und Ursula Schneider-Stiftung made a three-month stay at the Herzog August Library in Wolfenbüttel possible, in spring and summer of 2010. During the time spent in the wonderful surroundings of the library, I was able to work with important sources and engage in discussions with fellow scholars from around the world – about Leibniz's theology, Augustine's theodicy or Germany's national soccer team. A further grant from Prof. Dr. Dominik Perler's Leibniz-Prize Research Group of the Humboldt University in Berlin allowed me to finish the work without any financial concerns. I have also benefited greatly from the discussions about several chapters of this work within the Leibniz-Group's colloquium. The members of the colloquium offered extensive and valuable suggestions for improvement. I thank Jana Burbach for proofreading the manuscript. I am grateful to Ivo Romein, history editor at Brill, who accompanied, patiently and encouragingly, the process of edition of this work, as well as to Professor Han van Ruler, editor-in-chief of *Brill's Studies in Intellectual History*, for welcoming this book in this prestigious series. For their helpful comments on all or part of this book, I would also like thank the three anonymous reviewers invited by Brill in order to evaluate my manuscript before publication, as well as Dinah Rapliza for her professional assistance during the publishing process.

I am deeply indebted to Prof. Dr. Dominik Perler, my *Doktorvater* and philosophy professor at the Humboldt-Universität in Berlin, Germany. I would like to thank him for his generosity and his continuous support and his invaluable advice on my research.

Introduction

Two events that mark significant milestones in the development of early modern European philosophy determine the theoretical and the temporal frameworks of the present work. The first one is the publication of Gottfried Wilhelm Leibniz's *Theodicy* in 1710. This book is the only extensive philosophical work that the German polymath published during his lifetime. It contains the main theses and arguments of what began to be known already in the eighteenth century as 'optimism' (or – as I will also refer to it in the forthcoming chapters – 'philosophical optimism'): a rationalist theory about God's goodness and his wisdom, about divine and human freedom, the nature of the created world, and the origin and meaning of evil. This theory is often summarized with the famous – and frequently ill-interpreted – Leibnizian thesis that this world, despite the wickedness and suffering that it contains, is 'the best of all possible worlds'.

The second event occurred on November 1, 1755. On that day, an earthquake accompanied by a tsunami destroyed a great part of the city of Lisbon in Portugal, one of the richest, most splendid and important European port cities in the eighteenth century.[1] According to a popular account in the history of ideas, philosophical optimism suffered its first and probably most definitive crisis as the result of the myriad of literary and philosophical attacks on the doctrine of the 'best world' published after the earthquake, beginning with Voltaire's *Poème sur le désastre de Lisbonne* (1756) and *Candide, ou l'optimisme* (1759).[2] Modern historians have labelled the earthquake the "great upheaval" of optimism (Wolfgang Lütgert), the "cataclysm of enlightened Europe" (Horst Günther) or the "debacle of the perfect world" (Wolfgang Breidert). Others have talked about the "death of optimism" (Theodore Besterman), thus creating an aura of drama that surrounds the earthquake until the present day.[3] According to them, the fundamental intellectual crisis of the idea that the world is the best among all possible worlds began with Voltaire's reactions, passing in

---

1 On eighteenth-century Lisbon, the earthquake, and its main material consequences see Barreira de Campos 1998; Braun & Radner 2005; Eifert 2002; Kemmerer 1958; Kendrick 1956; Lauer & Unger 2008; Löffler 1999; Lütgert 1901; Paice 2008; Poirer 2005; Shrady 2008.
2 Important advocates of this picture are Besterman 1956; Braun & Radner 2005; Breidert 1993; Eifert 2002; Günther 2005; Kemmerer 1958; Kendrick 1956; Lauer & Unger 2008; Löffler 1999; Lütgert 1901; Marquard 2007; Neiman 2002; Paice 2008; Rohrer 1933; Shrady 2008; Weinrich 1986. However, this traditional account has been challenged in Strickland 2019.
3 On the celebration of the 250 years of the earthquake in 2005, see for example: Rothstein 2005; Wenzel 2005.

the last decades of the eighteenth century through David Hume's *Dialogues Concerning Natural Religion* (1779) and Immanuel Kant's treatise on the failure of philosophical theodicy, *Über das Misslingen aller philosophischen Versuche in der Theodizee* (1791), and reaching its philosophical climax, one century after the first publication of the *Theodicy*, in Arthur Schopenhauer's philosophy of pessimism, expounded, among others of his works, in *Die Welt als Wille und Vorstellung* (*The World as Will and Representation*, 1819). According to this 'standard picture' philosophical optimism enjoyed a rather untroubled predominance in the first half of the eighteenth century, a predominance which came to be questioned radically only after the Lisbon catastrophe.

Despite the widespread acceptance of this picture of the earthquake of 1755 as the ruin of optimism, a careful re-examination of the intellectual atmosphere succeeding the publication of the *Theodicy* makes it clear that the standard picture is problematic. In recent years scholars have shown not only that Leibniz's optimism was already the subject of philosophical debate in the first half of the eighteenth century, but also that early criticisms are both theoretically and historically relevant in view of a correct understanding of the development of Leibnizian thought.[4] Unfortunately, these enquiries, in spite of their undisputable relevance, are either very general overviews of the early critiques (as is the case with Wolfgang Hübener's and Luca Fonnesu's papers), or more comprehensive reviews (as is the case with Stefan Lorenz's valuable report) that, nonetheless, seem to lose sight of the necessity to point out the common philosophical motivation, as well as the theoretical, thematic, and methodological motives and approaches shared by the early critics. This is central for any intellectual investigation that aims to be not only historically but also philosophically authoritative.

The main purpose of the present work is, therefore, to examine with as much theoretical attentiveness as possible the critical reaction to philosophical optimism in the first half of the eighteenth century, or more exactly: between the publication of the *Theodicy* in 1710 and the Lisbon Earthquake in 1755. The question whether there were philosophically stimulating criticisms of optimism in that period is unproblematic: as the mentioned commentators have shown, there were indeed early critical reactions to optimism. This I will call in the next chapters the 'counter-optimist' reaction or 'counter-optimism'. The more particular objectives of this work, however, go quite a bit further.

---

4 To my knowledge, the main studies of the critical philosophical reaction to Leibnizian optimism in the first half of the eighteenth century are Fonnesu 1994 and 2006; Hübener 1978; Lorenz 1997. An interesting examination of the early literary reaction to optimist motives, which also involves Leibniz, and will thus be referred later on in this work, is Hellwig 2008.

The next chapters will examine, on the one hand, the motivations, the nature, the consistency, and possible problems of the theses and arguments offered by selected and representative counter-optimist authors. On the other hand, this work examines the question whether early critiques share relevant theoretical interests and approaches, in order to establish to what extent it is possible to give the general concept of 'counter-optimism' a content that would allow us to recognize, categorize, and understand the struggle between optimism and its critics in the first half of the eighteenth century adequately.

This task is significant in several aspects. First, regarding the general study of the history of philosophical ideas in the first decades of that prolific and influential period that was the European eighteenth century; secondly, regarding the understanding of the nature of the early reception of Leibnizian rationalist thought, particularly the reception of philosophical optimism.[5] And finally, in what concerns its theoretical significance, this work wants to examine an aspect of the way in which philosophical rationalism – an intellectual attitude that obviously survives until our days, and of which Leibniz was a major exponent – has come to be challenged.

Four early criticisms will be examined in the next chapters. Their authors are the German Lutheran theologians and philosophers Johann Frank Budde and Georg Christian Knoerr, who published in 1712 the first major criticism of optimism; the French Jesuit Louis-Bertrand Castel, reviewer of the *Theodicy* for the *Journal de Trévoux* in 1737 and coiner of the term 'optimism'; the influential German philosopher and theologian Christian August Crusius, whose critique of optimism is contained in his principal work on metaphysics, of the year 1745; and the private scholar Adolf Friedrich Reinhard, champion of a polemical contest on optimism of the Prussian Academy of Sciences in Berlin, held in 1755.

Of course, these are not the only authors who wrote against Leibnizian optimism in the chosen period. In 1741 the Wolffian philosopher Friedrich Christian Baumeister (1709–1785) published the *Historia doctrinae recentius controversae de mundo optimo* (1741), which can be called the first chronicle of 'counter-optimism', recording a number of works – mostly minor and long forgotten academic contributions – devoted to the condemnation of optimism.[6] Yet, there are good reasons for choosing precisely the mentioned authors as case

---

5 The continental reception of Leibniz's philosophical thought in the seventeenth and eighteenth centuries has of course been examined masterfully by several notable authors. See for example Barber 1955; Heinekamp 1968; Heinekamp & Robinet 1992; Rateau 2009; Wilson 1983. However, the particular reception of optimism, as it has been maintained previously, has been a rather neglected aspect of Leibnizian hermeneutics.

6 On Baumeister's account see Hübener 1978: 229.

studies in this work. As we will see in the next chapters, these authors deliver the most extensive and/or comprehensive criticisms of optimism before the Lisbon Earthquake. Further, given their intellectual provenance, they represent very different fronts and genres from which optimism is challenged in the eighteenth century (from the academic theological dissertation by Budde and Knoerr to the prize-contest contribution by Reinhard, passing through Castel's critical review and Crusius's systematical treatise). And thirdly, either because of their philosophical standing (Budde, Crusius) or because of the context in which they criticize optimism (Castel, Reinhard), the criticisms by these authors were quite influential both within the demarcated period as well as after 1755.

Chapter 1 presents a general, analytical picture of philosophical optimism. We will see that the system of 'the best of all possible worlds' is an integral element of Leibnizian metaphysics, that follows directly from Leibniz's characteristic rationalist presuppositions. The first chapter examines the central theses of optimism, its main assumptions, and points out a most important and problematic issue that will be present throughout the subsequent chapters: the question concerning the nature of divine freedom.

Chapters 2 to 5 survey the particular criticisms of the four authors mentioned above. These chapters will examine, on the one hand, the significant and problematic aspects of optimism that those critics underline, for example the attributes of Leibnizian eternal ideas, the scope of the Principle of Sufficient Reason, the theoretical solidity of optimism, the meaning of evil, the moral character the world, and, of course, the conflicts supposedly provoked by Leibniz's understanding of God's freedom of choice, among others. On the other hand, these central chapters will point out the problems of the critiques themselves. These primarily concern questions of the viability of the alternatives to Leibniz's belief in a rational God that the examined critics offer, as well as their own understanding of what it means that God is free. Two fundamental notions introduced in Chapter 1 that refer to Leibniz's and his critics' contradictory positions – namely the concepts of 'intellectualism' and 'voluntarism' – play a major role in the presentation and analysis carried out in Chapters 2 to 5.

Finally, Chapter 6 reflects on the general nature of the conflict between optimism and its early critics. After reviewing critically the main arguments against optimism, this chapter examines the problem of how to classify the conflict in order to give the vague term 'counter-optimism' a more concrete and philosophically enriching content. The mentioned concepts of 'intellectualism and 'voluntarism' are central for this discussion. The chapter ends by giving a brief look at some of the advantages and handicaps of Leibniz's optimism and the antagonist arguments of 'counter-optimism'.

CHAPTER 1

The *Theodicy* and Leibniz's Philosophical Optimism

The *Essais de Théodicée sur la bonté de Dieu, la liberté de l'homme et l'origine du mal* (*Essays on Theodicy on the Goodness of God, the Freedom of Man and the Origin of Evil*, 1710) is the one major philosophical book that appeared in print during Gottfried Wilhelm Leibniz's lifetime, and one of the main sources of knowledge of Leibnizian philosophical thought throughout the eighteenth century.

The *Theodicy* was written as a kind of literary memorial to the Queen Sophie Charlotte of Prussia (1668–1705), one of the most attentive, and certainly one of Leibniz's most charming intellectual counterparts since their first encounter in Berlin in 1698,[1] who would also prove to be instrumental in the fulfillment of the philosopher's project of creating an Academy of Sciences in Berlin. (The Academy was established in 1700 with Leibniz as its first president. In Chapter 5 we will meet once more the Prussian Academy of Sciences – though not precisely as an advocate of Leibnizian philosophy.)

Leibniz himself gives an account of the circumstances of the emergence of the *Theodicy* in a letter of 1710 to the Scottish Thomas Burnett. He explains that the greatest part of the book was conceived during the time of his conversations with Sophie Charlotte about Pierre Bayle's polemical theses, particularly regarding the paradoxes to which the presence of evil in the world seems to lead:

> The greater part of this work was composed in bits and pieces, when I was at the court of the late Queen of Prussia, where these topics were often raised on the occasion of Mr Bayle's *Dictionary* and other writings, which were much read there. In our discussions, I usually replied to Mr Bayle's objections, and showed the Queen that they were not as strong as certain anti-religious people wanted to be believed. Her Majesty often commanded me to put my replies down in writing, so that she could consider them carefully. After the death of this great Princess, friends who knew about these writings encouraged me to put them together and

---

[1] On Leibniz and Sophie Charlotte see Ross 1999, as well as the correspondence betwee Leibniz and both Queen Sophie Charlotte of Prussia and her mother, Electress Sophie of Hanover, in: LTS.

expand them, and I turned them into the work I mentioned above, which is a reasonably large octavo.

LEIBNIZ TO BURNETT, October 30, 1710/GP III 321[2]

Pierre Bayle (1647–1706) was fundamental for the reactivation of the ancient question concerning the nature and meaning of evil and suffering in the world, the so-called 'problem of evil', at the end of the seventeenth century. The French Calvinist theologian, radical philosopher, brilliant polemicist, and Richard Popkin's "supersceptic",[3] was the author of the *Dictionnaire historique et critique* (*Critical and Historical Dictionary*, 1697),[4] one of the most original and seditious works of modern thought. In the final years of the seventeenth century Bayle 'relaunched' the classical Epicurean question of evil and its problematical relationship to a good and omnipotent God, and inflamed one of the most persistent and absorbing intellectual debates of that century and the following. Although the concern with the phenomenon of moral and physical evil is present in all of Bayle's works,[5] his most popular theses on the matter can be found in two articles of the *Dictionary* devoted to two heterodox dualist sects of the third and fourth century: "Manicheans" and "Paulitians".

The basic argument that underlies both entries is to be found at the beginning of "Manicheans", note D. There Bayle intends to show that the monotheistic, Judeo-Christian hypothesis of *one* omnipotent, good, and omnipresent God is certainly *a priori* better than others as an explanation of the existence of the universe. However, when it comes to giving account of the empirical world, or rather: of one particular phenomenon of the empirical world, namely *evil*, the dualist doctrines that maintain the existence of two morally contradictory principles of existence seem to be superior. Further, in the *Dictionary* and in other works like the *Réponses aux questions d'un provincial* (*Replies to the Questions of a Country Gentleman*, 1704–1706), Bayle criticizes the traditional Christian, i.e. Augustinian explanation of evil,[6] which Leibniz accepts and adopts, and which will be examined in the forthcoming section.

---

2 Throughout this book, references to Leibniz's works are made in parenthesis in the main body of the text, following the standard editions of the original texts (e.g. GT). Whenever possible, the quotes correspond to the available English translations. Full publication details of both the standard editions and translations may be found in the Bibliography.
3 *Cf.* Popkin 2003.
4 Two editions of the *Dictionary* appeared during Bayle's life. Both were published in Rotterdam, in 1697 and 1702.
5 *Cf.* Jossua 1977.
6 On Bayle's critique of traditional theodicy, see Caro 2012; Kreimendahl 2009; Mori 1999.

Bayle's paradoxes were undoubtedly a crucial motivation behind Leibniz's concerns regarding the problem of evil and God's justice. But it must be noted that Leibniz's interest in these topics can be traced back to his very first writings, most notably to the *Confessio philosophi* (1673) – which has even been called Leibniz's "first theodicy" (Sleigh 1996).[7] Further, as has been stressed by Donald Rutherford and as we will be able to see later, Leibniz's theodicy plays an essential, if not a *central* role within his rationalist metaphysics.[8] Bayle's arguments, it would seem, simply magnified Leibniz's interest towards the problem of evil. Indeed, Bayle's arguments themselves occur within a broader theological framework, namely the reactivation of Augustinian thought and the so-called 'Jansenism controversy' during the seventeenth century.

This controversy was ignited by the publication in 1640 of the three-volume work *Augustinus* by the theologian Cornelius Jansen (1585–1638). Jansen promoted the return to the original Christian, Augustinian teachings, particularly to Augustine's doctrine of grace, according to which only a certain portion of humanity is predestined to be saved. This clearly went against the Catholic faith by denying the central role of free will in the recognition, acceptance, and enjoyment of divine grace, since Jansenism maintained that God's decision of granting the gift of grace, i.e. of delivering salvation, is independent of human acquiescence. Some of the most important seventeenth-century European intellectuals were involved in one way or another in the heated debate concerning the righteousness of Jansenism (the doctrine was condemned by the Pope on several occasions: first in 1642, last in 1713): Pascal, Descartes, Arnauld, Malebranche, and, of course, Bayle and Leibniz. It is in this rather complex setting, which will not be examined here, that the early modern discussion concerning evil, God's fairness, and human and divine freedom, takes place.[9]

Although Leibniz's "reasonably large octavo", the *Theodicy*, is of course not the only major philosophical work provoked by the controversy regarding the nature of grace and freedom, and particularly by Bayle's enigmas regarding evil, it is one of the most famous and powerful among them. The *Theodicy* was published anonymously in Amsterdam in 1710. This explains the rather strange fact that some readers of the first edition took the word 'theodicy' to be the pseudonym of the author. (In the second edition from 1712 Leibniz's name was added to the title.) In fact, as is well known, the term derives from the Greek '*theos*' ('God') and '*dikēk*' ('justice'), and was coined by Leibniz himself.

---

7 On the historical and theoretical development of Leibniz's theodicy, see Rateau 2008.
8 *Cf.* Rutherford 1995a.
9 On Jansenism and the relation to it of some of the mentioned philosophers, see for example Abercrombie 1936; Forget 1913; Laywine 1999; Nadler: 2008b; Schmaltz 1999.

As Leibniz explains to Bartholomew Des Bosses (1668–1738), the *Theodicy* is "like a certain kind of science, namely the doctrine of the justice (that is, of the wisdom together with the goodness) of God" (Leibniz to Bartholomew Des Bosses, February 1712/GP II 437).

The book is divided in three main parts, preceded by a "Preface" and a "Preliminary Dissertation on the Conformity of Faith with Reason". It also features three appendices: "Summary of the Controversy, Reduced to Formal Argument", "Reflections on the Work that Mr. Hobbes Published in English on 'Freedom, Necessity and Chance'", and "Observations on the Book Concerning 'The Origin of Evil', published recently in London" (that is, William King's *De origine mali* [1702], the first major 'theodicy' of the eighteenth century).

In the present investigation of early criticisms of so-called Leibnizian philosophical optimism, although I will of course refer to several of Leibniz's works, my focus will be on the text of the *Theodicy*, as well as the criticisms directed specifically against this work.[10]

The *Theodicy* is of essential importance for the present work for at least two reasons. First, the book was not only an enormously popular and discussed philosophical treatise in the eighteenth century, but basically Leibniz's best known work during the first half of the century. Together with his correspondence with Samuel Clarke from 1715 to 1716 (published for the first time in English in 1717[11]) and the *Monadology* of 1714,[12] the *Theodicy* was the main source of knowledge of Leibnizian thought for Leibniz's contemporaries. Thus, the greatest part of the critics examined in the present work had the *Theodicy* in mind when arguing against Leibniz.

This is precisely the second reason for the relevance of the *Theodicy* in this work. Without any doubt, Leibniz's description of the *Theodicy* as a "work composed in bits and pieces" is not merely an expression of modesty on the author's part. The book *is* indeed more an articulated collection of fragments

---

10   For a recent, multiperspectival introduction to Leibniz's *Theodicy*, see the essays collected in Jorgensen & Newlands 2014.
11   *A Collection of Papers, which passed between the late Learned Mr. Leibnitz, and Dr. Clarke, In the Years 1715 and 1716* (London: James Knapton). The first French and German translations both appeared in 1720: *Recueil de pièces diverses sur la philosophie la religion et l'histoire par Leibnitz, Clarke et Newton* (Amsterdam: Duvillard & Changuion), translation by Pierre Desmaizeaux, and *Merckwürdige Schriften welche [...] zwischen dem Herrn Baron von Leibniz und dem Herrn D. Clarke über besondere Materien der natürlichen Religion* (Frankfurt-Leipzig: Johann Meyer), translation by Heinrich Köhler, with a preface by Christian Wolff.
12   First published in the German translation by Heinrich Köhler in 1720: *Lehrsätze über die Monadologie* (Frankfurt-Leipzig: Johann Meyer). The first Latin translation, by Michael Gottlieb Hansch, was published in the *Acta Eruditorium* (VII: 500–14) in 1721.

and digressions than a completely solid whole, a quality that can render its reading somewhat weary.[13] Nonetheless, the *Theodicy* is undoubtedly the best and – albeit in Leibnizian terms – most systematic exposition of Leibniz's treatment of the problem of evil (*If God, the creator of this world, is good and omnipotent, where does evil come from?*) and the solution to it: what is known since the mid-eighteenth century as '*philosophical optimism*',[14] i.e. the Leibnizian rationalist system of 'the best of all possible worlds'.

In the first section of this chapter I will introduce two central tenets of philosophical optimism: the doctrine of the best of all possible worlds and Leibniz's views concerning the nature and the meaning of evils in the world. In the second section I will examine the question of the theoretical foundations of the system of optimism, particularly the Leibnizian concept of a rational God and the idea of the existence of principles of reason, to which even God is subjected. In the last section I will address a central problem related to optimism and Leibnizian thought in general – the problem of divine freedom – and will present Leibniz's challenging solution to it.

At the very first page of the "Preliminary Dissertation" Leibniz announces that the *Theodicy* shall begin with the question of the conformity of faith with reason, "because it has much influence on the main subject of my treatise, and because M. Bayle introduces it everywhere" (GP VI 49).[15] Although I will not examine in detail the "Preliminary Dissertation", as we will see throughout this and the next chapters, the idea of the conformity of faith and reason and, moreover, the conviction of the essential rationality of God's nature, his behavior, his creation, etc., is fundamental to optimism.

1 Philosophical Optimism: The System of the Best and the Meaning of Evil

1.1 *The Best of All Possible Worlds*

In informal terms 'optimism' is usually understood as some kind of positive attitude towards life and the future, which entails the belief or the hope that things are and will keep on being good (whatever 'good' may mean). Accordingly, optimism is related to outlooks like the fashionable idea of 'positive thinking' or popular metaphors like the half-full-glass-analogy, which express a kind

---

13 On the fragmentary style of the *Theodicy* see Aiton 1985: 298ff.; Antognazza 2009: 479ff.
14 On the coinage of the term 'optimism' see Chapter 3.
15 For a brief account of the contents of the "Preliminary Dissertation" see Aiton 1985: 298–300, Franke 1992.

of, well ... precisely *optimist* attitude towards life. But Leibnizian optimism is something rather different. Later on in this work (Chapter 3), I will examine the question whether Leibnizian optimism can *also* be understood as a kind of popular, positive-thinking-optimism. For the moment, however, philosophical optimism will be examined in a very specific manner, namely as the system that can be summarized in the – at first glance rather neutral – claim that this world is *the best of all possible worlds.*

Leibniz does not quite express that claim in a straightforward fashion, only one time in the *Theodicy* does he talk about his "fundamental assumption that God has chosen the best of all possible worlds" (T, §168/GP VI 210). Yet the *idea* that this is, or rather: that this *must be* the best of all possible worlds is stated innumerable times throughout the work. At the beginning of the *Theodicy* Leibniz writes, for example:

> As in mathematics, when there is no maximum nor minimum, in short nothing distinguished, every-this is done equally, or when that is not possible, nothing at all is done: so it may be said likewise in respect of perfect wisdom, which is no less orderly than mathematics, that if there were not the best (optimum) among all possible worlds, God would not have produced any.
> T, §8/GP VI 107[16]

And in an important letter to Des Bosses:

> In my opinion, if there were no best possible series, God would have certainly created nothing, since he cannot act without a reason, or prefer the less perfect to the more perfect.
> LEIBNIZ TO DES BOSSES, September 7, 1711/GP II 424–5

What does it exactly mean to say that the world is the *best possible* world? In what does the superiority or perfection of the created world consist? Or in other terms: Given that Leibniz's God acts upon objective reasons – as we shall observe in different places throughout this work – which are the objective reasons or criteria that determine God to chose this world?

Leibniz offers a number of descriptions of what it means to be a perfect world. In recent years, Leibniz's statements regarding the criteria that permit us to maintain that our world is the best of all possible worlds have been interpreted in two main directions.

---

16 *Cf.* T, §§52, 117, 119, 124, 130, 167f./GP VI 131, 167f., 169ff., 178f., 182ff.

On the one hand, it has been argued that, according to Leibniz, God chose this world because through it he could obtain the best possible *balance* between simplicity of laws (or order) and richness (or variety) of phenomena. This is the position of commentators like Nicholas Rescher.[17] For him, given God's infinite benevolence, the choice of the world certainly aims at the maximizing of goodness. Now, according to Rescher's reading, this maximization is defined by the *optimizing* of the combination of the variables of simplicity and variety. The chief criterion of the world's perfection or goodness, i.e. what makes this world appear as the best possible alternative to God, is thus determined by the balance between the profusion of phenomena and the simplicity of the rules that govern the world. Leibniz writes for example:

> But God chose [to create] the most perfect order, that is, the order that is at once simplest in general rules and richest in phenomena.
> DM, §6/GP IV 43[18]

As Rescher explains, the best world, i.e. the most perfect of all possible worlds is that which exhibits the greatest variety of contents (abundance of phenomena), consonant with the greatest simplicity of governing rules. According to this interpretation, in the structure of all possible worlds there exist two factors that are opposed to one another, that are in "a state of mutual tension": order and variety (Rescher 1979: 29–33).[19] God's achievement through the creation of our world is the attainment of stability between both conflicting factors. This stability or balance, which God attains by comparing and weighing possible worlds,[20] defines the perfection or goodness of the created world. Through the balancing of variety and richness of phenomena, on the one hand, and lawfulness or order on the other, Leibniz's God manages to maximize existence, i.e. to create as much as possible, which is his wish upon producing the world, within the most regular order possible. According to Rescher, then, for Leibniz the maximization of the goodness of the world does not depend on what Rescher calls a "monolithic, single-factor criterion" (Rescher 2003: 152), but is determined by a "single two-factor standard" (Rescher 1979: 33). Maximization of goodness, or the perfection of possible worlds, is to be understood as an

---

17 *Cf.* Rescher 1979: 28ff.
18 *Cf.* PNG, §10/GP VI 603; M, §58/GP VI 616; T, §§204–205, §208/GP VI 238, 241.
19 As Rescher also writes, these two "operative factors", so to speak, "pull in opposite directions" (Rescher 2003: 27).
20 *Cf.* T, §§225–6/GP VI 253f. and Chapter 2, 2.

optimizing of the balance and combination between the abundance of creatures and the simplicity of laws that govern them.[21]

A critical alternative to Rescher's interpretation of Leibnizian perfection as balance or 'optimization' (or maximization of goodness as optimizing of variety and simplicity) has been advocated by commentators such as Donald Rutherford.[22] In Rutherford's account, the maximization of goodness is defined by a "single-factor criterion" (although, as we will see, this reading is no less complex than Rescher's): the perfect world has the greatest *quantity* of perfection or, as Leibniz writes, of "essence" or "reality".[23] Against Rescher and others Rutherford argues that the superiority and, hence, desirability of the best world is not defined only by attaining the best balance between the variables of diversity of creatures and simplicity of rules. First and foremost, the amount of perfection is for Leibniz a determining criterion of the superiority of the world. Leibniz writes for example:

> [W]hat I have said implies not only that the world is physically (or, if you prefer, metaphysically) most perfect, i.e. the series of things that has been produced is the one that brings the greatest amount of reality into existence, but also that the world is morally most perfect, because moral perfection is really physical perfection with respect to minds.
> UOT/GP VII 306

According to Rutherford, Leibniz does not consider that variety and order are competing factors in the design of a world. The fundamental criterion for defining the superiority of the world is the "maximization of perfection" (Rutherford 1995a: 26). Leibniz identifies the perfection of the world with the amount of essence. This does not mean, of course, that the criterion of balance of order and variety is not central for the election of the world. For Leibniz, the world with the greatest quantity of essence is *also* the world with the largest number of phenomenal things, the largest number of monads, and the simplest working laws. For this reason it is also the world with the most harmony. Rutherford explains:

---

21 For a positive review of the theory of balance between variety and simplicity as criterion of perfection see for example Blumenfeld 1995: 383–93.
22 *Cf.* Rutherford 1995a and 1995b.
23 Leibniz writes for example: "[P]erfection is just the amount of essence. This makes it obvious that of the infinite combinations of possibilities and possible series, the one that exists is the one through which the most essence or possibility is brought into existence" (UOT/GP VII 303).

> It follows that the most harmonious world is at once the one with the most phenomenal entities, the most monads, and the greatest quantity of essence. This brings together in a simple way a variety of Leibnizian theses: the best world = the most harmonious one = the one that satisfies the variety/simplicity criterion = the one with the most phenomenal individual and the most monads = the one with the most reality, or essence.
> RUTHERFORD 1995b: 394

Therefore, the world is the best possible because it contains the greatest quantity of essence *and* is the most appropriate means of obtaining the best equation between simplicity of laws and variety of phenomena.[24] As Rutherford explains, there is still another aspect concerning perfection that must be included in this interpretation. In a letter of 1715 to Christian Wolff he defines perfection as:

> the degree of positive reality, or what comes to the same thing, degree of affirmative intelligibility, so that something more perfect is something in which more things worthy of observation are found [...]. The more there is worthy of observation in a thing, the more universal properties, the more harmony it contains [...].
> GW 161, 170–1; quoted in Rutherford 1995b: 395

Perfection is thus the degree of intelligibility or "contemplability" of a created world. The more contemplability a world has, the more harmony (or "order, regularity") it contains. This, as Leibniz explains, is precisely the "degree of essence, if essence is calculated from harmonizing properties [...]" (GW 170–2; quoted in Rutherford 1995a: 35). And there is more. According to Leibniz the best possible world also contains the greatest possible *happiness* of rational beings. In the *Discourse on Metaphysics* he writes:

> [H]appiness is to people what perfection is to beings in general. And if the ultimate explanation of the existence of the real world is the decree that it should have the greatest perfection that it can, then the ultimate aim for the moral world – the city of God, the noblest part of the universe – should be to infuse it with the greatest possible happiness.
> DM, §36/GP IV 462[25]

---

24   See also Jolley 2005: 161–6.
25   *Cf.* T, "Observations on the Book Concerning *The Origin of Evil*", §22/GP VI 426.

How can this be made compatible with the claims about the perfection, harmony, contemplability, greatest quantity of essence, etc. of the created world? Rutherford's suggestion is to argue that the greatest happiness is made possible by the greatest degree of contemplability, i.e. of harmony of the world. This is thus because happiness is precisely a lasting "state of pleasure sustained through the exercise of reason", which follows on perception, i.e. from the contemplability of the qualities of perfection and harmony.[26] Therefore,

> [t]he world with the most harmony offers the greatest potential for happiness, a potential, we may add, which will be realized provided that this world contains enough spirits who love God and are deserving of happiness. [...] Therefore, the world with the greatest harmony will also contain the greatest possible happiness.
> RUTHERFORD 1995b: 402

Rutherford's account of the Leibnizian notion of the perfection of a possible world is rather sophisticated. In contrast to Rescher's credible 'two-factor standard' theory of perfection, Rutherford offers a "monolithic, single-factor criterion" (Rescher 2003: 152) that nevertheless would seem to offer a more dynamic conception of perfection – namely as a *potential* for happiness – and thus to embrace more elements of Leibnizian metaphysics and his complex theory of happiness. Indeed, as I believe, Rutherford's interpretation does not dismiss Rescher's two-factor-theory, but actually *integrates* it in a more comprehensive account of what it means for a world to be perfect. In Rutherford's opinion, the game between variety and simplicity certainly plays a central role in the definition of perfection. This criterion is, however, only one more among the complex set of elements that are interconnected in the concept of the most perfect world. In Leibniz's system, this interconnection takes place in a way that is not necessarily empirically evident to us, limited human beings, but which implies a markedly rationalist approach and the assumption of a markedly rationalist understanding of God. But before examining this, we must take a look at the background and nature of Leibniz's account of evil in order to attain a more complete picture of philosophical optimism.

1.2 *Evil and Evils in the Best of All Possible Worlds*

Leibniz's doctrine of the best world can be described as the final stage or the 'last thesis' of a rather complex answer to the problem of evil, which includes both a typology of evils, as well as an account of the 'meaning' of the presence

---

26   *Cf.* Rutherford 1995a: 49ff.

of those evils in this world, created by a good and omnipotent God – i.e. Leibniz's justification of God or his theodicy, properly speaking.

What do we mean exactly when we talk about evil? According to Leibniz, evil can be understood in three ways, all related to one another. These he calls 'metaphysical', 'moral', and 'physical' evil:

> Evil may be taken metaphysically, physically and morally. *Metaphysical evil* consists in mere imperfection, *physical evil* in suffering, and *moral evil* in sin. Now although physical evil and moral evil be not necessary, it is enough that by virtue of the eternal verities they be possible. And as this vast Region of Verities contains all possibilities, it is necessary that there be an infinitude of possible worlds, that evil enter into divers of them, and that even the best of all contain a measure thereof. Thus has God been induced to permit evil. [...].
> T, §21/GP VI 116

In his tripartite definition Leibniz follows what could be called the traditional orthodox Christian answer to the problem of evil, which, as is well known, was systematized mainly by Augustine of Hippo (354–430 AD), perhaps the most influential theologian in Christian history.

The preoccupation with the problem of evil is a constant in Augustine's thought. Accordingly, there is not one particular passage or treatise which Augustine devotes particularly to explaining evil. Yet it is possible to draw a comprehensive picture of traditional theodicy from his main works of maturity: *De libero arbitrio* (387/388 AD), *Confessiones* (397–401 AD), *De civitate dei* (412–426 AD), and *De fide spe et caritate* (*Enchiridion*) (421/422 AD). In a rather interesting parallel to Leibniz's own rejection of Bayle's provocations, Augustine's account of evil is to a large extent an attempt to face up to the intellectual challenge resulting from his final rejection of the heresy of Manichaeism, that is to justify evil within the Christian monotheistic framework against the Manichean dualistic model.[27]

This justification can be summarized – very sketchily indeed – in three premises that deal with the central issues that constitute the classical problem of evil (the metaphysical character of evil, its source or sources, and the place, if any, that evil occupies within the created order), and constitute the basic structure of what I call here the 'traditional' or 'Augustinian theodicy':

---

27 On Augustine's dismissal of Manichaean dualism and its intellectual consequences, see *Conf.* 7.7.11ff.; Brown 1967: Chapters 5 and 16; Kirwan 1999: 60ff.

i)   Viewed from an ontological perspective, evil is the absence or privation of proper being.
ii) So-called 'evil' is either sin, i.e. the wrongdoing of free rational agents ('moral evil'), or the just punishment inflicted on sinners by God ('physical' or 'natural evils').
iii) Particular evils are constituent elements of the universe seen as a whole. They contribute to the order and beauty of creation, as well as to the emphasizing and bringing forth of goodness.

This is not the place to examine Augustine's account of evil and the problems and paradoxes implied by it in detail. However, we must take a brief look at it, in order to see to what extent Leibniz's system of the best corresponds to tradition, and to recognize which are the particularly Leibnizian rationalist traits of philosophical optimism.[28]

To begin with, Augustine's thesis of *evil as privation* or deficiency of being has a distinguished intellectual history. On the one hand, it corresponds to the Judeo-Christian dogmas of creation *ex-nihilo* and the inherent goodness of the created order, and on the other, it is heir to both Neo-Platonism and to early patristic.[29] It is, therefore, possible to talk about a traditional Christian, or even a *Western* view of evil as privation of being.[30] And yet, it is in Augustine's work that this view is expounded within a methodical account of evil for the first time. Furthermore, it was the Augustinian version of evil as privation that influenced all subsequent thought on the subject most decisively.[31] A summary delineation of the theory is: God, the pinnacle of being and goodness, created

---

28   Of course, the traditional Christian handling of the question of evil and its relationship to divine and human freedom is not an *exclusively* Christian account. Fundamental assumptions by Augustine and other classical Christian theologians can be found in earlier doctrines, most notably in Stoicism and Neo-Platonism. On this respect, see for example Bobzien 1998; O'Meara 2010.

29   For the biblical foundation, see, aside from the first chapter of the *Book of Genesis*, *John* 1:3; *Acts* 4:24, 14:15 and 17:24; *Corinthians* 8:6. Augustine's most notable philosophical influence on the subject of evil is perhaps Plotinus, for whom evil has "no place among Beings or in the Beyond-Being" and it can only be situated "in the realm of non-Being" or defined as "some mode of the Non-Being [...]" (*Enn.* 1.8.3). On Augustine's Neo-Platonic influence see, for example, *Conf.* 7.9.13; Alfaric 1918; O'Meara 1982. In the Christian world before Augustine, the theory of evil as absence of being was held by Origen, Athanasius, Basil, Gregory of Nyssa, and Ambrosius. For a brief pre-Augustinian history of the dogma of evil as negation, see Journet 1961: 16–25.

30   See, for example, Flasch 1994: 111–7, Hick 1966: 41–9, 179–87; Labrousse 1983: 66.

31   For a general survey of the development of the theory after Augustine see Hick 1966: 90ff; Schönberger 1998. For the specific case of medieval philosophers, see Kent 2007. Cress 1989 presents an interesting contemporary defense of Augustine's privation account.

the world out of nothing. As the work of omnipotent goodness, everything that exists is wholly good. Because being *is* goodness, evil – the contrary of goodness – cannot possess the metaphysical attribute of being. Consequently, in ontological terms evil is to be defined as non-being. Augustine articulates the thesis in several passages. For example in the *Confessiones*, while reporting on his youth as a follower of the Manichean sect: "I did not yet know that evil was nothing but a privation of good (that, indeed, it has no being)" (*Conf.* 3.7). Later: "Evil, then, the origin of which I had been seeking, has no substance at all; for if it were a substance, it would be good" (7.12). And in *De civitate dei*: "There is no such entity in nature as 'evil'; 'evil' is merely a name for the privation of good" (*Civ.* 11.22).

Augustine's denial of the substantial existence of evil obviously does not imply that he (or Christian tradition, or Leibniz for that matter) maintains that there is no evil in the world. It does mean, though, that there is neither, in the order of non-created beings, an iniquitous substance or a supernatural entity behind the behavior and the distress that we call 'evil' (a 'pure evil' or a Manichaean antagonist to God, whence all 'empirical evils' emanate) nor, in the realm of creation, something that could be considered inherently devoid of goodness or simply defective.

Now, if evil is not the expression of some corrupt substance, how does it – in its quality of malfunctioning of something good – enter the order of creation? According to Augustinian tradition, evil enters creation through free human choice. The source of evil is to be found exclusively (i.e. without any reference to a possible divine blameworthiness) in the voluntary turning away of free rational beings from the good. Augustine claims that "an evil will is the cause of all evils" (*Lib. arb.* 3.17.48). This statement must be taken literally, for according to classical Christian theology, both moral and physical or natural evil are to be attributed directly or indirectly to misused freedom.

The direct identification of moral evil with voluntary wrong choice or sin has been called by contemporary philosophers of religion the 'Free Will Defense':[32] In order to be morally good and, thus, produce goodness, rational

---

32   The most famous advocate of the Free Will Defense is Alvin Plantinga, who introduced the notion. He writes: "A world containing creatures who are significantly free (and freely perform more good than evil actions) is more valuable, all else being equal, than a world containing no free creatures at all. Now God can create free creatures, but He can't *cause* or *determine* them to do only what is right. For if He does so, then they aren't significantly free after all; they do not do what is right *freely*. To create creatures capable of *moral good*, therefore, He must create creatures capable of moral evil; and He can't give these creatures the freedom to perform evil and at the same time prevent them from doing so. As it turned out, sadly enough, some of the free creatures God created went wrong in

beings need to have free choice of the will. By creating them free, God, through an act of his infinite love, has made possible for rational creatures to do good. As Augustine explains: "Since, indeed, a good God made me, I cannot do any good except by my will. It is quite clear that a good God gave me the will for this purpose" (*Lib. arb.* 3.1.3).

Free will for Augustine is an "intermediate good" (*Lib. arb.* 2.50.191) that allows the accomplishment of virtue. But precisely because of its quality as intermediate good, free will also allows evil in the form of deliberate wrong acts: "[W]hen the will abandons what is above itself, and turns to what is lower, it becomes evil – not because that is evil to which it turns, but because the turning itself is wicked" (*Civ.* 12.6). Through the misuse of their freedom rational creatures introduce evil into the world.

The Free Will Defense is the backbone of the traditional theodicy. Indeed, as can be seen from the argumentative structure of *De libero arbitrio*, it is for purposes of theodicy that Augustine develops his account of human sin. Through it, two pillars of the traditional Christian response to the problem of evil are stated unambiguously: the innocence of God and the exclusive guilt of the creature. The importance of the Free Will Defense regarding the problem of evil becomes still more evident when one takes into consideration its second aspect, namely its applicability to the problem of physical evil. Indeed, for the Augustinian tradition moral evil depends on us, as it is to be identified with the malicious particular voluntary acts of rational agents. What about evils such as poverty, natural catastrophes, disease, and death, which are out of our control? Are they not pointless suffering? No, they are not. For Augustine natural evils depend on us as well, as the outcome of our willful wrongdoing; there is then in fact *no* pointless suffering. Augustine writes for example:

> For we use the word "evil" in two senses: first, when we say that someone has *done* evil; and second, when we say that someone has *suffered* evil. [...] But if you know or believe that God is good – and it is not right to believe otherwise – then he does no evil. On the other hand, if we acknowledge that God is just – and it is impious to deny it – then he rewards the good and punishes the wicked. Those punishments are certainly evils for those who suffer them. Therefore, if no one is punished unjustly – and

---

the exercise of their freedom; this is the source of moral evil. The fact that free creatures sometimes go wrong, however, counts neither against God's omnipotence nor against His goodness; for He could have forestalled the occurrence of moral evil only by removing the possibility of moral good" (Plantinga 1974: 30). The most important critics of the Free Will Defense in the past century were John L. Mackie (1955) and Antony Flew (1973).

we must believe this, since we believe that this universe is governed by divine providence – it follows that God is a cause of the second kind of evil, but in no way causes the first kind.

Lib. arb. 1.1.1–2

This extension of the Free Will Defense thus rules out any possible charges of divine responsibility concerning evil, in this case human suffering or death. Natural evils are fair divine punishment for sin – a kind of causal outcome of moral evil. Death, the gravest of all evils, is the principal effect of the first sin committed by Adam and Eve. Physical or natural sufferings surely exist, but due to the fact that they are an indirect consequence of our own sinning (or our innate guilt) in the end nothing in them is actually *natural*. For Augustine, therefore, there is strictly speaking no genuine problem of natural evil: we get what we deserve.

Returning to Leibniz, his theory of evil seems to follow quite faithfully the traditional Augustinian account, Free Will Defense included. According to Leibniz's definition of evil, from a metaphysical viewpoint, it is the essential limitation of creatures *qua* creatures. He describes this so-called '*metaphysical evil*' as "mere imperfection" in creatures (T, §21/GP VI 115), as the "original imperfection" that created beings, so to speak, carry with themselves for the reason of being precisely creatures (and not infinite, omnipotent, unlimited substances, i.e. God). Leibniz writes:

> The question is asked first of all, whence does evil come? *Si Deus est, unde malum? Si non est, unde bonum?* [...] The answer is, that it must be sought in the ideal nature of the creature, in so far as this nature is contained in the eternal verities which are in the understanding of God, independently of his will. For we must consider that there is an *original imperfection in the creature* before sin, because the creature is limited in its essence; whence ensues that it cannot know all, and that it can deceive itself and commit other errors.
>
> T, §20/GP VI 115

The (surely thorny) idea that evil "must be sought in the ideal nature" of creatures, which is "contained in the eternal verities" will be examined in more detail in Chapter 2, when we take a nearer look at Leibniz's theory of eternal truths. There I will also comment on some of the criticisms of the Leibnizian concept of metaphysical evil by early and modern interpreters, particularly on the idea that Leibniz's metaphysical evil in fact does *not* really correspond to the Augustinian concept of evil as the *privation* of a perfection that a thing should have according to its nature (a privation which, in itself, does not necessarily render the thing evil). According to this criticism, the Leibnizian notion would seem to refer rather to a *negation* or absence of a perfection, a fundamental lack of something that makes creatures prone to evil.[33] At this place, however, the most relevant aspect of metaphysical evil is the fact – wholly compatible with the traditional Augustinian theodicy – that, according to Leibniz, this essential metaphysical imperfection of creatures is what makes possible the other two types of evil, moral and physical evil. That is how we must understand Leibniz's claim that from metaphysical evil "ensues that it [the creature] cannot know all, and that it can deceive itself and commit other errors".

Just as for Augustine, *moral evil* is equivalent to sin for Leibniz: the abuse of freedom by rational creatures.[34] Due to its original imperfection the free, rational creature can deceive itself, for example by considering something to be good which, in fact, is only a minor good or no good at all. Why does God permit evil? Leibniz's answer should not surprise us: first, because in order to prevent sin, God would have had to deny his creatures' freedom of choice (and this, according to Leibniz and the Augustinian tradition, is a bigger crime than moral sin itself); and second, because the order of the best of all possible worlds requires, or better: *includes* the presence of evil. As I will explain in more detail in the following section, God always does the best (he is, in fact, obliged to always do the best). For Leibniz, a different world would have not been the best world. Such a world, for example, could perhaps have had less evil than the actual world, but its laws would have been more complex. In order to make the most harmonic possible world real, God is thus obliged to permit moral evil, or as Leibniz explains:

> God cannot prevent it without acting against what he owes to himself, without doing something that would be worse than the crime of man, without violating the rule of the best; and that would be to destroy divinity, as I have already observed. God is therefore bound by a moral necessity, which is in himself, to permit moral evil in creatures.
>
> T, §158/GP VI 204

Just as the 'ideal nature' of things gives rise to metaphysical evil, moral evil belongs to the best of all possible plans: a world without moral evil would have not been better than the actual world, i.e. a *better* world without evil would is

---

33 See Chapter 2, 1, 1.1.
34 *Cf.* T, §§21, 81, 107/GP VI 116, 146, 162.

not possible in Leibniz's view. (This, as we will soon see is one of Leibniz's main strategies when trying to justify evil in the worlds.) God, Leibniz argues further, "who has power to do all that is possible, only permits sin because it is absolutely impossible to anyone at all to do better" (T, §165/GP VI 208).

As for *physical evil*, the third sense in which the concept of evil can be understood and which refers to suffering in general – disease and pain, natural disasters, death, and eternal damnation – Leibniz describes it in Augustinian manner as the just divine penalty for sin. Physical evil is therefore the consequence of moral evil:

> Now at last I have disposed of the cause of moral evil; *physical evil*, that is, sorrows, sufferings, miseries, will be less troublesome to explain, since these are results of moral evil. [...] One suffers because one has acted; one suffers evil because one does evil. *Nostrorum causa malorum / Nos sumus.*
> T, §241/GP VI 261[35]

The Augustinian and Leibnizian solution to the problem of evil, inasmuch as it identifies, directly or indirectly, the entrance of evils in the world with the abuse of freedom by rational agents, is primarily a 'moral solution'. But there is an aspect of it, in which the morality of rational creatures does not seem to be the main topic of discussion. This aspect could be called a 'cosmological solution', since it focuses less on the problem of the origin or nature of evil than on the question concerning the role – if any – that evils (sin, suffering, catastrophes, death) play within the system of the created world. The cosmological solution maintains basically that evil plays a positive role in the operation and general composition of the created order.

As we saw previously, according to the Augustinian tradition, evils are constitutive elements of the universe as a whole. They contribute both to the order and beauty of creation, as well as to the emphasizing and bringing forth of goodness. Augustine writes for example in the *Enchiridion*:

> [Not all things] were created supremely, equally, nor immutably good. Still, each single created thing is good, and taken as a whole they are very good, because together they constitute a universe of admirable beauty. In this universe, even what is called evil, when it is rightly ordered and kept in its place, commends the good more eminently, since good things yield greater pleasure and praise when compared to the bad things. For the

---

[35] *Cf.* T, §155/GP VI 202. On the Leibnizian division between metaphysical, moral, and physical evil, and some problems connected with it, see for example: Rateau 2008: 577–87.

Omnipotent God, whom even the heathen acknowledge as the Supreme Power over all, would not allow any evil in his works, unless in his omnipotence and goodness, as the Supreme Good, he is able to bring forth good out of evil.

Ench. 3.10–1

At least two key themes of what I call the cosmological approach can be recognized in this passage. On the one hand, evil is a constituent element of the general makeup of the universe; on the other, only through the experience of evil can the good in the world be, so to say, highlighted. The former assumption has been termed by some commentators the 'aesthetic theme' of Augustine's theodicy:[36] Seen in its totality (i.e. from God's standpoint), the universe is good and beautiful, evil is (simply) one more element of that perfectly ordered totality. From our limited perspective, Augustine claims, "some things, because they do not harmonize with others, are considered evil", but from the divine viewpoint "there is no such thing as evil", since "those same things harmonize with others and are good, and in themselves are good (*Conf.* 7.13.19).[37]

---

36 See for example Billicsich 1938–59, vol. II: 182 (who talks of "aesthetic optimism"); Hick 1966: 82ff; Whitney 1994. About the significance of the aesthetic theme in Augustine's thought, Adolf von Harnack writes: "Augustine never tires of realizing the beauty (*pulchrum*) and fitness (*aptum*) of creation, of regarding the universe as an ordered work of art, in which the gradations are as admirable as the contrasts. The individual and evil are lost to view in the notion of beauty. [...] Even hell [...] is an indispensable part of the work of art" ([Harnack 1886–1890] cited in Hick 1966: 82).

37 *Cf. Civ.* 11.23: "The whole universe is beautiful, if one could see it as a whole, even with its sinners, though their ugliness is disgusting when they are viewed in themselves". The most appealing aspects of the aesthetic theme are perhaps the idea of the divine artist or architect who *designs* his creation according to the rational principles of order and beauty, and the related notion of the 'perspective of God', from which particular evils evidence themselves to be contributing organically to the complex and, again, *rational* perfection of the whole. Like the privative theory of evil, these allegories are of Platonic and Neo-Platonic lineage, and indeed rather archetypal similes of Western thought. *Cf.* Plato's *Laws*, 10.903 and specially Plotinus' *Enneads*: "The Reason-Principle is sovereign, making all: it wills things as they are and, in its reasonable act, it produces even what we know as evil [...]. We are like people ignorant of painting, who complain that the colours are not beautiful everywhere in the picture: but the Artist has laid on the appropriate tint to every spot [...]" (*Enn.* 3.2.11). Augustine uses this same metaphor explicitly in *De Civ Dei* 11.23 and *De Vera Religione* 40.76. The 'aesthetic' conception of evil, as Hick notes (1966: 83, n. 2), appears, between Plato and Augustine, in Epictetus' *Discourses*, I.12 and Marcus Aurelius' *Meditations*, 6.42. Of course, Leibnizian optimism also makes use of these metaphors, and the idea of the perspective of God is a fundamental theoretical premise of Leibniz's theodicy.

The second main theme of the 'cosmological' solution is closely related to the idea that evil is an essential ingredient of the general picture of creation, but it goes quite further, maintaining that evil can in fact contribute, as Augustine writes, to the "bringing forth" and emphasizing of goodness in the world ("since good things yield greater pleasure and praise when compared to the bad things") – a kind of empirical contrast-medium to bring to light the best part of creation. This argument has hence been labeled the 'contrast theory of evil' or the 'necessary contrast solution'.[38] According to this account, God permits evil, among other reasons, in order to guarantee the order of the universe (taken as a whole), to emphasize (through contrast) the goodness of creation, and to bring forth good (for example through the righteous deeds of previously punished sinners). Thus, Augustine counters the foreseeable objection regarding the injustice of divine penalty in the form of natural evils by writing: "Hence the penal state is imposed to bring into order, and is therefore in itself not dishonorable. Indeed it compels the dishonorable state to become harmonized with the honor of the universe. So that the penalty of sin corrects the dishonor of sin" (*Lib. arb.* 3.9.26).

As for Leibniz's case, to define evil as an imperfection or privation on the one hand, and to give responsibility for its presence exclusively to rational creatures, are of course already ways of playing down, if not the reality, then the weight of evil. But there are also explicit strategies by Leibniz directed to show that evils are in some way meaningful within the created order. And as it was the case with his typology of evils, Leibniz's strategies to justify the existence of evil in the world also evoke the Augustinian approach. Leibniz's many claims about the non-absurdity of evils can be grouped in at least three main ideas:

i) Particular evils are necessary for the order, harmony or beauty of the universe. Given our perceptual and intellectual limitations, we cannot discern that order. From God's perspective, however, the world *is* a perfect order and evil a constitutive brick of that harmonious building. Thus we read in the *Theodicy*:

> The part of the shortest way between two extreme points is also the shortest way between the extreme points of this part; but the part of the best Whole is not of necessity the best that one could have made of this part. For the part of a beautiful thing is not always beautiful, since it can be extracted from the whole, or marked out within the whole, in an

---

38 See Hick 1966: 89; Matthews 2005: 111. Once more a Platonic theme, the contrast theory first appears in Plato's *Theaetetus* 176A.

irregular manner. If goodness and beauty always lay in something absolute and uniform, such as extension, matter, gold, water, and other bodies assumed to be homogeneous or similar, one must say that the part of the good and the beautiful would be beautiful and good like the whole, since it would always have resemblance to the whole: but this is not the case in things that have mutual relations.

T, §213/GP VI 245–6

But one must believe that even sufferings and monstrosities are part of order; and it is well to bear in mind not only that it was better to admit these defects and these monstrosities than to violate general laws, as Father Malebranche sometimes argues, but also that these very monstrosities are in the rules, and are in conformity with general acts of will, though we be not capable of discerning this conformity. It is just as sometimes there are appearances of irregularity in mathematics which issue finally in a great order, when one has finally got to the bottom of them: that is why I have already in this work observed that according to my principles all individual events, without exception, are consequences of general acts of will.

T, §241/GP VI 261

A world without evils would seem to be *possible*. And it would also seem to be *better* than our actually created world. But Leibniz does not consider this to be the case. Seen as a whole, the created world is the best because it has such and such traits, to which particular evils belong unavoidably. As Leibniz maintains – somewhat counter-intuitively, it must be said, but then: that is *precisely* the whole idea of *philosophical* optimism – a world without sin and suffering would have been worse than the created world:

> Some adversary not being able to answer this argument will perchance answer the conclusion by a counter-argument, saying that the world could have been without sin and without sufferings; but I deny that then it would have been *better*. For it must be known that all things are *connected* in each one of the possible worlds: the universe, whatever it may be, is all of one piece, like an ocean: the least movement extends its effect there to any distance whatsoever, even though this effect become less perceptible in proportion to the distance. Therein God has ordered all things beforehand once for all, having foreseen prayers, good and bad actions, and all the rest; and each thing *as an idea* has contributed, before its existence, to the resolution that has been made upon the existence of

all things; so that nothing can be changed in the universe (any more than in a number) save its essence or, if you will, save its *numerical individuality*. Thus, if the smallest evil that comes to pass in the world were missing in it, it would no longer be this world; which, with nothing omitted and all allowance made, was found the best by the Creator who chose it.
T, §9/GP VI 107–8[39]

ii) Considering the pertinence of evil, evils, even moral evils, contribute to the obtaining of good. They, Leibniz believes, are always connected with greater goods:

Thus the evil, or the mixture of goods and evils wherein the evil prevails, happens only *by concomitance*, because it is connected with greater goods that are outside this mixture.
T, §119/GP VI 170

For this reason, and because in some cases, by preventing a good, God would in fact give rise to worse evils, God permits the existence of sin:

Concerning sin or moral evil, although it happens very often that it may serve as a means of obtaining good or of preventing another evil, it is not this that renders it a sufficient object of the divine will or a legitimate object of a created will. It must only be admitted or *permitted* in so far as it is considered to be a certain consequence of an indispensable duty: as for instance if a man who was determined not to permit another's sin were to fail of his own duty, or as if an officer on guard at an important post were to leave it, especially in time of danger, in order to prevent a quarrel in the town between two soldiers of the garrison who wanted to kill each other.
T, §24/GP VI 117

In the case of physical evils, Leibniz emphasizes the idea of evil as a way of attaining the good and avoiding bigger evils ("One may say of physical evil, that God wills it often as a penalty owing to guilt, and often also as a means to an end, that is, to prevent greater evils or to obtain greater good. The penalty

---

39   *Cf.* T, §130/GP VI 183: "Now since physical evil and moral evil occur in this perfect work, one must conclude (contrary to M. Bayle's assurance here) that *otherwise a still greater evil would have been altogether inevitable*. This great evil would be that God would have chosen ill, if he had chosen otherwise than he has chosen".

serves also for amendment and example"), and as a kind of contrast medium for the recognition of the good ("Evil often serves to make us savor good the more; sometimes too it contributes to a greater perfection in him who suffers it [...]" [T, §23/GP VI 116]).

iii) There is indeed more good than evil in the world (despite what experience may suggest):

> But it will be said that evils are great and many in number in comparison with the good: that is erroneous. It is only want of attention that diminishes our good, and this attention must be given to us through some admixture of evils.
> T, §13/GP VI 109

> I answer that since God chooses the best possible, one cannot tax him with any limitation of his perfections; and in the universe not only does the good exceed the evil, but also the evil serves to augment the good.
> T, §216/GP VI 247[40]

This is also valid of moral evil:

> I think that in reality, properly speaking, there is incomparably more moral good than moral evil in rational creatures; and of these we have knowledge of but few. This evil is not even so great in men as it is declared to be [...]
> T, §§219–220/GP VI 249

Leibniz thus offers an account of evil that comes from a reputable tradition of Christian theodicy. We will see next which are the representative rationalist assumptions and traits that render the Leibnizian interpretation of tradition nevertheless quite original, with regard to classical theodicy.

---

[40] Also: "I would dare to maintain that even in this life goods exceed evils, that our comforts exceed our discomforts, and that M. Descartes was justified in writing (vol. 1, Letter 9) 'that natural reason teaches us that we have more goods than evils in this life'. It must be added that pleasures enjoyed too often and to excess would be a very great evil" (T, §§251–252/GP VI 266–7). And against Bayle: "Bayle continues: 'that man is wicked and miserable; that there are everywhere prisons and hospitals; that history is simply a collection of the crimes and calamities of the human race.' I think that there is exaggeration in that: there is incomparably more good than evil in the life of men, as there are incomparably more houses than prisons" (T, §148/GP VI 198).

2 The Foundations of Philosophical Optimism

Is philosophical optimism, with its two central claims about the superiority of the created world and the meaningfulness of evils, (merely) some kind of *dogmatic* postulation, or is it the conclusion of a philosophical argument and in this sense a *system* of thought? In other words: Theoretically, how well- or ill-founded is optimism? Naïve or mistrustful as they might sound, these questions are important for the understanding of the theoretical nature of optimism, as well as due to the fact that in the next chapters I will examine early criticisms of optimism and specifically their argumentative weight.

It is possible to find assertions in the *Theodicy* that could seem to justify the idea that optimism, and particularly the doctrine of the best world, is a dogma, the expression of a doctrinaire belief on the part of Leibniz. For example:

> [S]o it may be said likewise in respect of perfect wisdom, which is no less orderly than mathematics, that if there were not the best (*optimum*) among all possible worlds, God would not have produced any.
> T, §8/GP VI 107

> It is true that one may imagine possible worlds without sin and without unhappiness, and one could make some like Utopian or Sevarambian romances: but these same worlds again would be very inferior to ours in goodness. I cannot show you this in detail. For can I know and can I present to you and compare them together? But you must judge with me *ab effectu*, since God has chosen this world as it is.
> T, §10/GP VI 108

> Is it possible, said Mr. Bayle, that there is no better plan than that one which God carried out? One answers that it is very possible and indeed necessary, namely that there is none: otherwise God would have preferred it.
> T, §226/GP VI 253

All these statements seem to amount to one and the same thing: our world is the best possible *because God created it*. Certainly, every reader of early modern philosophy *must* accept the fact that God as creator is a fundamental concept within every philosophical system of the time. And yet, it seems to be obvious that, at least for Leibniz, there is more to optimism than just the reformulation of the belief in God's greatness. Surely, optimism is *that*, but it is also more. Thus, for example, in the *Monadology* Leibniz offers a brief account that gives an idea of the kind of concepts and assumptions that seem to underlie optimism:

> Now, since in the ideas of God there is an infinity of possible universes, and since only one can exist, there must be a sufficient reason for God's choice of that one – a reason that leads him to choose one rather than some other of the possible universes. And this reason can only be found in the suitability or degrees of perfection that these worlds contain, with each possible world's right to claim existence being proportional to the perfection it contains. And that is the reason for the existence of the best, which God's wisdom brings him to know, his goodness brings him to choose, and his power brings him to produce.
>
> M, §§53–5/GP VI 615f.

Which are exactly the assumptions that constitute the theoretical basis of the claim that our world is the best possible? Which is, if any, the genealogy of the system of the best?[41]

2.1   *The Theoretical Genealogy of Optimism*

In a paper entitled "Leibnizian Optimism" Catherine Wilson talks about a "standard interpretation" of what could be called the theoretical genealogy of Leibniz's doctrine of the best of all possible worlds. According to that traditional interpretation, optimism follows directly from the application of two principles fundamental to Leibnizian metaphysics: the Principle of Sufficient Reason and the so-called Principle of Plenitude. Wilson writes:

> The first, the principle of sufficient reason, entails that God's choice among possible worlds must have been made according to some criterion. This criterion then emerges as the principle of plenitude, the principle that a world with greater variety is superior to any world with less. A world with both men and lions is thus preferable to a world with men only, whatever the particular disadvantages of lions.
>
> WILSON 1983: 767

---

41   In Chapter 4 I will return briefly to the idea of the nature and possibility of a theoretical 'proof' of optimism. On this respect see for example Look 2020, Rateau 2008: 510ff. And as we will in the next chapters the question regarding the theoretical strength of optimism and its possible dogmatic character will accompany us throughout the whole work.

According to this view God identifies among all possible worlds the one that better corresponds to what contemporary commentators have called the Principle of Plenitude. Both this identification and the subjection to the Principle of Sufficient Reason determine God to create our world.[42] The Leibnizian God thus creates the world (for that matter: always acts) for a reason – a *good* reason. It is of course possible to argue about the exact reasons, for which God chooses one possible world over all others. One could say, for example, that it is not necessarily the validity of the Principle of Plenitude (or at least not in the specific way in which Wilson states it) that gives God sufficient reason to choose this particular world, but instead the fact that through this world God could maximize goodness in some way (for example either, as Rescher suggested, by optimizing the balance between simplicity and variety or as Rutherford claimed, by maximizing the amount of essence – or perfection, or goodness – that the world contains) or fulfill the requirements of a given principle or set of principles. However, I believe this modification of the second principle that gives rise to optimism would not alter radically the original sense of standard interpretation, namely that optimism follows from the assumption of the Principle of Sufficient Reason and some other proposition or principle that establishes the objective superiority of the world.[43]

Catherine Wilson rejects the standard interpretation and suggests an alternative genealogy of optimism. Optimism, she claims, follows not from the two rational principles above mentioned, but is grounded on a different double presupposition. On the one hand, the assumption of a particular notion of *God*, and, on the other, of a specific understanding of what the *goodness* of the best of all possible worlds means. She writes:

> [T]he true basis for Leibniz's optimism lies not in his attachment to his two principles, but in his appropriation of a conception of God as divine strategian from his immediate predecessor Malebranche. Secondly, as a consequence of its origins, Leibnizian optimism is necessarily directed

---

42 *Cf.* Scribano 2003: 178: "The entire proof that this is the best of all possible worlds reduces thus to the establishment of its existence and to the validity of the principle of sufficient reason. If this world exists, it must be the best, otherwise God would not have been determined to action and nothing would exist, and if this best world exists, it is possible [...]".

43 The standard interpretation has a respectable tradition. As Wilson notes, some of the commentators that advocate this reading are Broad 1975: 139ff. Lovejoy 1936: 144ff. and 208f., and Russell 2005: 36f. As we will see later the standard conception of the theoretical foundations of optimism is also stated explicitly by some of the critics examined in this work, Christian August Crusius (Chapter 4) and Adolf Friedrich Reinhard (Chapter 5).

> toward an aspect of the world which is not directly available to perception and the sum of subjective pleasure is not in the end a good measure of its excellence. [...] I shall try to make plain [...] that, for Leibniz, the fact that the world is the creation of a supremely powerful, wise, and benevolent being implies that it is governed according to a system of laws that are the most beautiful and harmonious possible in a Malebranchean sense.
>
> WILSON 1983: 767

Here we understand that Leibniz assumes a notion of God as a 'divine strategian'. As will soon become clear, this means that Leibniz – following Malebranche – considers that God is a being that thinks and acts *rationally*, i.e. taking into account and weighing reasons for his actions (as we already saw when examining Rescher's and Rutherford's conflicting interpretations of the concept of the perfection of the world). Further, according to Wilson, to say that the world created by the divine strategian is the best of all possible worlds implies an understanding of the goodness of the world in non-hedonistic terms. This means that Leibniz believes that the goodness of the world cannot be identified with the pleasure of rational creatures. This notion of goodness, Wilson considers, focuses on an aspect of the world that cannot be accessed through empirical perception.

As I believe, both accounts of the origins of optimism – on the one hand the standard interpretation or the idea that optimism follows from the application of the two mentioned rational principles, and on the other Wilson's claim that optimism depends on a particular conception of God – do not necessarily exclude each other. In fact, I think that only an account that manages to articulate both genealogies/interpretations can do justice to Leibniz's thought. In the following sections, I will offer an overview of the two fundamental assumptions of philosophical optimism and will account for both genealogies. First, I will explain briefly the centrality of the notion of a *rational God* within Leibniz's metaphysics. Secondly, I will examine the assumption of the existence and universal validity of objective *principles of reason*, to which God himself is subject in his decisions and actions.

2.2 *Leibniz's God*

For any reader of Leibniz's works the thesis 'The concept of God occupies a fundamental place in Leibnizian thought' will not only appear indisputable, but even strikingly obvious. Indeed, within Leibniz's metaphysics, it is virtually impossible to talk about the nature of the world, the human soul or the problem of freedom without referring to God's attributes and his primordial role as creator. As modern as Leibniz might have been, Nicholas Rescher is right when he claims that Leibniz's system, "like the theories of the medievals for whom he [Leibniz] had such great respect, [...] put God as the *author of creation* at the focal position in metaphysics" (Rescher 1979: 13).

The mere structure of the *Discourse on Metaphysics* and the *Theodicy* are good examples of this. There Leibniz's reasoning goes from God to the substantial world and back to the kingdom of the spiritual. The fact that the world is "regular and orderly", indeed "the most perfect" world (DM, §6/GP IV 431) depends directly on the fact that God is an "absolutely perfect being" (who always chooses what he considers to be the best, etc.):

> The most widely accepted and sharpest notion of God that we have can be expressed like this: *God is an absolutely perfect being* [...]. [P]ower and knowledge are perfections, and God has them in unlimited form. It follows that the actions of God, who is supremely – indeed infinitely – wise, are completely perfect. This is not just metaphysical perfection, but also the moral kind. His moral perfection, so far as it concerns us, amounts to this: the more we come to know and understand God's works, the more inclined we shall be to find them excellent, and to give us everything we could have wished.
> DM, §1/GP IV 427

At the beginning of the *Theodicy*, building up to the 'proof' of the proposition that this must be the best of all possible worlds (T, §§8ff./GP VI 107f.), Leibniz's very first step is to establish that:

> *God is the first reason of things*: for such things as are bounded, as all that which we see and experience, are contingent and have nothing in them to render their existence necessary [...]. Therefore one must seek the reason for the existence of the world, which is the whole assemblage of *contingent* things, and seek it in the substance which carries with it the reason for its existence, and which in consequence is necessary and eternal.
> T, §7/GP VI 106

As Leibniz goes on to explain, God, this one necessary and eternal cause of the world, must also be intelligent, i.e. it must have an *understanding*, by virtue of which it identifies one world among the infinite possible worlds as the very best. By virtue of the *will* God "fixes upon" and chooses the one world that the understanding recognizes as the best possible. Through God's *power* his will is then "rendered efficacious".[44] In very general terms this is the foremost assumption of Leibniz's system (and particularly of philosophical optimism): the idea that the world was created by an all-powerful, all-intelligent God, who chose and created the world because he considered it to be the best of all possible alternatives.[45]

But what kind of God is Leibniz's God? What kind of God exactly is the God that created the best of all possible worlds? As we saw previously Catherine Wilson talks about Leibniz's God as a "divine strategian". This is a God who examines and compares infinite alternative possible worlds and chooses among them the one he considers the best (whatever criteria he follows). I added that this means that God is essentially rational, that he acts in an essentially rational manner. But what does it exactly mean to be an 'essentially rational' God? Steven Nadler offers a helpful characterization of this 'rational God' (which for Nadler is, in the seventeenth century, the God of Malebranche and Leibniz[46]). In very general terms, the divine strategian is a being who acts for "an intelligible and objective purpose". In short: a being whose actions respond to *reasons* – that is what makes him a rational being. The reasons that prompt this rational agent to action are determined teleologically by aims, in other words, his decisions and actions are motivated by so-called *final causes* – a notion that is fundamental to Leibniz's theory of action and freedom of choice, but which is, neither in the seventeenth century nor nowadays, obvious or unproblematic.[47] In any case, according to Leibniz, God acts in the pursuit of final causes, that is, he acts with a particular purpose. This particular purpose

---

44 *Cf.* M, §48/GP VI 615: "In God there is: (i) power, which is the source of everything, then (ii) knowledge, which contains every single idea, and then finally (iii) will, which produces changes in accordance with the principle of what is best".

45 *Cf.* Schmidt-Biggemann 2009: 56: "The famous proposition, *The world is the best of all possible worlds*, is deduced by Leibniz from his concept of God, in which love and justice, omniscience and omnipotence are reunited. This God is omniscient not only regarding the reality of the world but also – since he existed before the world did – regarding its possibility. […] God conceived, he planned the world before he created it […]. In his omniscience he represented to himself an infinite amount of possible worlds and examined them according to their compossibility. He then chose the metaphysically and morally best of all logically possible worlds and created it. This is for him the process of the '*Fiat*' – 'So be it'".

46 The specific affiliation and similarities between Malebranche's and Leibniz's God are examined in detail in Scribano 2003; Wilson 1983. Here I will only focus on the general attributes of Leibniz's 'rational God'.

47 Representative of the polemical character of final causes in the seventeenth century is Spinoza's rejection of the concept in his *Ethics*, book 1, Appendix. On the problematic history of final causes in early modern thought, see Schmid 2011.

is something that the agent recognizes as being good, in some way "desirable in its own right". Further, the rationality of this being is instrumental, whereby he is capable of "selecting means toward his desired goal", given that he considers that "those means are the most efficient to it" (Nadler 2011b: 168).

God, then, in Leibniz's worldview, acts following reasons. These reasons are final causes, aims that God considers desirable to attain and which determine God to action. In fact, God's aim, the final cause that always determines divine activity, is of course always one and the same: goodness. Leibniz explains quite clearly the way in which God's decisions and actions take place:

> Some people – including Descartes – hold that there are no rules of goodness and perfection in the nature of things, or in God's ideas of them, and that in calling the things God made 'good' all we mean is that God made them. I am far from agreeing with this. [...] [I]t seems that any act of the will presupposes some reason for it – a reason that naturally precedes the act – so that God's choices must come from his reasons for them, which involve his knowledge of what would be good; so they can't be the sources of the goodness of things.
>
> DM, §2/GP IV 428

God acts for the purpose of doing good. Put schematically, this means the following: the divine will acts upon the perceptions or representations of the good provided to it by the understanding.[48] (Or as we saw previously: God identifies, by virtue of his understanding, the aim that he considers to be the best possible – for the case of creation: God identifies one world among all infinite possible worlds as the very best. By virtue of his will informed by his understanding, God 'fixes upon' the world identified as the best and creates it by virtue of his infinite power.) As Leibniz writes:

> There is always a prevailing reason which prompts the will to its choice, and for the maintenance of freedom for the will it suffices that this reason should incline without necessitating. [...] The will is never prompted to action save by the representation of the good, which prevails over the opposite representations.
>
> T, §45/GP VI 127–8

---

48 Jolley 2005: 128: "For Leibniz, it is the nature of the will, whether divine or human, to be guided by the intellect, and its perfection consists in being guided by perceptions of the intellect that are clear and distinct".

Steven Nadler has called the particular concept of the divine nature defended for example by Leibniz (and Malebranche) a 'rationalist' notion of God. According to Nadler, the rationalist concept is one of three 'concepts of God' which are representative for early modern philosophical-theological European thought. The other two are what he calls an 'anti-rationalist' or 'voluntarist' concept (advocated for example by Descartes and Arnauld) and Spinoza's God.[49]

The two first concepts of God – which will be fundamental in the present investigation – are characterized by Nadler in the following terms:

> The rationalist conception of God regards God as an analogous to a rational agent endowed with will and understanding and acting, very much as we act, on the basis of practical reasoning. According to the anti-rationalist, or voluntarist, conception, God's understanding is not distinct from His will, and in the very structure of His being and agency God transcends practical rationality altogether. On the first conception, God always acts for good reasons; on the second, God's will is absolute and completely unmotivated by (logically) independent reasons.
>
> NADLER 2011a: 525–6

As I believe, Nadler's opinion concerning the existence of disagreeing 'concepts of God' that contribute fundamentally to determining the conflicts between early modern metaphysical systems, as well as his typology of those concepts, are by and large adequate and very useful when examining the history of modern philosophical ideas and particularly the conflict between optimism and its early critics. However, I also think that his *terminology* could be misleading. Indeed, even though Descartes's notion of God and his understanding of divine freedom may drastically differ from Leibniz's, it would be bizarre to deny the former's stature as a *rationalist* thinker – at least concerning his views about the nature of man's mind and the universe, the possibility of knowing reality as it is, the precedence of intuitive knowledge, etc. (The same can be seen, although perhaps with less clarity, in the case of some of the critics I will examine in the following chapters: even though they criticize Leibnizian rationalist optimism, within the traditional schema 'rationalism-empiricism [and perhaps, as a common antagonist: skepticism]', they could still be described as – *some kind of* – rationalist thinkers.)[50]

---

49 See Nadler 2008b, 2011a, 2011b, as well as Chapter 2.
50 Of course, the traditional characterization of 'rationalist' thinkers through their opposition to 'empiricist' thinkers – regarding particularly the Cartesian case – is itself

For this reason, I will prefer to refer to the concepts of 'intellectualism/ intellectualist' and 'voluntarism/voluntarist' throughout this work. Again, the distinction between voluntarism and intellectualism is itself not fully unproblematic, since it – just as every drastic distinction – cannot account for the nuances within the views of particular authors. And yet, I believe it provides a suitable framework for understanding an essential aspect of the conflict between Leibnizian optimism and its early critics.

In rather general terms, intellectualism is to be understood, following Nadler's outline, as the theory that defends some kind of priority or guidance on the part of the intellect or the understanding over the will, and maintains that God (or any rational being) acts according to reasons. Voluntarism, on the contrary, rests upon the claim that the will of rational beings is never determined by their understanding, either because the will is in some manner prior to understanding or because both are simply identical. Thus, whereas for intellectualists (Nadler's 'rationalists') rational beings are always motivated by reasons, voluntarists (Nadler's 'anti-rationalists') claim that the will is undetermined, uninfluenced in his actions by the understanding or by anything different to the will itself.[51]

Now, at least from a certain point of view (having established our vocabulary, we can now say: at least from a *voluntarist* point of view) the Leibnizian theory of divine agency seems to have very problematic consequences. In the present context, the most important of them is the problem of divine freedom. In the Leibnizian system, God as an agent is, strictly speaking, never completely *indeterminate*. As I have explained, God is always guided by representations in his actions – more exactly, by the representation of the good – that determine him to act in a specific manner. This means that the will is always guided, regulated by reasons. Moreover, as we will see later, for Leibniz, the very definition of a decision or an act of the will implies that it is impossible, absurd, that the will is *not* determined by reasons. To put in simple terms: for Leibniz, if there were no reasons to act, then we would simply not act.

For the particular case of divine creation the situation is clear: In deciding how to act, God can *only* choose what his wisdom determines as being 'the best'. In creating the world, God can *only* create the best possible world. Now if God is not able to do *anything* he wants, how is it then possible to say that God

---

quite problematic and has been in past years matter of intense debate. On the history, the meaning, and the problems of the rationalism-empiricism-model see for example Cottingham 1988: 1–4; Doney 1983; Engfer 1996; Perler 2003. On the ambivalence of the term 'rationalism', see Kondylis 1981: 36ff.

51   On the distinction between intellectualism and voluntarism, see also Schneewind 1996: 25ff.

is free? If the will is always determined by the representation of the good, how can we reasonably affirm that God has a *free will*?

As we will see throughout this work this is one of the main questions – indeed probably *the* main question – that trouble early critics of optimism and one of the fundamental motors of their criticisms. At the end of this chapter I will present briefly Leibniz's response to the question of how to make the Leibnizian concept of God compatible with a satisfactory account of divine freedom.

Before doing that, however, let us examine the other chief theoretical assumption of optimism: the idea of the existence of objective principles of reason to which rational beings and nature are subjected, and which establish both the direction of God's actions as well as the nature of the created world.

2.3   *The Principles of (Divine) Reason*

A central tenet of Leibniz's theory of divine agency – which was not stated explicitly in the previous section but is contained in what has been said about the Leibnizian concept of a rational God – is the idea that God acts following what Leibniz describes as 'first principles', 'propositions of eternal truth' or simply 'eternal truths'. Among them we find what I will call here 'principles of reason'.

Unlike philosophers like Descartes or Arnauld – or, as we will see in Chapter 2, Budde and Knoerr – Leibniz does not believe that the eternal truths were created by God and can be modified by acts of his will. For Leibniz the eternal truths, that is, the necessary and immutable principles that determine the essential nature of things – "the laws of the universe" (NE IV, 11.14/GP V 429) – are uncreated, independent of God's decrees. Indeed, according to the Leibnizian account, the eternal truths offer the moral and logical framework in which God's actions take place. As well as the created world, its creatures, the sciences, morals, etc., for Leibniz, God himself is also subjected to the parameters established by the eternal truths. As he writes in the *Theodicy*:

> The dominion of his [God's] will relates only to the exercise of his power, he gives effect outside himself only to that which he wills, and he leaves all the rest in the state of mere possibility. Thence it comes that this dominion extends only over the existence of creatures, and not over their essential being. God was able to create matter, a man, a circle, or leave them in nothingness, but he was not able to produce them without giving them their essential properties. He had of necessity to make man a rational animal and to give the round shape to a circle, since, according to his eternal ideas, independent of the free decrees of his will, the essence

of man lay in the properties of being animal and rational, and since the essence of the circle lay in having a circumference equally distant from the center as to all its parts. This is what has caused the Christian philosophers to acknowledge that the essences of things are eternal, and that there are propositions of eternal truth; consequently that the essences of things and the truth of the first principles are immutable. That is to be understood not only of theoretical but also of practical first principles, and of all the propositions that contain the true definition of creatures.

T, §183/ GP VI 224ff.[52]

Certain theoretical and practical "first principles", "propositions of eternal truth", thus establish the framework inside which God's actions (can) take place. Leibniz's God cannot just *want anything*; he cannot *do anything* that contradicts those eternal truths. The idea mentioned before – that the divine will is always determined by the representation of the good – corresponds to the general theory that God is always bound in his decisions and actions to the parameters founded by those eternal propositions or principles of reason.

This account could seem problematic. What does it mean to say that eternal truths are not created, that God is subjected to them, that, given the existence of such first principles, God cannot just want and do *anything*? Does this mean that Leibniz's universe must be understood as some kind of Platonist order in which even God must be subject to eternal forms? As I believe, Leibniz would answer by saying that God is not following anything *external* to himself when following the eternal truths. He is following *himself*, or, in other words, his own wisdom. Indeed, as Leibniz claims, the eternal truths exist in or, more exactly, are "the object of the divine intelligence" (T, §42/GP VI 126), of God's understanding.[53] And yet, as we will clearly see later, the doctrine of the eternal truths will be an important point of tension between Leibniz and his early critics.[54]

But which are those first principles or principles of reason exactly? This issue does not seem to be completely clear. There are two well known references by Leibniz that establish those principles as being (at least) two. In the *Theodicy* Leibniz writes:

---

[52] *Cf.* UOT/GP VI 305: "In reality we find that all things in the world take place according to the laws of eternal truths, not only geometrical but also metaphysical [...]".

[53] *Cf.* T, §20/GP VII 115; DM, §2/GP IV 428.

[54] For a more detailed examination of Leibniz's account of the eternal truths, as well as of the thorny discussion between the – apparently Cartesian – critics Budde and Knoerr and Leibniz concerning the nature of the eternal truths, see Chapter 2, 1, 1.2.

> [T]here are two great principles of our arguments. The one is the principle of *contradiction* [...], the other principle is that of the *determinant reason* [*principe* [...] *de la raison déterminante*].
>
> T, §44/GP VI 127

And similarly, in the *Monadology*:

> Our reasonings are based on two great principles: the *principle of contradiction* [...]. And the *principle of sufficient reason* [*de la raison suffisante*] [...].
>
> M, §§31–32/GP VI 612

According to Leibniz's explanation, the *Principle of Contradiction* states that "of two contradictory propositions the one is true, the other false" (T, §44/GP VI 127), or more particularly, permits us to judge as false "anything that involves contradiction" and as true "whatever is opposed or contradictory to what is false" (M, §31/GP VI 612).

The *Principle of Sufficient or Determinant Reason* (as we will see later, this distinction, apparently harmless for Leibniz, is used by a critic of optimism, Christian August Crusius, to fashion a somewhat subtle alternative to Leibnizian metaphysics[55]), as is well known, establishes that "*nothing is without a reason* (*nihil est sine ratione*) or *there is no effect without a cause*" (Look 2020), or as Leibniz writes, that "nothing ever comes to pass without there being a cause or at least a reason determining it". That cause gives a reason why something is "existent rather than non-existent", and why it is "in this wise rather than in any other". According to Leibniz, the Principle of Sufficient Reason "holds for all events, and a contrary instance will never be supplied". It therefore "suffers no exception", and even if we are often "insufficiently acquainted with these determinant reasons, we perceive nevertheless that there are such" (T, §44/GP VI 127).

Although the formulations of the Principle of Contradiction and of Sufficient Reason in both the *Theodicy* and the *Monadology* emphasize the importance of the two principles as principles of thought, Leibniz evidently thinks that they are valid in absolutely *all* aspects. Regarding particularly the Principle of Sufficient Reason, he thus writes to Clarke that "the move from mathematics to natural philosophy requires a further principle, namely the principle of the need for a sufficient reason, which says that for anything that is the case there is a reason why it should be so rather than otherwise." (LC,

---

55   *Cf.* Chapter 4.

L.II.1/GP VII 356). And as he had already written in 1679, the principle "must be considered one of the greatest and most fruitful of all human knowledge, for upon it is built a great part of metaphysics, physics, and moral science" (GP VII 301/Loemker 227). The Principle, as we will see in the following, is of central relevance for the theory of the best of all possible worlds. And as we will learn throughout this work and particularly in Chapter 4, Leibniz's theory of the universal validity of the Principle of Sufficient Reason will be strongly censured by critics of philosophical optimism.

Now, according to other commentators, Leibniz admits to more than only two fundamental principles. For Nicholas Rescher[56] there are *three* first principles in Leibniz's philosophy: the Principle of Sufficient Reason, the Principle of Identity (or Contradiction), and the so-called Principle of Perfection (or of the Best). And according to Brandon C. Look there are even more additional principles to which Leibniz bestows a central place in his thought. According to him:

> To these two great principles [of Sufficient Reason and of Contradiction] could be added four more: *the principle of the best, the predicate-in-notion principle, the principle of the identity of indiscernibles*, and *the principle of continuity*.
>
> LOOK 2020[57]

Given my main interest is to show that the concept of a rational God, which lies at the basis of the system of the best, implies that God is subjected to certain principles, I shall briefly examine the question which of those principles are essential to the theoretical foundation of optimism and I will suggest how those principles are connected to one another within this system.

According to what has been said previously, a kind of relaxed 'argumentative structure' of the proof of Leibniz's doctrine of the best world would look like something like this: The world exists and was created by God, who chose

---

56   *Cf.* Rescher 1979: 21ff.

57   The relationship among these principles, Look admits, is rather complicated: "Leibniz sometimes suggests that the principle of the best and the predicate-in-notion principle can be said to ground his 'two great principles'; at other times, however, all four principles seem to work together in a system of circular implication. And while the principle of the identity of indiscernibles is often presented in contemporary discussions in analytic metaphysics as a stand-alone axiom, Leibniz tells us that it follows from the two great principles. Finally, the principle or law of continuity is actually a principle that Leibniz takes from his work in mathematics and applies to the infinite hierarchy of monads in the world and to the quality of their perceptions; it appears to derive only tenuous support from the principle of sufficient reason" (Look 2020).

it among infinite possible worlds. According to Leibniz, God always acts for a reason. The creation of the world must therefore also respond to a reason. As has been said before, on different occasions, the reason for God's actions (or more exactly: the purpose of God action's – since the reasons for the actions of rational beings are final causes), is always the achievement of what is good, more specifically, of what is best. The world God chose among infinite possibilities must, therefore, be the best of all possible worlds.

This formulation depends on at least two propositions (apart from the 'evident facts' of the existence of our world and the reality of God): 'God always acts for a reason' and 'The reason for God's actions is always the achievement of what is best'. The first is clearly an instance of the Principle of Sufficient Reason. As I said before, Leibniz maintains the universal validity of the Principle – this means that the Principle of Sufficient Reason is also valid with regard to God. The second proposition corresponds to Rescher's third fundamental principle of Leibnizian philosophy: the *Principle of Perfection* or *of the Best*.

What the Principle of the Best states is obvious: God always acts in the best way possible. More refined versions could be: "God acts for the objectively best" (Copleston 1999: 288), or perhaps: "[A]s omnibenevolent (impeccable, all-perfect), God is bound by the principle of perfection (henceforth, POP) to *never prefer a less perfect ø over a more perfect ø*" (Steinberg 2007: 124). Leibniz believes that the statement 'God always acts in the best way possible' expresses a norm to which God is necessarily bound in his actions. At the beginning of the *Discourse on Metaphysics* Leibniz offers a kind of 'deduction' of the Principle of the Best from the notion of God as a perfect being. He writes:

> God is an absolutely perfect being. [...] [P]ower and knowledge are perfections, and God has them in unlimited form. It follows that the actions of God, who is supremely – indeed infinitely – wise, are completely perfect. This is not just metaphysical perfection, but also the moral kind.
> DM, §1/GP IV 427

And in other places he explains:

> God is supremely perfect, from which it follows that in producing the universe he chose the best possible design [...].
> PNG, §10/GP VI 603

> The love that we owe to God, above all things, is based (I think) on our grasp of the great truth that God always acts in the most perfect and desirable way possible.
> DM, §4/GP IV 429

> So it is enough to be sure of this about God: that he does everything for the best [...].
>
> DM, §5/GP IV 430[58]

The Principle of the Best represents an objective criterion for God's actions. It is, as Rescher comments, the "philosophic formulation of the theological principle of God's goodness" (Rescher 1979: 33). In accordance with Leibniz's theory of eternal truths the Principle is wholly independent of the divine will, i.e. God is so to speak *obliged* by his own nature to do what is objectively good or the best. Clearly, Leibniz opposes here the Cartesian idea that things are good *because* God creates them or decides that they are good.[59] For Leibniz things are good or the best objectively, in their own right. And the Principle of the Best stipulates that God subscribes in his actions to a "rule of goodness and perfection" (DM, §2/GP IV 427).[60]

Philosophical optimism, thus, assumes at least two 'great truths'. Or more exactly: Leibnizian philosophical optimism presupposes the reality of a God/'divine strategian'/creator whose actions are subjected to at least two 'great truths'. These are the Principle of Sufficient Reason and the Principle of Perfection or of the Best. The first is a logical principle that applies to all things possible and existent, including God himself. The second, which is an ethical principle, establishes a particular criterion of behavior for God. Philosophical optimism maintains that our world is the best of all possible worlds. How come? According to what has been said, the answer to that question must be something like this: God never acts without a reason (Principle of Sufficient Reason). That is, "since in the ideas of God there is an infinity of possible universes, and since only one can exist, there must be a sufficient reason for God's choice of that one – a reason that leads him to choose one rather than some other of the possible universes" (M, §53/GP VI 615f.). This reason, as we have seen in the previous lines, is always the achievement of the best (Principle of the Best). Given the factual existence of the world, the world must be the best of all possible worlds. For, as Leibniz writes, "if there were not the best

---

[58] See also DM, §19/GP IV 444ff., as well as the appendix to the *Theodicy* "Summary of the Controversy, Reduced to Formal Arguments", VIII/GP VI 385ff.

[59] On this respect see Chapter 2, 2.

[60] Rescher examines the question whether the Principle of Perfection/of the Best is just a version of the Principle of Sufficient Reason. For several commentators (among the ones mentioned by Rescher are Couturat and Russell) consider the pair of principles constituted by Sufficient Reason and Contradiction complete. For Rescher this is not the case: in his view the Principle of Sufficient Reason "requires merely *that* a contingent true be analytic; the Principle of Perfection shows *how* this is the case" – the Principle of Perfection, so to speak, is a principle of "definiteness" that complements the Principle of Sufficient Reason (Rescher 1979: 34f.).

(*optimum*) among all possible worlds, God would not have produced any" (T, §8/GP VI 107).

Now, if we remember Catherine Wilson's depiction of the 'standard interpretation' of optimism, the system of the best world depends on two principles: the Principle of Sufficient Reason and what she calls the *Principle of Plenitude*. What about that? Interestingly enough, the Principle of Plenitude does not appear in the lists of the 'fundamental principles' of Leibnizian philosophy I have mentioned so far. And still, for some commentators an additional principle seems to be required if we are to explain adequately the theoretical foundations of optimism. Thus, we have for example Wilson's account of the standard interpretation. ("The first, the principle of sufficient reason, entails that God's choice among possible worlds must have been made according to some criterion. This criterion then emerges as the principle of plenitude [...]" [Wilson 1983: 767]), as well as more drastic statements, like Arthur Lovejoy's straightforward claim:

> The foundation, then, of the usual eighteenth-century argument for optimism was the principle of plenitude.
> LOVEJOY 1936: 215

In its most summarized form, the Principle of Plenitude can be described as a principle according to which the best world is the 'fullest' world. The concept of 'Principle of Plenitude' was coined by Lovejoy in his famous classic *The Great Chain of Being* (Lovejoy 1936) in order to label a doctrine that, according to him, is one of the guiding ideas of Western thought since Plato. As Lovejoy explains, he uses the term to cover

> not only the thesis that the universe is a *plenum formarum* [fullness of forms] in which the range of conceivable diversity of *kinds* of living things is exhaustively exemplified, but also any other deductions from the assumption that no genuine potentiality of being can remain unfulfilled, that the extent and abundance of the creation must be as great as the possibility of existence and commensurate with the productive capacity of a 'perfect' and inexhaustible Source, and that the world is the better, the more things it contains.
> LOVEJOY 1936: 52[61]

---

61   *Cf.* Mercer 2001: 180ff.

As we saw previously, Wilson depicts the Principle as maintaining that "[a] world with both men and lions is [...] preferable to a world with men only, whatever the particular disadvantages of lions" (Wilson 1983: 767). Certainly, the Principle is not really *about* men and lions (at least not directly), but Wilson's point is manifest: according to the Principle, the more creatures and phenomena in the world, the better the world. Or as she explains in another place: the best universe is the one that is "as full as possible" (Wilson 2018).

Together with the *fullness* of the universe the Principle also seems to establish the *variety* of creatures as a criterion of the superiority of the world. According to Leibniz:

> [I]f there were only rational creatures, there would be less good. Midas proved to be less rich when he had only gold. And besides, wisdom must vary. To multiply one and the same thing only would be superfluity and poverty too. To have a thousand well-bound Vergils in one's library, always to sing the airs from the opera of Cadmus and Hermione, to break all the china in order only to have cups of gold, to have only diamond buttons, to eat nothing but partridges, to drink only Hungarian or Shiraz wine – would one call that reason? Nature had need of animals, plants, inanimate bodies; there are in these creatures, devoid of reason, marvels which serve for exercise of the reason. [...] Therefore, since God's wisdom must have a world of bodies, a world of substances capable of perception and incapable of reason; since, in short, it was necessary to choose from all the things possible what produced the best effect together, and since vice entered in by this door, God would not have been altogether good, altogether wise if he had excluded it.
>
> T, §124/GP VI 179

Lovejoy refers to other passages in which Leibniz addresses the idea that in his decision to create the world, God was guided by the principle that a world that contains the most possible existences is better. In a letter of 1714 Leibniz writes: "The actual universe is the collection of all possible existences, that is, of that which composes the richest arrangement [*composé*]" (Letter to Bourguet, December 1714/GP III 573). And in a letter of 1679 to Malebranche, Leibniz had stated even clearer:

> We must also say that God makes the most things he can, and what obliges him to seek simple laws is precisely the necessity to find a place for as many things as can be put together; if he made use of other laws, it would

> be like trying to make a building with round stones, which makes us lose more space than they occupy.
>
> LEIBNIZ TO MALEBRANCHE, June 22, 1679/GP I 331/Loemker 211

The Principle of the Best can be understood as a specification of the Principle of Sufficient Reason (God's sufficient reason is the realization of the best).[62] In turn, according to what has been said the Principle of Plenitude seems to be a kind of specification or concretization of the Principle of the Best. God, according to this principle, always acts for the best. But what does 'the best' exactly mean for Leibniz's God? If the Principle of Plenitude subsists, if it is right, and if Leibniz really accepts it as a fundamental principle that institutes a rule for the divine election of the world, then the best world is the fullest world, the world that contains the "most things" that God could create. Lovejoy explains this very clearly when he concludes that for Leibniz:

> The 'good', then, for the sake of which, and by reason of which, things exist, is simply existence itself – the actualization of essence; and the world that in the eternal nature of things was necessitated to be, was the world in which 'the quantity of existence is as greatest as possible'.
>
> LOVEJOY 1936: 179–80

"The greatest possible quantity of existence" says Lovejoy. Now Leibniz also talks in his letter to Malebranche about "simple laws" that govern that richest arrangement of things. And this we have heard before: it obviously reminds us of Nicholas Rescher's definition of the 'best' or 'most perfect world' as the world which "exhibits the greatest variety of its contents (richness of phenomena), consonant with the greatest simplicity of its laws" (Rescher 1979: 29). For Rescher, indeed, this is *the* criterion that determines which world must be actualized by God (although Rescher does not speak of it as an additional principle). For commentators like Christa Mercer the Principle of Plenitude (or, as she names it: the "Principle of Harmonized Plenitude") must be understood exactly in this way, as maintaining that the best world is not only the one in which the quantity of existence is as greatest as possible, but also the one in which the governing rules are the simplest. The Principle, she explains, "assumes that the goodness of the world is partly a function of the variety of the beings within it, partly a function of the sum of the goodness of the beings within it, and partly a function of the order among those beings [...]"

---

62   *Cf.* Rescher 1979: 34f.

(Mercer 2001: 184). And in a paper written together with Robert C. Sleigh Jr. Mercer clarifies more extensively Leibniz's understanding of plenitude:

> In an important essay of 1676, entitled "On the Secrets of the Sublime" he [Leibniz] proclaims: "After due consideration I take as a principle the harmony of things: that is, that the greatest amount of essence that can exist does exist" (A VI iii 472). In order to attribute as much goodness as possible to the universe, Leibniz assumes that essences are good and then reasons that the more (compatible) essences in the world the better. It is important that Leibniz is not just after the greatest possible number of essences, he wants to make every positive aspect of the world as full as possible. He states: "It follows from this principle that there is no vacuum among forms; also that there is no vacuum in place and time [...] From which it follows that there is no assignable time in which something did not exist nor is there a place which is not full" (A VI iii 473). Although he is uncertain about the exact consequences of this "plenitude of the world", he thinks that "it is true that any part of matter, however small, contains an infinity of creatures, i.e., is a world" (A VI iii 474). It becomes clear in the course of the essay that this commitment to plenitude is only a part of the principle of harmony and that proper maximization will occur only within the context of a divinely arranged elegant simplicity. [...] The suggestion is that God's creation combines the greatest possible elegance with the greatest possible variety.
> MERCER & SLEIGH 1995: 86

According to the interpretation that includes the so-called Principle of Plenitude in the list of fundamental principles of optimism, the system of the best (or better: God's decision of creating the world) rests therefore not on two but rather on three propositions: i) God always acts for a reason (Principle of Sufficient Reason); ii) God's reason for acting is the achievement of the best (Principle of the Best); iii) for the particular case of creation, the best world is the world with the greatest amount of existence possible and the simplest governing laws (Principle of Plenitude). *This* is what it means that Leibniz's God, as 'divine strategian', chooses the best world among all worlds possible, guided by principles of reason that determine how chooses.

And yet it must be clear that this account is just a possible interpretation of the exact theoretical nature of philosophical optimism. As we saw previously, Donald Rutherford offers an interpretation of the notion of the best world that goes somewhat further than the variety-order-combination-theory. This interpretation seemed to be more complex than that two-factor standard-theory of perfection. If Rutherford's reading is right, then the Principle of Plenitude is only one more element that God takes into consideration when identifying the best possible world, but not a definitive and sufficient 'third principle' of optimism.

And there are of course other questions concerning the status and scope of the Principle of Plenitude. For example: does the Principle imply that God created *everything* that was possible, i.e. does it imply that there are no non-actualized possibilities?[63] And why must actuality necessarily be better than potentiality? And which is the exact relationship between the Principle of Plenitude and the so-called Principle of Continuity, which maintains that there are no leaps in nature, no abrupt transitions of level in the hierarchy of beings in the universe?[64] I will not examine these questions in this work, as they do not concern my main interest directly. Indeed, as we will see in the forthcoming chapters, early critics of philosophical optimism either direct their arguments against the *general* idea that God's will is bounded by the representation of the good and by principles of reason, or, if they manifest a particular disgust towards a particular principle of reason, this is, of course, the Principle of Sufficient Reason – evidently the chief offender in the question concerning divine freedom. This question was mentioned in the previous section, and now, after examining the idea of principles of reason to which God himself is subjected, it comes to the fore again with particular strength. To this question and Leibniz's answer to it, I will direct my attention in the next and final section of this chapter.

3   The Problem of Freedom and Leibniz's Theory of Hypothetical Necessity

3.1   *Is Leibniz's God Really Free?*

In the preceding sections I mentioned a special problem that seems to follows from Leibniz's account of God: the problem of divine freedom. As we will see in Chapter 2 Leibniz believes the human mind imitates God's mind, claiming that human beings are "mirrors of God" (DM, §9/GP IV 434). In view of that, in the context of Leibnizianism, the problem of freedom obviously applies to rational creatures as well. Nevertheless, given the aims of this work and the fact that early critics of philosophical optimism underline in particular the *theological* menaces of Leibniz's thought – as we will see in the next chapters –

---

63   This is at least what Lovejoy seems to suggest. *Cf.* Lovejoy 1936: 52.
64   On the relationship between both principles see Anapolitanos 1999: 60ff.; Lovejoy 1936: 55ff.

I will focus on the questions and paradoxes concerning specifically *God's* freedom of choice.

In the last two sections, after examining Leibniz's account of divine nature, we arrived at a series of claims about the way in which Leibniz's God operates. Some of these claims are:

– Leibniz's God is an essentially rational being. This means that his actions are always determined by reasons.
– In particular, given God's nature, his will is always determined by the perception of the good provided by the divine intellect. The achievement of the best is always God's reason to act.
– The idea that God is an essentially rational being implies, thus, that God is subjected to what has been called 'principles of reason' – eternal truths which are wholly independent of the divine will and are universally valid.
– Regarding the particular case of the creation of the world, God's actions take place in the framework established by the Principle of Sufficient Reason, the Principle of the Best, and – according to some interpretations – the so-called Principle of Plenitude.

These claims amount to the same thing: God, as a rational being, is determined to act according to certain principles, one of them explicitly specifying that God's actions always follow reasons. Once God, by virtue of his understanding, identifies the best possible world among an infinite series of possible worlds, he is obliged (by virtue of his own nature and the mentioned principles of reason) to decide to create *this* world, since as Leibniz writes: "the will of God is not independent of the rules of wisdom" (T, §193/GP VI 231). Once he identifies it, God *can neither want nor create another world* different from the best – he has, literally speaking, no other choice.

For Leibniz, the view that God or any other rational being acts according to reasons is uncontroversial. For him, as I mentioned previously, the whole idea of a rational agent who is undetermined in his actions is absurd, the notion of an act completely indifferent to the will meaningless. This kind of indeterminacy of the will that Leibniz rejects is called by him *'indifference of equipoise'*. He writes about it in the *Theodicy*:

> There is therefore a freedom of contingency or, in a way, of indifference, provided that by 'indifference' is understood that nothing necessitates us to one course or the other; but there is never any *indifference of equipoise*, that is, where all is completely even on both sides, without any inclination towards either.
>
> T, §46/GP VI 128[65]

---

65   *Cf.* T, §§132, 199ff., 302ff./GP VI 183f., 234ff., 296ff.

Against some later Scholastics, like the Molinists, who according to Leibniz maintain the complete arbitrariness of actions,[66] against Descartes's theory of eternal truths that depend on God's decrees,[67] or against Bayle's skeptical comments concerning the incompatibility between the concept of freedom and a theory of action similar to Leibniz's,[68] Leibniz argues that an agent following no reasons at all in his decisions, whose will was not 'guided', 'directed', 'inclined' in some way or another by his knowledge, would not be able to decide or act, since nothing could steer his will in one specific direction.

> It is not to be imagined, however, that our freedom consists in an indetermination or an indifference of equipoise, as if one must needs be inclined equally to the side of yes and of no and in the direction of different courses, when there are several of them to take. This equipoise in all directions is impossible: for if we were equally inclined towards the courses A, B and C, we could not be equally inclined towards A and towards not A. This equipoise is also absolutely contrary to experience, and in scrutinizing oneself one will find that there has always been some cause or reason inclining us towards the course taken, although very often we be not aware of that which prompts us [...]
> T, §35/GP VI 122f.

> But, as I have declared more than once, I do not admit an indifference of equipoise, and I do not think that one ever chooses when one is absolutely indifferent. Such a choice would be, as it were, mere chance, without determining reason, whether apparent or hidden. But such a chance, such an absolute and actual fortuity, is a chimera which never occurs in nature.
> T, §303/GP VI 296f.

Leibniz's point seems to be – at least – reasonable: A will without inclination would be a will without content: it could not want anything at all. Further, Leibniz maintains, even when we think we are acting without reasons, with complete indifference, we are always following an inclination: indifference is only *apparent* indifference.[69]

'Determined', 'subjected', 'obliged', 'guided', 'directed', 'inclined', etc. This is then the situation, according to Leibniz, in which a rational agent finds himself

---

66 *Cf.* Chappell, Della Rocca & Sleigh 1998.
67 See for example DM, §2/GP IV 428.
68 See for example T, §§227ff., 302ff./GP VI 253ff., 296ff.
69 See for example NE, II, 21.47/GP V 183.

when deciding how to act, or more exactly, the kind of relationship between the rational agent's decision and his knowledge of what is good. It should, therefore, come as no surprise that Bayle or Clarke, or for that matter almost all the critics that will be examined in the next chapters, consider either that Leibniz's theory of rational agency is problematic or that it leads ultimately to the denial of freedom. Their concerns *also* seem to be – at least – reasonable: If God is always determined in his actions, if his will is always subjected to rational principles and the perception of the best, if – for the particular case of creation – once God identified the best among all possible worlds he could not but create this world, is God *really* free?

For Leibniz, he definitely is. Leibniz explains, for example:

> The decrees of God are always free, even though God be always prompted thereto by reasons which lie in the intention towards good: for to be morally compelled by wisdom, to be bound by the consideration of good, is to be free.
>
> T, §236/GP VI 258–9

That an agent is 'free' does not mean, for Leibniz, that he does not act for (good) reasons. The criticism according to which Leibniz denies freedom, because he maintains that the actions of rational agents are never undetermined, never indifferent, seems to presuppose that the only alternative for an agent to be free is for his will to be completely undetermined. But for Leibniz that is precisely the problem: for him 'freedom' is not a synonym of 'indifference' and to be free is not contrary to be determined:

> I would not take 'free' and 'indifferent' for one and the same thing, and would not place 'free' and 'determined' in antithesis. One is never altogether indifferent with an indifference of equipoise; one is always more inclined and consequently more determined on one side than on another: but one is never necessitated to the choice that one makes. I mean here a *necessity* absolute and metaphysical; for it must be admitted that God, that wisdom, is prompted to the best by a *moral* necessity. It must be admitted also that one is necessitated to the choice by a hypothetical necessity, when one actually makes the choice.
>
> T, §132/GP VI 184

As we have seen, there is always a "prevailing reason which prompts the will to its choice". The will, as Leibniz writes, "is never prompted to action save by the representation of the good, which prevails over the opposite representations. This is admitted even in relation to God, the good angels and the souls in bliss".

And even though the will of rational creatures is guided by the knowledge of what is good, "it is acknowledged that they are none the less free" (T, §45/GP VI 127–8). Indeed, according to Leibniz's understanding of the notion of freedom, to be bound, guided, prompted, etc. by the representation of the good is *exactly* what it means to be free:

> The decrees of God are always free, even though God be always prompted thereto by reasons which lie in the intention towards good: for to be morally compelled by wisdom, to be bound by the consideration of good, is to be free; it is not compulsion in the metaphysical sense.
> T, §236/GP VI 258–9

> For when a wise being, and especially God, who has supreme wisdom, chooses what is best, he is not the less free upon that account: on the contrary, it is the most perfect liberty, not to be hindered from acting in the best manner.
> LC, L.V.7/GP VII 390

There *is*, therefore, a kind of necessity in God's actions, namely a:

3.2 *Moral or Hypothetical Necessity*

Leibniz, as has been explained before, is certain of the existence and the universal validity of objective and immutable principles of reason, to which even God is subjected in his decisions and actions. Indeed the whole idea of the essential rationality of God, his creatures, and the world – in which Leibniz believes resolutely – lies in the acceptance of the existence of such principles. The Principle of Sufficient Reason establishes that *nothing is without a reason*; it "holds for all events" and "suffers no exception" (T, §44/GP VI 127). Thus, God's actions also happen for a reason (according to the Principle of the Best, this reason is simply the achievement of the best) and given that, in the case of the creation of the world, the existence of a best world is a fact for Leibniz, God's actions are in that sense *necessary*. Now, as Leibniz explains in the passages referred earlier, it is not a necessity or compulsion in the "metaphysical" or "absolute" sense we are dealing with here. God – indeed every rational agent – is "prompted to the best by a *moral*" or "hypothetical necessity" (T, §132/GP VI 184).

Given his rationalism and, more exactly, his acceptance of the Principle of Sufficient Reason, Leibniz must also accept the necessity of divine actions: If God's decision to create the world did not follow from some reason, if it "did not issue from some type of necessity" then, as Kenneth Seeskin correctly explains, it would be impossible to explain God's actions, "his decision would be wholly arbitrary and the existence of the world unintelligible" (Seeskin 1994: 324). That is, neither God nor the world could be described as rational. Further, as I commented earlier, Leibniz holds that, if there were no reason for God's actions, God would not, indeed *could* not, act at all. And yet, Leibniz believes, God *is* free. Leibniz therefore *needs* an additional or, so to speak, alternative kind of necessity that, in spite of rendering actions necessary, guarantees in some manner (at least from a Leibnizian point of view) the contingency of those actions. This is the role of moral necessity.

Leibniz describes the kind of necessity that God's actions imply as follows:

> God is prompted to all good; the good, and even the best, inclines him to act; but it does not compel him, for his choice created no impossibility in that which is distinct from the best [...] There is therefore in God a freedom that is exempt not only from constraint but also from necessity; for it is a moral necessity that the wisest should be bound to choose the best.
>
> T, §230/GP VI 255

> To get straight about this we must distinguish between absolute necessity and hypothetical necessity. We must also distinguish between the necessity something has because its opposite implies a contradiction (called 'logical', 'metaphysical', or 'mathematical' necessity) and the moral necessity that is at work when a wise being chooses the best and when any mind follows its strongest inclination. [...] As for moral necessity: this doesn't detract from freedom either. For when a wise being, and especially God, who has supreme wisdom, chooses what is best, he is not the less free upon that account: on the contrary, it is the most perfect liberty, not to be hindered from acting in the best manner.
>
> LC, L.V.4ff./GP VII 389ff.

God's actions, therefore, seem to be 'only' morally necessary, because God always chooses what is best. As has been explained, God cannot but choose the best – he can choose only the best. According to Leibniz, it is *precisely because* God has no other option but choosing the best once he has identified it, that the necessity of his actions is not absolute. Does this make any sense at all?

At least for Leibniz, it does. The secret lies in the way in which one decides to interpret the proposition 'God can do only what is best'. Critics of the Leibnizian theory of freedom of choice stress the concept of *'only'*. Rather, Leibniz would seem to want to say, we must focus upon *'the best'*. This becomes clearer when we examine *what kind of reason or cause* the perception of the good/the best is.

For Leibniz the hypothetical or moral character of the necessity of actions lies in the fact that those actions are not determined by efficient or moving causes, but by *final causes*, that is, by the aim or purpose of those actions – the best. Teleological aims, as determining causes of actions, surely introduce a kind of necessity into actions. For Leibniz, however, this is not an absolute necessity that completely erases both the possibility of other courses of action and the internal, individual self-determination of the agent.

Leibniz's distinction between absolute (or logical, or metaphysical) and hypothetical (or moral) necessity explains how it is possible that within a system governed by the Principle of Sufficient Reason, the choices of the will can still be described as contingent and, thus, as free. Metaphysical necessity, Leibniz writes, is "absolutely necessary and its contrary implies a contradiction". For its part, hypothetical or moral necessity "is not necessary nor absolutely, but only *ex hypothesi*, and, so to speak, accidentally. It doesn't bring us to *It is necessary that P*, but only to *Given Q, it follows necessarily that P* [...]" (DM, §13/GP IV 437).[70] Its contrary doesn't imply a contradiction. Rational agents act for the purpose of achieving the good and for this reason, Leibniz maintains, their actions are free.

But let us examine this more closely. According to Leibniz, three conditions are required for freedom: intelligence, spontaneity, and contingency.[71] God's decision to create the world is *intelligent*, since the action of seeking the good is based on the perception of the good provided by the understanding. It is also a *spontaneous* action, as it follows God's *decision* to achieve the good. As Leibniz explains, the actions of rational agents are spontaneous since their "source is in him who acts" (T, §301/GP VI 295): we are masters over our actions.[72] Further, God's actions are *contingent*. But why, one can ask, if for example in the case of the creation of the world only one course of action was possible? Leibniz's explanation seems to be: actions are contingent because their non-occurring is nevertheless possible. Certainly, God could not decide

---

70   *Cf.* T, §349/GP VI 321.
71   See for example: T, §288/GP VI 288. *Cf.* Blumenfeld 1994; Jolley 2005: 125ff.
72   Certainly this 'mastery' over our own actions is ambivalent, as Leibniz admits: "Thus it is that our actions and our wills depend entirely upon us. It is true that we are not directly the masters of our will, although we be its cause; for we do not choose volitions, as we choose our actions by our volitions. Yet we have a certain power also over our will, because we can contribute indirectly towards willing another time that which we would fain will now, as I have here already shown: that, however, is no *velleity*, properly speaking. There also we have a mastery, individual and even perceptible, over our actions and our wills, resulting from a combination of spontaneity with intelligence" (T, §301/GP VI 295).

to create another world – and yet another world is *possible* in itself. The contingency of actions thus seems to consist in the fact that, for every action, another course of action would have been possible in itself. As Leibniz writes in an appendix to the *Theodicy*:

> Nevertheless, although his will is always indefectible and always tends towards the best, the evil or the lesser good which he rejects will still be possible in itself. Otherwise the necessity of good would be geometrical (so to speak) or metaphysical, and altogether absolute; the contingency of things would be destroyed, and there would be no choice. But necessity of this kind, which *does not destroy the possibility of the contrary*, has the name by analogy only [...] This necessity is called moral, because for the wise what is necessary and what is owing are equivalent things; and when it is always followed by its effect, as it indeed is in the perfectly wise, that is, in God, one can say that it is a happy necessity.
> T, "Summary of the Controversy, Reduced to Formal Arguments" VIII/GP VI 386; my italics[73]

The fact that the cause of rational actions is the *purpose* of achieving the good guarantees the presence of the three stated conditions of freedom: the desire of achieving the good results from the *intelligence*, that is from the knowledge of the good (for the case of creation: the identification of the best possible world); that knowledge makes possible the decision of attaining the good, i.e. makes possible the *spontaneity* of the action; and given that the existence of the best and its perception does not exclude the possibility of a lesser good or of evil (or of another possible world), actions are *contingent*. God's decision is therefore free. It seems to be in this way that we have to understand Leibniz's talk about the way in which final causes "incline" but do not "compel" an agent to act:

> The free substance is self-determining and that according to the motive of good perceived by the understanding, which inclines it without compelling it: and all the conditions of freedom are comprised in these few words.
> T, §288/GP VI 288[74]

---

[73] *Cf.* DM, §30/GP IV 454: "Absolutely speaking, our will is in a state of indifference, as opposed to necessity: it has the power to do otherwise, or to suspend its action altogether, each alternative being and remaining possible."

[74] *Cf.* T, §45/GP VI 127–8; NE, II, 21.12, 49/GP V 162, 184.

The Leibnizian concept of moral or hypothetical necessity, this major notion in Leibniz' theory of freedom and rational agency, has been the subject of countless controversies and criticisms, which cannot be examined here.[75] Moral necessity, of course, is itself not unproblematic. The thorny question at the end remains always the same: does the introduction of the complex concept of moral necessity really satisfy the requirements of freedom? No matter how we try to 'minimize' the character of the necessity of divine actions, if, at the end of the day, God, when creating the world, had only *one* option, can he really be described as a free agent? For Leibniz, as I pointed out previously, hypothetical necessity is not only *compatible* with freedom. For him, to be determined by the purpose of the best is exactly what it *means* to be free ("The decrees of God are always free; even though God be always prompted thereto by reasons which lie in the intention towards good: for to be morally compelled by wisdom, to be bound by the consideration of good, is to be free [...]" [T, §236/GP VI 258–9][76]).

And yet, as we will see throughout the following chapters, the problem of divine freedom remains a key concern for Leibniz's critics, perhaps even *the* main concern behind early criticisms and rejections of philosophical optimism.

---

75 For both clarifying and critical discussions of Leibniz's theory of necessity and contingence, as well of the concept of hypothetical/moral necessity, see for example Blumenfeld 1994; Johnson 1954; Adams 1994: 9–52 and 2005; Murray 2005; Seeskin 1994.
76 *Cf.* T, §132/GP VI 183–4; NE, II, 21.49/GP V 184.

CHAPTER 2

Eternal Truths, the Choice of the Best, and the Almighty Reality of Sin: Budde and Knoerr's *Doctrinae orthodoxae de origine mali* (1712)

The first extensive critique of Leibniz's philosophical optimism is the theological dissertation *Doctrinae orthodoxae de origine mali contra recentiorum quorundam hypotheses modesta assertio* (*A Modest Statement of Orthodox Doctrine Concerning the Origin of Evil, in Opposition to Certain Recent Hypotheses*), published in Jena just two years after the publication of the *Theodicy*. The work was written by Georg Christian Knoerr (or "Knörr") (1691–1762), who after his theological studies in Jena would eventually become librarian under Ludwig Rudolph, Duke of Brunswick-Lüneburg and later court counselor under Emperor Karl VI in Vienna.[1] Knoerr wrote under the supervision of the great Lutheran theologian and philosopher Johann Franz Budde (1667–1729), who worked as professor of moral philosophy in the University of Halle until 1705, when he began teaching theology in the University of Jena.

Budde's views in philosophy have been described as 'eclectic'.[2] He recognized Descartes's central role in the development of modern philosophy and, apparently following Christian Thomasius (1655–1728), opposed radically the doctrine of Spinoza, considering him – very much in the spirit of his time[3] – an atheist. Out of the same religious concern, Budde also rejected Leibniz's and Wolff's rationalism, and wrote a series of criticisms against the latter, to which Wolff responded. They were published in 1724 as *Bedencken über die Wolffianische Philosophie mit Anmerckungen von Christian Wolffen* (*Objections Against Wolff's Philosophy, With Remarks by Christian Wolff*).[4] It is not clear, however, to what extent the contents of the *Doctrinae* could have been influenced directly by Budde's own philosophical views, since Budde never wrote an important criticism of Leibnizian optimism or the *Theodicy*.

---

1 On Knoerr's life and works see Doering 1832, vol. 2: 145–6.
2 On Budde's life and works see Abashnik 2010; Frank 1876; Stolzenburg 1979.
3 *Cf.* Chapter 3, 2, 2.1.
4 For a brief but informative exposition of Budde's critical position towards Wolffianism see Israel 2002: 544ff.

The text of the *Doctrinae* is divided into three chapters.[5] The first two are devoted to the exposition of the authors' positive considerations regarding the origin of evil and to the reply of possible objections to those considerations. Budde and Knoerr's account of the origin and nature of the evils of the world correspond in its main lines to the traditional Christian, i.e. Augustinian solution to the problem of evil: Evil is ultimately the result of the misuse of freedom on the part of rational creatures. Moral evil, or sin, is the direct outcome of the abuse of freedom; physical evil is God's just punishment for the sinful actions of rational creatures. God permits the committing of sin in order to guarantee the freedom of his creatures. Yet, he is not directly responsible for the emergence of evil, as this responsibility falls solely on rational creatures. Thus Budde and Knoerr write: "*Unde ergo malum? Creaturis intelligentibus*" – "Where does evil come from? From intelligent creatures" (*Doctrinae*, I, §9 [8]).[6] Although this view shares important doctrinal premises with the Leibnizian theodicy, it also entails a spirited rejection of concepts central to Leibniz's thought like the notion of metaphysical evil and the best of all possible worlds, as well as of theoretical assumptions like the doctrine of uncreated eternal truths and a rationalist understanding of the divine nature. All of which results in a radical distancing from the optimist metaphysical mindset. The third chapter (pp.63–96) of the *Doctrinae* contains the examination of central tenets of the *Theodicy* and the critique of philosophical optimism. In this chapter I will focus on this part of Budde and Knoerr's treatise.

In the following section, I will examine what I consider are the three most important and intellectually challenging aspects of Budde and Knoerr's account: first, the critical evaluation of the concept of metaphysical evil, together with the rejection of the Leibnizian rationalist theory of uncreated eternal truths. This rejection, as we will see, implies from Budde and Knoerr's side an understanding of eternal truths and of the divine nature that resembles a Cartesian approach to those problems – although they never mention the possible sources of their theological and metaphysical views. Second, the critique of the theory of the divine choice of the best world among possibles. And third, Budde and Knoerr's counter-optimistic considerations regarding the spoiled character of the world after the emergence of evil through human sin and the pertinence of describing our world as the best of all possible worlds.

---

5 On the *Doctrinae* see Fonessu 1994: 137; 2006: 756, and especially Lorenz 1997: 105–20. Lorenz's presentation of Budde and Knoerr's arguments against Leibniz, though rather descriptive and even uncritical, has been very valuable for this chapter.
6 On Budde and Knoerr's answer to the problem of evil see Fabbianelli 2003: 300f.; Lorenz 1997: 110ff.

As we will observe, Budde and Knoerr's criticism of optimism responds to both theoretical and theological concerns that are intimately connected to one another. Budde and Knoerr believe that optimism results in the denial of God's freedom of choice (understood as complete indeterminacy and indifference of the will). Indeed, for them, optimism advocates a particular understanding of God (namely as a rational being that can be explained by rational means and using rational categories, etc.) that is at odds with the real divine nature and subjects God to parameters and concepts that, ultimately, only limit his omnipotence and his freedom. Further, Budde and Knoerr stress eloquently the real and overwhelming presence of evil in the world in a kind of empirical pessimism and reject optimism by considering that it ignores the essentially mischievous character the world acquired after the first sin.

In the last section of the chapter, I will briefly address the central topic, already mentioned in the previous chapter, of the two seemingly consistent and mutually exclusive conceptions of God that Leibniz and Budde and Knoerr defend. I will also examine the question of how justified a criticism of theoretical theses can be that rests upon dogmatic presuppositions – as seems to be the case with Budde and Knoerr's criticism of optimism.

1 Two Conceptual Hazards: Metaphysical Evil and Uncreated Eternal Truths

1.1 *Metaphysical Evil or the Necessity of the Bad*

As I explained in Chapter 1, according to Leibniz, evil may be spoken of in three ways: as moral, physical, and what he calls 'metaphysical evil'.[7] Following the traditional Christian, Augustinian account, Leibniz describes moral evil as sin – the abuse of freedom by rational creatures – and physical evil – death, disease, natural disasters – as the just divine penalty for sin, that is, as the consequence of moral evil.[8] As for metaphysical evil, Leibniz describes it as the "original imperfection", the essential limitation of creatures *qua* creatures, which, ultimately, is what makes moral and physical evil possible.[9]

---

7 On this distinction see: T, §21/GP VI 116.
8 On the definition of physical evil as the result of moral evil ("one suffers evil because one does evil") see: T, §241/GP VI 261.
9 In the *Theodicy* we read: "For we must consider that there is an *original imperfection in the creature* before sin, because the creature is limited in its essence; whence ensues that it cannot know at all, and that it can deceive itself and commit other errors" (T, §20/GP VI 115). *Cf.* Rutherford 1995a: 10.

Many commentators have criticized Leibniz for introducing the concept of metaphysical evil. For example, as Maria Rosa Antognazza explains, it has been claimed that Leibniz's metaphysical evil does not correspond exactly to the Augustinian or Thomistic idea that evil arises from the mere *privation* of a perfection that a thing ought to have according to its nature (a privation which, in itself, does not necessarily render the thing evil), but seems to be more, namely the *negation* or the absence of a perfection, the essential 'not-having' of something that makes the thing prone to evil.[10] The criticism is therefore that this Leibnizian concept seems to imply that creatures are fundamentally evil for the mere reason of *being*, and moreover, that in the best of all possible worlds evil is necessary, i.e. that once they were created, rational beings were doomed to commit evil. The concept of metaphysical evil therefore seems to imply that creatures, "simply in virtue of not being gods, are in some sense intrinsically and inescapably evil, and that this partially, yet necessarily evil nature is the ultimate cause of any other evil" (Antognazza 2010: 114).

Whether this oft-made criticism of Leibnizian metaphysical evil is fair or not cannot be examined here. Important for us is the fact that Budde and Knoerr also consider, for similar reasons, the notion of metaphysical evil problematic. For them, the notion of metaphysical evil implies that evil belongs to the created world essentially and necessarily. Even worse: it implies that God, as creator, is ultimately responsible for evil, since the order he chose produces evil, so to speak, automatically.[11] Therefore, they stress the truth of the traditional Augustinian account that evil results solely from the abuse of freedom by rational creatures:

> [T]he one and only guilt and origin reside in the Fall of the creatures, and none in the creator. Everything [...] is convenient for the creatures; God, however, allows them to think freely, to will freely.
>
> [*Vides ergo, in creaturis lapsus unicam & solam residere culpam & originem, in creatore nullam.* [...] *Deus tamen, ut libere cogitent, libere velint, permisit.*]
>
> *Doctrinae*, I, §20 [21]

---

10   *Cf.* Antognazza 2014. The most important critics of Leibniz on this point that Antognazza mentions are Broad 1975; Russell 2005; Theis 1987. *Cf.* Latzer 1994.

11   Budde stresses this point again in his criticism of Wolffian metaphysics of 1724, the *Bedencken über die Wolffianische Philosophie*. He writes there: "If God had to choose necessarily the best world and this best world contained evil, evil must necessarily come from God. What follows from the idea not only that God is the creator of evil, but that evil is necessary, can be reflected upon by anyone" (*Bedencken*, § 6 [56]).

Thus, Budde and Knoerr ban any reference to other possible sources of evil, to a universal constitution that necessarily produces the bad, or to any kind of metaphysical '*Ur*-evil':

> Hence we see that the world, in its current state, in no way flows from God's pre-established harmony [...] The opportunities to sin [...] do not spring from the harmony of things, nor from God's idea, but from the creatures' evil [...]
>
> [*Hinc videmus mundum, prouti nunc est, ex praestabilita harmonia Dei nequaquam fluere* [...]*Occasiones autem peccandi, quae iam huic magis, alteri minus obveniunt, non ex harmonia rerum, non ex Dei idea, sed ex malo creaturarum culpa attracto gignuntur, de qua re inferius.*]
> Doctrinae, I, §21 [22–3][12]

The dismissal of the concept of metaphysical evil is a relevant tenet of Budde and Knoerr's censure of optimism, since it manifests a fundamental conceptual rejection of Leibniz's explanation of the origin of evil. Behind that dismissal, however, there lies a theoretical discussion that, as I believe, is the really interesting aspect of Budde and Knoerr's criticism, namely the examination of Leibniz's account of the *origin* of metaphysical evil – of the origin of the origin of evil, so to speak. This is the doctrine of uncreated eternal truths.

1.2   *Eternal Questions on Eternal Truths*

If, according to Leibniz, metaphysical evil makes moral and physical evil possible, what makes metaphysical evil possible, where does the "original imperfection" of creatures come from? For Budde and Knoerr the Leibnizian reply to that question is highly problematic. Leibniz writes in the *Theodicy*:

> It [the source of evil] must be sought in the ideal nature of the creature, in so far as this nature is contained in the eternal verities which are in the understanding of God, independently of his will.
> T, §20/GP VI 115

---

[12]   As Stefan Lorenz puts it, Budde and Knoerr reject the Leibnizian concept of metaphysical evil because it leads to the conclusion "that evil belongs to the world in such a constitutive manner that it could not be removed unless one would modify the whole existing world" (Lorenz 1997: 114). For Budde and Knoerr the traditional Augustinian theory of evil as *privatio* refers only to the free act of sinning which results from a moral mistake, not from the essential imperfection of human being; physical evil is God's just penalty for moral evil. *Cf.* Fabiannelli 2003: 300f.

According to Leibnizian rationalism the essential nature of creatures is determined by the so-called *eternal truths*. Setting aside the particulars and possible problems of this theory, which I already mentioned in Chapter 1 – and such problems certainly exist –[13] some of the most important of Leibniz's claims regarding the eternal truths are that they determine the essential nature of things;[14] they contain the determining reason and regulating principle of existent things – "the laws of the universe, in short" (NE IV, 11.14/GP V 427–8), and are immutable and necessary.[15]

Furthermore, concerning the relationship between God and the eternal truths, Leibniz maintains that the eternal truths exist in or, more exactly, are the object of God's understanding.[16] However – and this is probably the most interesting (and for Budde and Knoerr, definitely the most menacing) aspect of the account that Leibniz defends – the eternal truths were not brought into being by a creative act of God's will. They are *uncreated*. As Leibniz writes, the eternal truths

> [...] do not depend upon God's decrees – whatever the Cartesians may say of it.
> LEIBNIZ TO ARNAULD, 14 July 1686/GP II 49

Against the view – described as Cartesian by Leibniz – that "the eternal truths of metaphysics and geometry, and therefore also the rules of goodness, justice and perfection, are brought about by God's will", Leibniz therefore argues that the eternal truths exist independently of God's volition: "no more depending on his will than his intrinsic nature does" (DM, §2/GP IV 428).[17] Since, as we will see next, the complete independence of the eternal truths from the divine will is for Budde and Knoerr a most problematic feature of Leibnizian rationalist metaphysics, it may be useful to quote Leibniz's account more fully:

---

13   On this respect see Nadler 2008b: 184–216; Schlüssler 1992: 94ff.
14   T, §20/GP VI 115; M, §43/GP VI 614.
15   T, §183/GP VI 224–6.
16   T, §§20, 42/GP VI 115, 166–7; DM, §2/GP IV 428.
17   Leibniz rejects Descartes's account of eternal truths as a product of the divine will on the grounds that, if eternal truths were created by a voluntary decision of God, this would mean that God resembles a tyrant who acts without reason – an assumption that for Leibniz is utterly absurd. On Leibniz's criticism of the Cartesian doctrine of eternal truths see Devillairs 1998; Lorenz 1997: 69ff.; Marion 2007: 116ff.; Nadler 2008b: 196–200; Schmidt 2009: 116ff.

> The dominion of his [God's] will relates only to the exercise of his power, he gives effect outside himself only to that which he wills, and he leaves all the rest in the state of mere possibility. Thence it comes that this dominion extends only over the existence of creatures, and not over their essential being. God was able to create matter, a man, a circle, or leave them in nothingness, but he was not able to produce them without giving them their essential properties. He had of necessity to make man a rational animal and to give the round shape to a circle, since, according to his eternal ideas, independent of the free decrees of his will, the essence of man lay in the properties of being animal and rational, and since the essence of the circle lay in having a circumference equally distant from the centre as to all its parts. This is what has caused the Christian philosophers to acknowledge that the essences of things are eternal, and that there are propositions of eternal truth; consequently that the essences of things and the truth of the first principles are immutable. That is to be understood not only of theoretical but also of practical first principles, and of all the propositions that contain the true definition of creatures. These essences and these truths emanate from the same necessity of nature as the knowledge of God.
>
> T, §183/ GP VI 224ff.[18]

The eternal truths, understood as theoretical and practical first principles (i.e. both moral and logical, mathematical propositions) that determine the nature of things, are for Leibniz wholly independent of God's will. In fact, the divine will is itself subjected to the eternal truths, as they constitute the framework for all that is and can be, including God's choices and actions (hence Leibniz's belief that God is also subjected to the Principle of Sufficient Reason, the Principle of the Best, etc.).[19] Concerning the problem of evil, this means that the "original imperfection of creatures" (metaphysical evil), that for Leibniz makes sin (moral evil) and suffering (physical evil) possible, is like everything else, determined in the "region of the eternal truths", established by eternal principles that settle on the nature of created things, independently of God's will. Thus Leibniz writes that in that region of eternal truths "is found not only

---

18   *Cf.* M, §46/GP VI 614.
19   *Cf.* UOT/GP VI 305: "In reality we find that all things in the world take place according to the laws of eternal truths, not only geometrical but also metaphysical [...]. And this is true not merely generally, with respect to the reason, already explained, why the world exists rather than not exists and why it exists thus rather than otherwise; but even when we descend to the details we see that metaphysical laws hold good in a wonderful manner in the entire universe [...]". *Cf.* Chapter 1, 2, 2.3.

the primitive form of good, but also the origin of evil [...]" (T, §20/GP VI 115f). The eternal truths are therefore the cause of good, but also of evil, insofar as evil arises from the fundamental imperfection of created beings.[20]

Leibniz's account of the origin of evil clashes with Budde and Knoerr's understanding of the divine agency. Or rather: the Leibnizian account of the *eternal truths* clashes with that theory. For Budde and Knoerr, if there are eternal truths – more exactly, if these truths are such as Leibniz describes them, then God is not completely free. The basic thought behind this conviction goes something like this: if good and evil (or, for that matter, the essential nature of everything that exists) are determined by the eternal truths; if these eternal truths are independent of God's will, then good and evil (and the nature of everything that exists) do not depend ultimately and exclusively on God's choices.

As I will examine in more detail later, Budde and Knoerr defend a God whose choices are completely arbitrary and undetermined. For this reason, Leibniz's account of the nature of the eternal truths is completely unacceptable to them. The existence of eternal truths that were not established by God; truths which, on the contrary, determine God's behavior by setting both logical and moral parameters to his will, means, for Budde and Knoerr, that God's will is determined by something *external* to itself and is, thus, not free. To claim that there are eternal truths to which God must adjust his behavior means nothing else than to admit that God's decisions are under constraint:

> God wants what he wants in a sacred manner and chooses thus what corresponds to his holiness and his wisdom. For this reason, everything what God chooses is the best in a moral way [...]. It is not morally the best for itself, but on account of God's choice. God would have had something coactive exterior to him, which would have impelled him in such way that he could have not acted otherwise. This results from the opinion of those who maintain that the eternal truths are the reason and origin of evil in so far as they made sin, first, possible, and second, necessary for the best world.

---

20 On metaphysical evil as dependent on eternal truths and the ensuing problem of divine understanding as being ultimately the principle of evil, see Rateau 2008: 570–7. Rateau explains why Leibniz can indeed maintain his theory of eternal truths as the origin of evil with relatively little risk, despite its supposedly problematical character with regard to the dogma of divine infinite goodness and justice.

> [*Interim Deus quod vult, sancte & sapienter vult, & sic suae sanctitati & sapientiae quod conveniens est, eligit. Hinc quidquid Deus elegit, est moraliter quoque optimum & non potest non esse optimum, quia Deus elegit. Sed non est optimum moraliter per se, sed ob Dei electionem. Alias enim Deus extra se habuisset aliquid cogens, quod ut aliter rem agere non potuisset, illum impulisset. Quod ex illorum sententia fluit, qui autumant, veritates aeternas esse causam & originem mali in tantum, in quantum (1) faciunt peccatum possibile, (2) ad optimum mundum necessarium.*]
> *Doctrinae*, III, §5 [72]

Certainly, the Leibnizian account of the nature of the eternal truths is not unproblematic. Regarding the issue of their complete independence of "God's decrees" and particularly the fact that they are uncreated, traditional thorny questions – some of which Leibniz himself was very conscious of[21] – emerge necessarily. If the eternal truths do not depend on God, what makes them *true*?[22] Does this mean the eternal truths make *themselves* true? And if so, are they therefore some kind of Platonic Forms that God contemplates and which determine – or more exactly *limit* – God's actions? And does this mean that God, in the end, is as limited as the Platonic Demiurge?[23] No doubt, these problems, as well as Leibniz's possible replies to them must be taken seriously by any examination of Leibniz's theory of the eternal truths. It is not my interest to offer that kind of examination here. As I commented in Chapter 1, Leibniz probably would have rejected those questions by maintaining that they result from a misunderstanding of God's nature: the eternal truths certainly determine God's actions. But that just means that God's rationality, God *himself*, determines his own actions.

Still, one can ask: Does Budde and Knoerr's criticism really do justice to Leibniz's claims about the workings of God? Does the existence of laws and first principles that model God's behavior but, nevertheless, are in *his* understanding, necessarily mean that there is "something coactive *exterior* to him"? One could say, and certainly Leibniz would say, that it is absurd to argue that because God's actions of will follow the parameters given by *his own*

---

21 *Cf.* T, §184/GP VI 226–7.
22 This problem is addressed explicitly by Budde and Knoerr: "Truth is a representation, [and] a representation [is] necessarily is grounded in some *thing*. Therefore, what grounds the eternal truths besides the divine will? Some necessity, a fate that is therefore outside of God? Some agreement of possible things? Where does this agreement come from? From the nature of things? The nature of things is grounded in God's will" (*Doctrinae*, III, §5 [73]).
23 These problems were suggested to me by Stephen Zylstra.

understanding, he is obliged by something *external*. God's understanding *is* also God. Further, as I commented earlier, for Leibniz God is free *precisely* because he is "prompted to action by the representation of the good" (T, §45/GP VI 127), provided to him in his understanding, "morally compelled by his wisdom" (T, §237/GP VI 258). Despite the real problems of the Leibnizian theory of the eternal truths, Leibniz's definition of freedom seems to be able to resist the criticisms of those who maintain that to say that God's will is determined implies the denial of divine freedom. (Of course, if we want to go further into the real nature of the conflict, we need only mention that for Budde and Knoerr, who define freedom as complete indeterminacy of the will, Leibniz's definition is simply nonsense. The important topic of inconsistent definitions and presuppositions will be examined at the end of the chapter.)

Thus, in a sense (in a *Leibnizian* sense at least) one might feel that Budde and Knoerr construct a Leibnizian enemy that does not correspond fully to Leibniz's own teachings or, more exactly, to the consequences of these teachings. This feeling will emerge again in the course of the next pages.

In any case, the theory of eternal truths presupposed by the Leibnizian genealogy of evil seems to be for Budde and Knoerr more noxious than the specific concept of metaphysical evil. To say that there are objective logical, mathematical, moral criteria that exist and are valid independently of God's will amounts, for them, to dangerously limitting the divine freedom of choice. Their solution is quite radical: if the divine will is to be free, that is – they would say – *really* free; if God is to be seen as the most perfect being, then the eternal truths (whose existence Budde and Knoerr are not willing to deny) cannot be independent of God's volition. "The nature of things is grounded in God's will" [*Rerum natura in Dei voluntate fundatur.*], they write (*Doctrinae*, III, §5 [73]). This must also apply to the eternal truths.[24]

Budde and Knoerr's position is reminiscent of the Cartesian account mentioned above of the eternal verities as divine creation. For Descartes, as well as for a Cartesian like Arnauld,[25] any theory that maintains that the eternal truths are independent of God's volition goes against the idea of an absolutely free God. Such a theory, Descartes writes, "can't be right, because it is grossly impious to suggest that anything could determine God, i.e. act on him or sway him or incline him or anything like that [...]" (Sixth Replies, 8). In the Cartesian view, the eternal truths are, or *must be* also created things. Descartes writes in a famous letter to Marin Mersenne:

---

24   *Cf.* Perler 2001: 260.
25   *Cf.* Nadler 2008a: 532f.; 2008b; 2011: 530–7.

> The mathematical truths that you call eternal have been laid down by God and depend on Him entirely no less than the rest of His creatures.
>
> DESCARTES TO MERSENNE, April 15, 1630/AT I 145

According to Descartes, as Steven Nadler has explained, not eternal, immutable, and independent laws, but *God* made it true that one plus one equals two. In the same manner, God could make a mountain without a valley, a triangle whose interior angles are more or less than 180 degrees, or even make it false that contradictories could *not* be true together ...[26] Now, just as God's complete freedom and wholly unlimited power applies to the laws of logic, mathematics or nature, it applies to the principles of morals. That is, in exactly the same manner as logical principles were, according to Descartes, created by God, the goodness or superiority of anything depends completely on his will. As Nadler explains, "whatever is true is true only because God has made it so, and [...] nothing is good unless God makes it good" (Nadler 2008b: 193). In this respect, Descartes argues:

> It is impossible to imagine that anything is thought of in the divine intellect as good or true, or worthy of belief or action or omission, prior to the decision of the divine will to make it so.
>
> SIXTH REPLIES, 6/AT VII 432[27]

And further:

> If in advance of all God's decrees there had been a reason for something's being good, this would have determined God to choose the things that it was best to do [...]. The real story runs in the other direction: precisely because God resolved to prefer certain things, those things are, as Genesis says, 'very good'; they are good because God exercised his will to create them.
>
> SIXTH REPLIES, 8/AT VII 435–6

Budde and Knoerr's point, as I understand it, goes in the same direction as the Cartesian account. According to their anti-Leibnizian approach, the nature of a created thing, its physical constitution, its goodness or evil, does not depend

---

26 Nadler 2008b: 191ff. *Cf.* Perler 2006: 203ff.
27 This and other translations from Descartes' works are from *The Philosophical Writings of Descartes* (3 vols., ed. and trans. John Cottingham, Robert Stoothoff & Douglas Murdoch), Cambridge: Cambridge U.P., 1985.

on eternal immutable truths, independent of God's ruling, but are established directly by God. Just as God is obliged by no principle of morality or rationality different from him (or, more exactly, from his will), the fact that something is good or evil is not established by eternal principles that determine the essential nature of things independently of God's writ. Further, everything that God creates is good, or as Budde and Knoerr write, "morally the best", but not "for itself" – i.e. by virtue of uncreated eternal truths – but only "on account of God's choice" (*Doctrinae*, III, §5 [72]).[28]

The consequences of this view regarding the alleged superiority of the created world are clear. According to Leibniz, God chose our world among all possible worlds because he identified it as the best possible. He recognized that this world, "objectively and in its own right" (Nadler 2008b: 200), is better than any other; the inherent superiority of the world was God's reason for choosing it.[29] For Budde and Knoerr, as for Descartes, the truth is the other way around: the world which God decided to create was not good independently of the fact that it was God's creation. The 'objective' goodness of the world (determined by the eternal truths) was not God's reason for creating it. In fact, according to this view, God did not even have an 'objective' reason for choosing our world. If this world is in some way good, or if it is the best of all possible worlds – as we shall see later in this chapter, Budde and Knoerr do not wholly believe this to be the case – it is simply *because God created it*:

> The morality of things is the object of eternal truths; but the ground of such truths does not lie only in the divine intellect but also in his will, as well as in his sanctity and his wisdom. But the physical good depends upon the divine will as well. If creatures have everything what, according to the Creator's will, correspond to their nature, they are physically good. And so it is evident in any case that God did not choose the world because the world is the best, but rather this is the best world because God chose it.
>
> [*Nam quae Deus facit, omnia voluntarie facit. Ratio autem de veritatibus aeternis, ab objecto externo non dependentibus & in intellectu divino extra eius voluntatem subsistentibus quid dicit? Nihil. Nam quod statim cum vel*

---

28 Does this mean that evil also exists because God wants it? Not necessarily. Budde and Knoerr would surely answer that question by resorting to the traditional Augustinian theodicy: God created rational beings free, they abused that freedom, fell into sin, etc. *Cf. Doctrinae*, I, §§20–1 (21–3).

29 *Cf.* T, §§8, 171, 225/GP VI 107, 215–6, 252. See also Rescher 2003: 31ff.

> *ipse, vel alter peccat, nouerim peccatum hoc esse, ex insita notitia etiam veritatum practicarum fluit. Sed ratio non urget, ut concludam per aeternas veritates, in intellectu divino tantum existentes, esse aliquid bonum, aut malum. Veritates aeternae de moralitate rerum sunt: non tantum autem in intellectu, sed in voluntate etiam divina cum sanctitate & sapientia conjuncta, fundamentum habent. Sed physicum quoque bonum itidem, in voluntate divina se fundavit. Si enim creaturae ea habent omnia, quae creator naturae earum convenientia esse voluit, physice bonae sunt. Et sic quidem clarum est, Deum non elegisse mundum, quia optimus, sed esse optimum, quia Deus elegit.]*
>
> *Doctrinae*, III, §5 [74]

The world is good because it is God' creation, not good 'in itself'. For Budde and Knoerr the goodness of this world, indeed any attribute of anything that exists, is not determined by the eternal, independent truths that Leibniz poses, simply because such Leibnizian independent eternal truths do not exist. Everything that exists does so in virtue of God's will.

Before closing this section, I would like to address briefly the topic of Budde and Knoerr's view of the divine nature, a subject only rapidly mentioned during their criticism of Leibniz's theory of eternal truths. The idea of the complete dependence of the eternal truths on God's will implies a view of divine nature radically opposed to the Leibnizian model. Budde and Knoerr's criticism of the idea of the independence of the eternal truths, as I said previously, follows from the conviction that such an idea limits, or simply denies, divine freedom by subjecting God to external constraints. In general terms, in the case of God's willing and acting, these constraints are the logical and moral parameters that the eternal truths establish; in the specific case of the creation of the world, the constraint is the inherent goodness and superiority of the world, which constitutes God's 'objective' reason for choosing this and no other world.

Budde and Knoerr believe that God is not guided or determined in his volition and his actions by any canon or principle independent of his will. God's will is indifferent, his freedom consisting precisely in the complete independency of his will from any 'external' influence. They emphasize the sovereignty of God's decrees over everything possible and existing, including the eternal truths. With this in mind, Budde and Knoerr's account of divine agency could be described, according to the terminology explained in Chapter 1, as a typical voluntarist account, since it maintains the independence and indifference of the will in God's acting, i.e. it defends – against a position like Leibniz's, which stresses the rational guidance of the will by the understanding and the idea of the good, and was therefore called an intellectualist position – the complete functional independence of the will of *every* external or internal parameter different to the will itself.[30]

Now, Budde and Knoerr actually go further than simply arguing for the preeminence of the will over every other divine faculty. They point out an essential aspect of their view of the divine nature after criticizing the hypothesis of the independence of the eternal truths. They write:

> If there is something in the divine intellect which is not simultaneously in his will, then things are conceived in God which are external to him. For in God, will and intellect are one and the same thing. Everything God knows in himself, he must also want, and vice versa. But things which are external to him are capable of constituting a representation that God certainly knows, but does not want.
>
> [*Si aliquid est in intellectu divino, quod non in eius voluntate simul est, est conceptus in Deo de rebus, quae extra ipsum sunt. Nam in Deo voluntas & intellectus sunt unum idemque; quidquid enim Deus in se cognoscit etiam vult, & contra. Sed res extra ipsum, fundare possunt conceptum, quem Deus quidem cognoscit, sed non vult.*]
>
> Doctrinae, III, §5 [73]

Hence, Budde and Knoerr do not maintain the superiority of God's will over his understanding. What they maintain is the essential *simplicity* of God: his attributes do not admit a real distinction. It is not that God's will has priority over his understanding. It is that his will and his understanding are to be seen as *identical*. Whether this position can still be depicted as a voluntarist account of divine nature or not will not be discussed here. Since, however, the idea of the complete independence and preeminence of God's decrees regarding every external law or principle or eternal truth is still maintained strongly by Budde and Knoerr, it still seems to be reasonable to say that they defend a *sort* of voluntarism.[31]

---

30   On the voluntarism-intellectualism distinction, see Chapter 1, 2, 2.1, as well as the final section of the present chapter. On Descartes's voluntarism see for example Nadler 2008b; 2011; Perler 2001: 261.

31   The proposal of calling the Cartesian theology 'voluntarist' has been critized by authors as Jean-Luc Marion, who maintains that this label suggests a distinction between divine faculties, something that Descartes's the theology of simplicity rejects. However, as Steven Nadler argues – adequately in my opinion – against such criticisms, "the term, while misleading in this way, does serve well to highlight the fact that for Descartes, the eternal

Once again, this account reminds us of a Cartesian kind of theology, which maintains the essential simplicity of God and the identity of divine understanding and will. Descartes writes:

> In God, willing and knowing are a single thing in such a way that by the very fact of willing something He knows it and it is only for this reason that such thing is true.
> DESCARTES TO MERSENNE, May 6, 1630/AT I 149[32]

In Cartesian fashion, thus, Budde and Knoerr uphold the thesis of the fundamental simplicity of God. In the following section and at the end of the chapter, I will return to the examination of Budde and Knoerr's Cartesian theology of simplicity and its role within their critique of Leibniz.

We have seen so far that Budde and Knoerr reject the Leibnizian concept of metaphysical evil on the grounds that this concept, rather that explaining satisfactorily the question of the origin of evil, opens the door anew to the theological concern that makes evil in the world a problem: the possibility that creatures are in some way essentially evil and therefore God himself, as creator, is ultimately responsible for evil. By criticizing the doctrine of metaphysical evil, Budde and Knoerr seek to underline the apparent incompetence of optimism as an answer to the problem of evil.

Further, Budde and Knoerr criticize Leibniz's account of the nature of the eternal truths as being uncreated and wholly independent of the divine decrees, and defend the idea of the creation of eternal truths by God, and thus their complete dependence on his willing. In general terms, this view manifests a strong opposition to the Leibnizian worldview. With regard to optimism, it is a central aspect of the rejection of the very assumption – central to the Leibnizian philosophy itself – that lies at the basis of the system of the best: the idea that God acts according to reasons and following rational principles, and that he has chosen our world in this rational fashion.

In the following section, I will examine a further aspect of Budde and Knoerr's rejection of the Leibnizian doctrine of the rational nature of God presupposed by optimism: the criticism of the theory of the divine choice of the best world among infinite possibles.

---

truths are dependent on God's causal power, even if His willing those truths is identical with His understanding them" (Nadler 2008b: 275, n. 29).

32 See also Descartes to Mersenne, May 27, 1630/AT I 152f. On Descartes's doctrine of the identity of God's will and understanding, see 2008b: 194; Perler 2001: 258ff. On Arnauld's acceptance of the theology of simplicity, see Nadler 2008a: 531ff.

2 "God Did Not Identify Several Worlds, but Immediately the Best": Against the Divine Choice of the Best

Leibniz describes God's weighing of infinite possible worlds and the subsequent choice of the best with the following words:

> The infinity of possibles, however great it may be, is no greater than that of the wisdom of God, who knows all possibles. [...] The wisdom of God, not content with embracing all the possibles, penetrates them, compares them, weighs them one against the other, to estimate their degrees of perfection or imperfection, the strong and the weak, the good and the evil. It goes even beyond the finite combinations, it makes of them an infinity of infinites, that is to say, an infinity of possible sequences of the universe, each of which contains an infinity of creatures. By this means the divine Wisdom distributes all the possibles it had already contemplated separately, into so many universal systems which it further compares the one with the other. The result of all these comparisons and deliberations is the choice of the best from among all these possible systems, which wisdom makes in order to satisfy goodness completely; and such is precisely the plan of the universe as it is. [...] The careful consideration of these things will, I hope, induce a different idea of the greatness of the divine perfections, and especially of the wisdom and goodness of God, from any that can exist in the minds of those who make God act at random, without cause or reason.
>
> T, §§225–6/GP VI 253f.

In Leibniz's opinion, this depiction of the divine choice and creation of the best is the only one capable of giving a fitting account of God's infinite intelligence (by virtue of which God is capable of contemplating, examining, and comparing all infinite possibles), his infinite goodness and perfect will (by which he fixes upon the best among all possible worlds and chooses it), and his unlimited power (which renders the will efficacious through the creation of the best possible world).[33] Philosophical optimism is, thus, the most adequate account of God's rationality and greatness.

For Leibniz.

Of course, Budde and Knoerr think differently. They recognize that Leibniz believes that the system of the best shows most effectively God's rationality: Leibniz "admits that God is a rational being because there were several

---

[33] *Cf.* T, §7/GP VI 106.

possible worlds, which he identified and considered when choosing one of them" [*Nempe Deum esse ens intelligens probat, quia plures mundi fuerint possibiles, quos cognoverit, & ad quos respexerit, dum unum elegit.*] (*Doctrinae*, III, §4 [65]). However, Budde and Knoerr reject the theory of the choice of the best. As they observe, that theory:

> [...] will not satisfy everyone because, even though it is certain that matter has the potency to permit infinite realizations and therefore, with regard to matter, several worlds are indeed possible, this cannot be admitted with regard to God. That God had several [worlds] in his representation and his intellect is what most people will deny. God is the most perfect and wise being. The perfect wise builds at least perfect representations; and he who is omniscient does not inquire what is best, since he already knows the best. One can say: the illustrious gentleman wants God to have identified the numerous worlds and to have chosen one of them. I reply: God did not identify several worlds, but immediately the best.
>
> [*Nempe Deum esse ens intelligens probat, quia plures mundi fuerint possibiles, quos cognoverit, & ad quos respexerit, dum unum elegit. Ideo non omnibus satisfacient haec, quia licet certum sit, quod materia infinitorum motuum sit capax, & quod adeo respectu materiae plures mundi fuerint possibiles; vix tamen respectu Dei hoc concedent. Deum enim pluris uno in ideis & intellectu habuisse, id est, quod negabunt plurimi. Nam Deus est ens perfectissimum sapientissimumque. Perfecte sapiens perfectas saltem ideas format: nec exquirit ille, qui omniscius est, quid sit optimum, cum optimum iam, noscat. Dicas: hoc vult illustris vir, Deum nosse mundos possibiles plurimos, & unum elegisse. Respondeo: non dico Deum plures mundos nouisse, sed nouisse statim optimum.*]
>
> *Doctrinae*, III, §4 [65]

According to Leibniz, God, as a perfect, infinitely wise and good being, must be able to compare infinite possibles and choose the best alternative among them. On the contrary, Budde and Knoerr argue that *precisely* because God is a perfect, infinitely wise and good being, he does *not* need to compare infinite possibles in order to identify the best possible alternative. God already knows the best without having, as it were, to 'search for it' among infinite possible options.

The rejection of the theory of the divine choice seems to follow from the same concern that led Budde and Knoerr to reject Leibniz's description of the nature of the eternal truths, that is, the conviction that these doctrines result in the denial of God's freedom of choice. As was the case with the Leibnizian uncreated eternal truths, the idea of an infinite series of possible worlds from which God chooses one that – even worse – is the best by virtue of *its own* essential nature determined by the eternal truths, means for Budde and Knoerr, on the one hand, that there are things that do not depend on God's decrees, and on the other, that the divine choices are subjected to influences external to him. The only account that seems to be suitable to Budde and Knoerr's view of the divine nature maintains that God, when creating, did not have to consider different alternatives, but simultaneously knew, desired, and created the world – which is the best precisely because God created it. With this in mind, it does not come as a surprise that Budde and Knoerr write: "God chose this world immediately not among several worlds, but he chose only this one, since the existence of the universe depends only on him, not on a motive existing outside God himself" [*Deus vero statim hunc mundum non ex pluribus, sed hunc tantum elegit, quia existencia universi mere ab ipso dependet, non a causa extra ipsum.*] (*Doctrinae*, III, §4 [68]).

Now, Budde and Knoerr's interpretation of the theory of the divine choice is problematic. They seem to depict Leibniz as maintaining that God, as human beings would do, first contemplates and analyses a series of possible worlds, and then chooses one among them. This, however, must not be the case, and although Leibniz's own account could give the false impression that the process of divine choice takes place successively,[34] I believe it is clear that that account is merely the attempt of conceptualizing courses of action that, given the agent (God), occur non-temporally. We could speculate, then, that here – as in the case of the description of uncreated eternal truths as "something coactive exterior" to God – Budde and Knoerr either misinterpret or misrepresent Leibniz.

In spite of how inexact Budde and Knoerr's reading of Leibniz might be, the rejection of the theory of the divine choice speaks eloquently about the profound difference in attitude that separates the theologians from Leibniz. This is, in my eyes, the interesting aspect of their criticism of optimism. As Stefan Lorenz has commented, Budde and Knoerr's rejection of the Leibnizian theory of the divine choice responds to the desire of distancing themselves from a "hyper-rationalizing of God" (Lorenz 1997: 115) that subjects the divine attributes and actions to rational categories and laws that, at the end, have as an outcome the restriction of God's freedom of choice. This becomes even clearer when Budde and Knoerr mention what they consider to be the reason for the emergence of the optimist's theory of the choice of the best. Optimism

---

34   See for example T, §§225–6/GP VI 252f.

follows, they claim, from "anthropopathy" [*Anthropopathie*], i.e. the ascription of human attributes, traits, and actions to God.

This tendency of humanizing God by Leibniz can be found in the doctrine of the choice of the best or, for example, Budde and Knoerr claim, in the distinction between divine will and divine understanding and the ensuing supposed denial of their conviction in God's essential simplicity. Budde and Knoerr write:

> Certainly, that we should consider God's intellect and will as separate is anthropopathy. I do not say that the divine essence does not understand and will, but that, should we consider his intellect and will as separate, this at least results in anthropopathy.
>
> *Doctrinae*, III, §4 [67–68]

For Budde and Knoerr Leibniz, fixated on showing the essential intelligibility of God and the possibility of explaining the divine ways in a rational manner, judges God's behavior in comparison with or even in correspondence to the human way of acting, arriving through that way to theories that are highly dangerous, as they prepare the way for a denial of divine freedom. For Budde and Knoerr this methodological approach misses the point. They write:

> [T]he anthropopathy can have no place here, since in this manner of acting there is no similarity in the execution between the divine and the human intellect. God did not choose one world among several worlds that he knew, such as a wise man considers several and chooses one [...].
>
> [*Haec si ad praesens institutum adplicemus, video antropopathiam hic locum habere non posse, quia similitudo effectus inter intellectum divinum & humanum, in hoc negotio est nulla. Non enim Deus ex pluribus mundos, quos cognouit, unum elegit, prouti sapiens ex pluribus consideratis unum eligit* [...]]
>
> III, §4 [67]

The confusion arises, Budde and Knoerr continue, by "drawing a conclusion from a similar terminology, but not from a similar execution". That is: by thinking that when one says that God decides to create the world, this creation can be comparable to a human performance, something that according to Budde and Knoerr is definitely not the case.

Leibniz would no doubt consider Budde and Knoerr's objections misleading. Regarding the reproach of the denial of divine simplicity, in spite of the fact that Leibniz's handling of the distinction between divine understanding and will could seem perplexing,[35] it seems safe to say that Leibniz himself would never accept that this distinction implies in any way the negation of God's essential simplicity. As he writes in the *Monadology*:

> *Monads*, which I am going to talk about here, are nothing other than simple substances which make up compounds. By 'simple' I mean 'without parts'.
>
> M, §1/GP VI 607

> This God alone is the primary unity [or monad], or the original simple substance, which produces all created or derivative monads.
>
> M, §47/GP VI 614)

The distinction between attributes in God[36] is, Leibniz would probably say, a functional distinction, one that follows from the attempt of explaining rationally God's actions, but not a distinction that implies a real ontological partition of God's essential unity.[37]

Further, regarding the general charge of anthropopathy, Leibniz would no doubt reply that this charge has it all wrong. For Leibniz it is not that the divine behavior can be understood by 'projecting' the human workings into God, but on the contrary, it is man's nature which in certain manner reflects the nature of God (see below the idea of spirits as "images of God" and "minor deities"). The conviction underlying this idea is that only this approach can make a rational approach to God possible. From Leibniz's perspective, then, the charge of anthropopathy would therefore be still another instance of misrepresentation by Budde and Knoerr.

Now, once again, if we look at the big picture, Budde and Knoerr's criticisms, whether right or wrong, make evident that behind those criticisms there is a kind of approach to both theology and to the question concerning the relationship between God and the human being that differs fundamentally from the Leibnizian approach. According to Leibniz, the human mind imitates God's mind. If there is a difference between both, it is only a difference of degree,

---

35   For example: "Moreover, all these operations of the divine understanding, although they have among them an order and a priority of nature, always take place together, no priority of time existing among them" (T, §225/GP VI 252), or: "For it must be known that in God, as in every intelligent being, actions of the will are posterior in nature to actions of the intellect [...]" (Leibniz to Bierling, 20 June 1712).

36   *Cf.* T, §7/GP VI 106; M, §48/GP VI 615.

37   On Leibniz's notions of substance and God's simplicity see also Rescher 1979: 13ff.

not, so to speak, an essential difference. Thus Leibniz writes in the *Discourse on Metaphysics*:

> All effects express their causes, and so the essence of our soul is a particular expression, imitation or likeness of God's essence, thought and will, and of all the ideas contained in it.
> DM, §28/GP IV 453

And later in the *Monadology*:

> [S]pirits are also images of the divinity itself, or of the Author of Nature himself. They are capable of knowing the system of the universe, and can imitate it to a certain extent through their own small-scale constructions, since each spirit is like a minor deity in its own sphere of authority.
> M, §83/GP VI 621[38]

For Budde and Knoerr, in contrast, the divine and the human mind *cannot* be compared to one another. As they claim, "there is no such a similar execution" of divine and human thoughts, choices, actions (*Doctrinae*, III, §4 [67]). This is still another fundamental aspect of the great gap between the metaphysical and theological approaches of Leibniz and Budde and Knoerr, to which I shall return at the end of the chapter.

The following section is dedicated to Budde and Knoerr's assessment of the concept of the best of all possible worlds. Budde and Knoerr criticize Leibniz's theory of the divine choice of the best world and the views that give rise to that theory. However, interestingly enough, this criticism does not seem to entail the idea that a best world is *not* possible, in other words, it does not imply that the concept of a best world is contradictory or theoretically invalid. On the other hand, this does not exclude the fact that Budde and Knoerr, nevertheless, consider the notion of a best world, applied to *our* specific world, to be a highly problematic concept. In the following we will see how it is possible that Budde and Knoerr both accept *and* reject the concept of the best world.

3 Not a Wonderful World – The Best of All Possible Worlds after Sin

As we saw in the preceding sections, the first two points of Budde and Knoerr's criticism of optimism, the critique of Leibniz's account of eternal truths and

---

[38] On Leibniz's idea that creation is the "mirror of God", see Jolley 2005: 2ff.

of the theory of the divine choice of the best among infinite possible worlds, seem to follow directly from the conviction that those doctrines deny God's freedom of choice (understood as the absolute indeterminacy and independence of the divine will). Budde and Knoerr's view, therefore, seems to conflict with those fundamental tenets of the Leibnizian mindset mainly on theoretical grounds, namely the interest of defending an account of divine nature according to which, on the one hand, God's willing is completely independent of any external influence, and on the other, there is nothing whose existence does not depend from God's resolve. Further, there seems to be a deep gap between Budde and Knoerr's and Leibniz's approach to the divine nature. Whereas Leibniz believes that God is fundamentally rational and his behavior can be explained according to rational parameters, Budde and Knoerr seem to consider that God works in ways that go beyond any explanation that supposes that God acts like other rational beings (hence the problematic charge of antropopathy against Leibniz referred to in the last section).

The third stage of Budde and Knoerr's critique is the rejection of the idea that our world is the best possible world. Unlike the case of the eternal truths and the theory of the divine choice, Budde and Knoerr's criticism of the thesis of the best world does not seem to be motivated by the belief that this thesis entails some kind of theoretical difficulties regarding the concept of God. Rather, that criticism follows from the idea that the description of our present world as the best world goes against a fundamental doctrine of the Christian religion: the dogma of the *Fall of Man*.

As is well known, the term refers to Adam's and Eve's first sin as narrated in the book of Genesis (3:1–24). According to the Judeo-Christian tradition – and subsequently to the traditional, Augustinian theodicy – sin (moral evil), death (the most grievous kind of physical evil), and suffering in general entered the world as a result of the Fall. Humanity's condition of sinfulness resulting from the Fall is what is known as the original sin.[39]

The Augustinian tradition upholds that this fundamental change in human nature, which implies that all descendants of Adam are born in sin, can only be redeemed by divine grace. Jesus' first coming to the world, his ministry, and above all, his death on the cross, are the definitive redemption for the sin of mankind (whereby they are also an indirect result of the Fall). The central concern, then, on behalf of which Budde and Knoerr criticize the optimistic

---

39 The exact nature of the state of 'contamination' or inborn sinfulness that original sin represents has been characterised by the various Christian confessions in different ways which cannot be examined here. On this problem see for example Cross & Livingstone 2005; Hart 1997.

doctrine of the best world is the belief that the description of our world as the best possible is at odds with the doctrine of the Fall of Man and its dogmatic – and dramatic – consequences.

Budde and Knoerr's criticism is directed against at least three ideas: i) the view that this is the best of all possible worlds; ii) the conviction that a world without sin, pain, and sorrow would be in fact worse than ours; iii) the idea that in this best of all possible worlds there is more good than evil.

Regarding the first point, Leibniz famously writes:

> Now this supreme wisdom, united to a goodness that is no less infinite, cannot but have chosen the best. For as a lesser evil is a kind of good, even so a lesser good is a kind of evil if it stands in the way of a greater good; and there would be something to correct in the actions of God if it were possible to do better. As in mathematics, when there is no maximum nor minimum, in short nothing distinguished, everything is done equally, or when that is not possible nothing at all is done: so it may be said likewise in respect of perfect wisdom, which is no less orderly than mathematics, that if there were not the best (*optimum*) among all possible worlds, God would not have produced any.
> T, §8/GP VI 107

On the topic of the superiority of our world compared to other supposedly 'better' worlds:

> Some adversary not being able to answer this argument will perchance answer the conclusion by a counter-argument, saying that the world could have been without sin and without sufferings; but I deny that then it would have been *better*. For it must be known that all things are *connected* in each one of the possible worlds: the universe, whatever it may be, is all of one piece, like an ocean: the least movement extends its effect there to any distance whatsoever, even though this effect become less perceptible in proportion to the distance. Therein God has ordered all things beforehand once for all, having foreseen prayers, good and bad actions, and all the rest; and each thing *as an idea* has contributed, before its existence, to the resolution that has been made upon the existence of all things; so that nothing can be changed in the universe (any more than in a number) save its essence or, if you will, save its *numerical individuality*. Thus, if the smallest evil that comes to pass in the world were missing in it, it would no longer be this world; which, with nothing omitted and all allowance made, was found the best by the Creator who chose it.

> It is true that one may imagine possible worlds without sin and without unhappiness, and one could make some like Utopian or Sevarambian romances: but these same worlds again would be very inferior to ours in goodness. I cannot show you this in detail. For can I know and can I present infinities to you and compare them together? But you must judge with me *ab effectu*, since God has chosen this world as it is.
>
> T, §§9–10/GP VI 107–8

And finally, regarding the amount of good and evil in the world, we read in the *Theodicy*:

> But it will be said that evils are great and many in number in comparison with the good: that is erroneous. It is only want of attention that diminishes our good, and this attention must be given to us through some admixture of evils.
>
> T, §13/GP VI 109

> Bayle continues: 'that man is wicked and miserable; that there are everywhere prisons and hospitals; that history is simply a collection of the crimes and calamities of the human race.' I think that there is exaggeration in that: there is incomparably more good than evil in the life of men, as there are incomparably more houses than prisons.
>
> T, §148/GP VI 198[40]

Budde and Knoerr oppose the three optimist views – the created world is the best possible; the configuration of the created world is such that no other world cannot be better; there is more good than evil in the world – based on what could be called 'empirical' or perhaps 'empirical-theological' arguments.

Regarding the question whether the created world can be considered the best possible world, Budde and Knoerr maintain that, given the amount of evil, or better, given the mere presence of evil in the world, this cannot be the best possible world. As they had already argued at the beginning of the *Doctrinae*:

> [W]hich is the best species of world? I will say: That world in whose order there is no evil at all, whether moral or physical. I gather that the best world is that in which harmony is perfect/the best [*optima*]; and I do not

---

40 Leibniz refers here to Bayle's eloquent depiction of the evils of the world in the famous article "Manicheans", note D, of the *Historical and Critical Dictionary*.

deny that the world, inasmuch as the evil things are mixed together with the good ones, has nevertheless some harmony, and thus with some reason it is also good, but not the best [...]

[[Q]uaenam mundi species optima sit? Dicam: illa, in cuius serie plane malum est nullum, nec morale, nec physicum. Fateor, optimum esse mundum, in quo harmonia est optima, nec diffiteor mundum, prout bonis admixta sunt mala, aliquam tamen harmoniam habere, & sic aliqua ratione etiam bonum esse, sed non optimum.]
    Doctrinae, I, §6 [4]

And further:

In short, the best world is that in which there is no evil at all; or else, thus, it is fairly clear that, whatever you may say and imagine, if in some of its parts this universe is seen without harmony, the world would not be the best, in so far as some or many of its parts are evil, which in themselves also act in unison harmonically towards evil, never pursuing the good, and only accidentally steer toward the good.

[*Denique optimum mundum esse illum, in quo plane malum est nullum, vel inde satis patet, quod quicquid dicas fingasque, in tantum tamen, si extra hamoniam* [sic] *in partibus spectaretur hoc universum, non optimus esset mundus, in quantum partes eius nonnullae vel plures malae sunt, quae in se etiam harmonice ad malum conspirant, nunquam bona intendunt, & per accidens tantum ad bonum diriguntur.*]
    Doctrinae, I, §6 [6]

Thus, Budde and Knoerr's rejection of the Leibnizian identification of our world with the best possible world rests upon the conviction that only a world without evil can be rightfully called the best, something that naturally does not apply to our world.

    Speaking for Leibniz, one could ask if Budde and Knoerr are really justified in talking about a world without evil. Indeed, is an evil-free world even possible? Budde and Knoerr do seem to have good reasons (at least from their own perspective) to believe in the possibility of a world without evil, and, therefore, to reject the idea that our own world is the best possible. This can be better understood by taking a look at Budde and Knoerr's opinion about Leibniz's second claim, about the superiority of our world. They write:

[T]he illustrious man confesses that a world without sin and misery can certainly be imagined, but such world would be worse than ours [...]. The world before the Fall must be contrasted with the world after the Fall [...], because the state of the actual world cannot be derived harmoniously from the nature and the idea of the previous world. The best world is the one without sin, whose noble natures could be corrupted. When those natures fall into sin, this best, previous world must be distinguished from the subsequent world, which is naturally the worst. [Leibniz's] claim that a world without sin would be worse than ours has thus, I think, been refuted through convincing reasons. [...] [T]he world without evil is good in all its parts and hence all its parts promote together the good harmoniously, all of which results in the best world. In the world in which evil is present there are some parts that tend towards evil and open accidentally the possibility of goodness and produce dissension. But is there *here* some superior harmony?

[*Pergit vir illustris, se concedere, quod fingi possit mundus sine peccato & infortunio, sed talem mundum deteriorem fore nostro, si existerer, id quo ex effectu, quia infinita repraesentari & comparari non possint, sit concludendum. [...] Utique enim mundus ante lapsum, mundo post lapsum opponendus est [...] quia praesentis mundi status non ex natura antecedentis aut eius idea harmonice fluit. Quia enim ille mundus est optimus, qui peccatum non habet, ut tamen in peccata labi, potuerint creaturae eius nobiliores, hinc si labuntur, recte distinguitur a priori mundo optimo posterior mundo, utpote deterioris, conditio. Quod autem dicit: mundum sine peccato deteriorem fore nostro, id hactenus argumentis, ut puto, non spernendis a nobis negatum est. Nec omnibus forte satis caute concludere videbitur, quod ab effectu concludendum esse putat, quia si ab effectu ad causam concludimus, nulla alia causa, nisi haec ad quam concludimus, cum ratione fingi aut esse debet. Sed, quod mundus ita comparatus sit, non omnes hanc allegabunt causam, quia optimus est, sed cum scriptura sacra etiam multi hanc dabunt, quia optimus mundus talis fuit, qui corrumpi potuit. Quod autem dicit ab effectu esse concludendum, quia duo infinita repraesentari & inter se invicem comparari non possint; id quidem in huius rei probatione locum non invenire existimo: quod patebit, si modo duo indefinita haec, prouti harmonice spectantur, in conceptu generali secundum harmoniam examinentur. Sic mundus, qui sine malo est, in omnibus partibus bonus est, & consequenter partes omnes ad bonum harmonice conspirant, id quod optimum mundum facit. In mundo, ubi malum est, partes nonnullae malae*

sunt, quae per se ad malum inclinant, per accident boni occasionem dant & disharmoniam efficiunt. Num hic harmonia optima?]
   Doctrinae, III, §7 [78–81]

Hence, for Budde and Knoerr a best world without evil is not only possible; in fact, such a world already existed and was indeed the world that God originally created.

The doctrine of the Fall of Man forces (or allows) us to assume that there is a fundamental difference between the world (or the state of the world) before and after the first sin of humankind. The Leibnizian doctrine of the best possible world is for Budde and Knoerr necessarily unfeasible as an adequate description of *our* world because for them the dogma of the Fall is necessarily true. Certainly, the concept of the best of all possible worlds refers to the world that God created (and how could it be otherwise?). However, it does not refer to the *actual* state of that world. The best possible world is, or rather *was* the prelapsarian world, the paradisiacal state of creation as described in the Bible.

In Budde and Knoerr's opinion, through the coming of evil into the world as a result of the first sin, the world was altered and corrupted in such a way that, in the strict sense, it is not possible to consider that the world *ante lapsum* and the world *post lapsum* are the *same* world. According to this view, there has been an essential fracture in the evolution of the world caused by the first sin; a fracture which every rational examination of the world should try to account for. Leibnizian optimism, in Budde and Knoerr's opinion, would seem to favor an approach to the problem of evil that is based on the reflection on the timeless nature of God and human beings.[41] According to Budde and Knoerr, this approach ignores the fact that sin corrupted both human nature and the world in an essential manner.

The outcome of the corruption of the paradisiacal state of creation, that is, our mischievous world, is no longer the best possible world God could have created. Hence, Budde and Knoerr's reply to Leibniz's third claim regarding the amount of good and evil in the world:

> In paragraph 13 the illustrious author examines the question whether there is more evil than good in this universe. He denies it and claims that there is more good than evil. [...] However, it must be said, following the

---

41   *Cf.* Fabbianelli 2003: 300–1; Fonnesu 1994: 137 and 2006: 756; Lorenz 1997: 110ff.

Scriptures, that after the Fall there is more evil than good in our world. See Gen. 6: 6; Rom. 5: 19–20.[42]

[*Subsequente §13 auctor illustris, iam se adcingit ad quaestionem: num plus mali, quam boni in hoc universe sit? Negat & adherit plus boni esse, quam mali.* […] *Sed in nostro mundo post lapsum omnino plus mali, quam boni esse, scriptura sacra praevia dicendum est. Confer.* Gen. 6:6. Rom. 5:19–20.]
   Doctrinae, III, §8 [81]

At the risk of falling into a terminological anachronism, it could be said that Budde and Knoerr uphold not only a 'counter-optimistic' position but, moreover, an empirical *pessimism* regarding the moral character of the existent world.[43]

In the same line of reasoning, Budde and Knoerr refer to another dogmatic assumption in order to underscore the fundamental invalidity of Leibniz's identification of our world with the best possible world. That assumption is the role of Jesus Christ in God's plan for the salvation of the world.

As I said previously, the dogma of the Fall of Man is connected to the Christian account of Jesus' incarnation and death as means for the redemption

---

42 Gen. 6:6: "The Lord regretted that he had made human beings on the earth, and his heart was deeply troubled." Rom. 5: 1920: "For just as through the disobedience of the one man the many were made sinners, so also through the obedience of the one man the many will be made righteous. The law was brought in so that the trespass might increase. But where sin increased, grace increased all the more". (Both quotes from: *Holy Bible*, New International Version, 2011.)

43 Budde and Knoerr's 'empirical pessimism' is manifest in several passages of the *Doctrinae*. For example: "[T]hat grievous saying is in everyone's mouth and voice, and it is thus the saddest of all: All of these things, completely, are full of evil, just as of evil men. […] Indeed, the genera of gathered calamities, the swarm of illnesses, the time that is imminent to all the dead – [all of these things] overwhelm anyone, and presses him very often. On the contrary, the complaints are of many things, much more of the evil and of the evil things that happen, than of the good and good things. The most holy boundaries of the divine word reveal that evil has invaded everything. That Fall of Satan and of man, which we call 'moral evil', has occurred, and that which we call 'physical evil' has thence flown necessarily […] [*Nam lugubre illus dictum in omnium ore ac voce est, adeosque tritissimum: haec universa malo abundare, prouti hominibus mali. Nempe ipsa ratio iniqua hominum facta pensitans, mala ea esse tam evidenter videt, quam damnum inde sentit respublica praesentissimum. Cumulata enim calamitatum genera, morborum caterva, mortisque hora omnibus imminens, premunt quemque, opprimunt saepissime. Imo plus mali & malos plures esse, quam boni sit, bonosque, querelae sunt plurium. Sacratissima divini verbi pomoeria malum omnes omnino invasisse, in limine statim ostendunt. Satanae hominumque lapsus illud, quod malum morale vocamus, invexit, & quod physicum dicimus inde necessario fluxir* […].] (*Doctrinae*, I, §2 [1]).

of humankind. For Budde and Knoerr the appearance of Christ in human history is, thus, further proof (or another aspect of the proof) of the fundamental corruption of the world after the Fall. And it is therefore a further step, or the ultimate step, in the refutation of the optimist idea that our world is the best possible world. They write:

> In fact, according to the testimony of the Scriptures, Christ came, sent by God, to take the best world back to the original condition, and to this refer the words that the fact that the world could be taken back to the condition of goodness only through Christ's death shows the extreme corruption of the world.
>
> [[S]ed Christus teste scriptura sacra ad optimum mundum per peccatum ante corruptum, denuo restaurandum venit, a Deo missus, & huc quidem dicta adducta pertinent; quod & mundi extremam corruptionem satis indicat, quippe qui, non nisi Christi morte restaurari ad bonitatem potuit.]
> Doctrinae, III, §7 [81]

The Leibnizian theodicy, as Stefan Lorenz has commented, seems to 'level' the world(s) *ante* and *post lapsum* by declaring our world the best possible world. Hence, optimism renders Christ's role in the history of humankind irrelevant by making our world a world which is "potentially in no need of redemption [*erlösungsunbedürftig*]" (Lorenz 1997: 112), since according to the rationalist-optimist's premises there cannot be any world which is better than this one.[44]

In sum, as I said before, Budde and Knoerr do not consider the concept of the best world unfeasible or contradictory. The concept of the best does not imply for them the kind of theoretical problems that the Leibnizian eternal truths or the theory of the divine choice of the best are supposed to entail. The only problem, they believe, is that such concept cannot be applied to our actual world. Budde and Knoerr certainly seem to share Leibniz's – or for that matter, Augustine's – belief that evil in the world promotes the good.[45] They do

---

[44] The notion of 'being in no need of redemption' ("*Erlösungsunbedürftigkeit*") is originally used by Wilhelm Schmidt-Biggemann to explain the situation in which the world is left by Leibnizian optimism. According to this account, the 'best world' of the *Theodicy* is "calculable" and "reliable"; the "stabilization of creation" that results from Leibniz's rationalist defense of God "reduces the necessity of salvific history". *Cf.* Schmidt-Biggemann 1988: 78.

[45] For example, Leibniz writes in the *Theodicy*: "A little acid, sharpness or bitterness is often more pleasing than sugar; shadows enhance colours; and even a dissonance in the right place gives relief to harmony. [...] And is it not most often necessary that a little evil render the good more discernible, that is to say, greater?" (T, §12/GP VI 109), or: "[G]od, by

not think, however, that this obliges us to accept the doctrine of the best world, i.e. to maintain that no other better world could have been – or, as we have seen, *was* – possible. In Budde and Knoerr's view Leibnizian optimism collides with the Christian dogma of the Fall of Man, with a hard interpretation of the concept of original sin, and with the idea of redemption through Christ. Since, for Budde and Knoerr, these dogmas are necessarily true, the Leibnizian system of the best must be fundamentally mistaken.

4 Final Comments and Open Questions

4.1 *On Useful Misunderstandings and the Two Gods*

At least three capital aspects of Leibniz's metaphysics of optimism have been seen as being misinterpreted or misrepresented by Budde and Knoerr: first, the Leibnizian theory of uncreated eternal truths; second, the theory of the divine choice of the best; third, Leibniz's description of divine attributes and actions, which Budde and Knoerr consider as "anthropopathy". These misunderstandings, as I noted earlier, seem to make it easier for Budde and Knoerr to criticize Leibniz, since they allow them to depict optimism as a system that is either absurd or wholly hazardous for the idea of God as a free and omnipotent being.

Regarding the first issue, Budde and Knoerr consider that the existence of eternal truths that do not depend of God's will, but to which even God's will is subjected, implies that God is not able to choose freely, since there are "coactive", "external" parameters that determine his behavior. As I argued previously,

> a wonderful art, turns all the errors of these little worlds [human beings] to the greater adornment of his great world. It is as in those devices of perspective, where certain beautiful designs look like mere confusion until one restores them to the right angle of vision or one views them by means of a certain glass or mirror. It is by placing and using them properly that one makes them serve as adornment for a room. Thus the apparent deformities of our little worlds combine to become beauties in the great world, and have nothing in them which is opposed to the oneness of an infinitely perfect universal principle: on the contrary, they increase our wonder at the wisdom of him who makes evil serve the greater good" (T, §147/GP VI 197–8). Budde and Knoerr agree: "In the meantime I do not deny that in this world every evil, whether moral or physical, is converted by God into a good, and indeed it is always like that. In fact, God does not intend the evil to occur, but if it does occur, God leads it into the good. [...] Through sin man becomes infected with disease, [and] he is evil; but while he dwells through disease, God intends him to know sin's vanity and damage." [*Interim non nego, quicquid mali in hoc orbe sit, vel moralis, vel physici in bonum a Deo verti & id quidem semper. Deus quidem malum, ut fiat, non intendit, sed si fit, ad bonum deducit. [...] Homo per peccatum morbum sibi contrahit, malum est sed dum in morbo versatur, peccati vanitatem, & detrimentum, ut inde cognoscat, Deus intendit.*] (*Doctrinae*, I, §29 [30]).

Leibniz does not agree which such an interpretation. For him, God is certainly subjected in his willing to the eternal truths, but that means nothing more than to say that God is subjected to his own understanding, i.e. to *himself* – as a rational being who acts upon reasons, etc. For this reason, and precisely for this reason, God *is* free, since he follows *his own* dictates. For Leibniz to say that God is not free because his will is not completely arbitrary and undetermined, is simply to misunderstand what God is and what it means to be free.

As for the theory of the divine choice, it would seem that Budde and Knoerr see Leibniz as claiming candidly that God chooses the best world as a human being would do: comparing and examining first a series of possible worlds, then choosing one among them, which he then creates. Certainly, Leibniz *writes* in this manner. However, as I consider, we are justified in believing that Leibniz would maintain that this is an explanation, or the attempt of an explanation, of something that happens simultaneously, in a non-temporary manner, since God of course is not a temporal being. That is, the attempt of explaining rationally how creation took place, why God created this and no other world, and why the world is the best of all possible alternatives.

Finally, regarding the charge of anthropopathy, Budde and Knoerr argue that Leibniz projects human traits onto God in order to explain how or why God acts in one way or another. For them any comparison between the ways in which God and human beings act is invalid, since, as it seems, they consider that God is essentially different to human beings and not to be grasped or explained by any categories that could also be applied to the behavior of rational creatures. Leibniz, as I explained, thinks the contrary: God and man *can* indeed be compared to one another, not because human attributes should be projected onto God's nature, but rather because, as I quoted earlier, human beings, in biblical manner, are "images of the divinity", "minor deities". Thus, it is not that Leibniz humanizes God. It is rather that he, in a certain manner, divinizes the human being. And since Leibniz thinks that God is essentially a rational being, it is obviously possible to detect some essential similarities between God and men.

As I have shown, it is definitely possible to read the Leibnizian theories that Budde and Knoerr consider hazardous in a way that does not necessarily result in an obvious denial of God's freedom or in the depiction of God as some kind of super-human, but still pseudo-human, and therefore limited, rational being. Now probably, this reading only works from a *Leibnizian* perspective. And indeed, it is interesting to stress that both Leibniz and Budde and Knoerr maintain stubbornly, as in some complicated relationship, that *their* way of seeing things (in this case: of describing what it means to be free and explaining the divine nature), is *the* right one, the only one that does justice to God and that can guarantee divine freedom. Precisely this situation, I believe, shows what kind of problem we are dealing with here.

Expressed in a rather obvious manner, this problem consists in the following: Leibniz and Budde and Knoerr advocate two opposed and possibly mutually exclusive theological models, i.e. Leibniz and Budde and Knoerr believe in two different Gods, and their theoretical claims about God follow consequently from those two different concepts. Thus, for example, despite the problems that a Cartesian theory of eternal truths like the one that Budde and Knoerr defend may have,[46] that theory, as modern commentators have shown, can indeed be made meaningful and shown to be consistent with the particular kind of voluntarism or better, with the somewhat voluntarist theology of simplicity that Descartes and Budde and Knoerr defend[47] – according to which God is a

---

[46] The most typical problem of the Cartesian theory of created eternal truths is stated by Marin Mersenne in the Sixth Objections to Descartes. Mersenne's complete question runs like this: "How can the truths of geometry or metaphysics, such as those you refer to, be immutable and eternal and yet not be independent of God? What sort of causal dependence on God do they have? Could he have brought it about that there has never been any such thing as the nature of a triangle? And how, may we ask, could he have made it untrue from eternity that twice four makes eight, or that a triangle has three angles? Either these truths depend solely on the intellect that is thinking of them, or on existing things, or else they are independent, since it seems that God could not have brought it about that any of these essences or truths were not as they were from all eternity" (Sixth Objections/AT VII 417). Descartes's theory of created eternal truths has also been considered to be highly problematic by a number of commentators, both early modern and contemporary, who have maintained that this account is "both internally inconsistent and detrimental to Descartes's system as a whole" (Kaufman 2005: 1). Leibniz himself, for example, claimed that Descartes's theory of the creation of eternal truths, in particular the creation of the rules of goodness and perfection in the nature of things, leads to quite awkward theological as well as theoretical difficulties and paradoxes (see DM, §2/GP IV 427–8). Alexandre Koyré considered the theory inconsistent with all of Descartes's philosophy and with the idea of science itself (see Koyré 1922: 19ff.). And contemporary authors have maintained that the idea of created eternal truths introduces the view that "the world may be inherently absurd", that "reality may not be rational" (Frankfurt 1977: 54), whereby it is "clearly […] a bizarre doctrine" (Curley 1984: 569).

[47] To my knowledge, some of the most interesting attempts to make sense of the Cartesian theory of the creation of eternal truths, which cannot be examined here, are: Frankfurt 1977; Curley 1984; Kaufman (2005). An informative overview of the proposals of these authors is: Cunning 2018. Dominik Perler (Perler 2001) argues that Descartes had good rational motives to claim that the eternal truths are the creation of God, and that his account does not simply follow from the idea of a completely arbitrary and – as Harry Frankfurt (1977) seems to think – irrational God. According to Perler, there are good conceptual and ontological reasons for Descartes to argue for the dependency of eternal truths: first, the concept of God as an essentially simple being; second, the concept of God as an almighty being; third, the Cartesian theory of substances.

completely arbitrary being who acts following no reasons provided by his understanding (since his will and understanding are identical, the talk about the guidance of the will by the understanding makes no sense in their Cartesian model), etc. Budde and Knoerr's anti-Leibnizian account of the nature of the eternal truths can thus be shown to be consistent with their theological views.

Does all this speak for the superiority of Budde and Knoerr's account over Leibniz's? Of course it does not. Leibnizian optimism can also be shown to follow coherently from particular theological and theoretical assumptions, like for example: God is essentially a rational being who acts according to rational principles (the Principle of Sufficient Reason, the Principle of the Best, etc.); God, good and omnipotent, always acts following reasons, i.e. his will is subordinated to the representations of the good provided by his understanding, etc. It just happens that these assumptions are contrary to Budde and Knoerr's presuppositions.

As I explained in Chapter 1, following Steven Nadler, these two conflicting sets of presuppositions and conceptions of God are – together with a third prominent concept of divine nature: Spinoza's pantheism – typical for early modern theological and philosophical thought. I called them an 'intellectualist' model on the one hand, and a 'voluntarist' model on the other (Nadler talks about a 'rationalist' vs. a 'anti-rationalist' model), explaining that whereas the first one claims that God is a rational agent who acts for reasons and whose willing is always guided by practical reasoning (in other words, is bound to the assistance of intellectual information), voluntarists maintain that God's willing is "absolute and completely unmotivated by (logically) independent reasons" (Nadler 2011a: 525–6). The most notable representatives of these theological conceptions are, obviously, for intellectualism Leibniz, but also Malebranche; and for voluntarism Descartes, Pierre Poiret, and, according to Nadler, also very probably Arnauld. As we have seen, Budde and Knoerr can also be counted among the apologists for (a Cartesian sort of) voluntarism.

Which one of these sets of assumptions is the right one? Which theology captures God's nature more adequately? With this question we clearly arrive at a problematic and interesting point: that of deciding which concept of God applies better to the nature of God. For the case of early modern philosophy, it would seem we have arrived at a dead end, since, for the present case we are ultimately left with two seemingly valid but clashing models of divine nature and two possible, seemingly coherent metaphysics that follow from each of them.

Is this really the case? In the last chapter of this work, I will return to this question. For the moment, as we will see in the following chapters, the conflict between these two conceptions of God (or between Leibnizian intellectualism and some kind of voluntarism, now radical, now temperate) will be a constant over the course of the present examination of early modern opposition to Leibnizian optimism. In a certain sense, then, it could be said that the clash between optimism and counter-optimism is also (if not necessarily in all cases) a clash, which has been rendered theoretical, between two different conceptions of God.

4.2   *On Dogmatic Assumptions and Theoretical Effectiveness*

As we saw in the third section of this chapter, Budde and Knoerr make at least two claims regarding the quality of the world: first, our world is not the best of all possible worlds; second, and of course intimately connected with the first claim, there is more evil than good in our world. Both claims, as I explained in that place, result from a dogmatic religious, Judeo-Christian assumption: the doctrine of the Fall of Man. From that assumption follows the conviction that sin corrupted the world created by God so much that it is clear that the amount of evil surpasses the amount of goodness in the world and therefore the world *post lapsum* cannot be identified with the Leibnizian best of all possible worlds.

As I observed in that section, this kind of reasoning could seem to be problematic. Budde and Knoerr's criticism of *theoretical* claims by Leibniz – this world is the best of all possible worlds, no other world could have been better, etc. – rests for the most part on nothing more than a *dogmatic-religious* assumption. What is then the strength, the effectiveness of Budde and Knoerr's critique (as a critique of theoretical claims) given that it is built on doctrinaire premises that no one is obliged to assume?

Disregarding the simple reality that virtually all philosophers of the early modern period seem to assume one or another concept of God and adopt a particular religious mindset, it is clear that this question addresses an issue that is essential to the philosophical activity and as old as philosophy itself: the plain fact that theories tend to presuppose premises that they are not always able (or obliged to, or willing) to prove. Thus, more than desiring to solve this issue, I want to point out once more that it is present in Budde and Knoerr's criticism.

But also in Leibniz's account. Indeed, it seems that such a question can also be applied to Leibnizian optimism and the thesis of the best of all possible worlds. As R.S. Woolhouse has commented, God is in Leibniz's philosophy "an abiding presence" (Woolhouse 1998: 41). Thus, strictly speaking, the thesis of the best of all possible worlds (i.e. the identification of our world as the best possible) could also be described as following from a kind of dogmatic conviction. This conviction rests upon, on the one hand, on the belief in the existence of a God who is intelligent (that is, who has understanding), has a will, is powerful, good, wise, is essentially rational, etc.[48] This theological conviction is combined, on the other hand, with the theoretical suppositions we have mentioned before: the universal validity of the Principle of Sufficient Reason, the so-called Principle of the Best, etc.

Of course, Leibniz's procedural method is not unproblematic. Leibniz has also been criticized for assuming a specific theology. As we have seen in this chapter and will continue to see in the following, one of the main points of early critics of optimism is precisely Leibniz's assumption of a rationalist concept of God (a God that is subjected to rational principles, whose decisions follow reasons, etc.), which differs drastically from the concept of God maintained by those authors. And there are also the criticisms by later commentators, like Bertrand Russell's well known claim that "the weakest part in Leibniz's philosophy, the part most full of inconsistencies" is the use it makes of the "lazy device of reference to an Omnipotent Creator" (Russell referred in Woolhouse 1998: 41). The question regarding dogmatic assumptions and theoretical effectiveness is definitely not foreign to Leibnizian optimism. In turn, Russell's criticism could obviously be applied to the religious-founded account on which Budde and Knoerr's rejection of optimism rests, and so on. Thus once again, we seem to be left in the situation previously mentioned: in the presence of two (or more) internally consistent theological models that seem to contradict each other.

---

48   See for example T, §7/GP VI 106.

CHAPTER 3

A Jesuit Attacks: Louis-Bertrand Castel's Review of the *Theodicy* in the *Journal de Trévoux* (1737)

The learned journals of the seventeenth and eighteenth centuries were one of the most vital agents of intellectual change, as well as a representative witness of the topics, fashions, and obsessions that gave life to the intellectual world in early modern Europe. Some of the most popular early periodicals in continental Europe were the *Journal de savants*, the first scientific journal published in Europe (1665–1792); the Italian *Giornale de' letterati* (1668–1683); the *Acta Eruditorum*, the first German learned journal (1682–1782), and the famous *Nouvelles de la république des lettres* (1684–1718 with interruptions), founded by Pierre Bayle. Among them the *Mémoires pour l'histoire des sciences et des beaux arts*, or *Mémoires* or *Journal de Trévoux*, as they are more commonly known, occupy a prominent place.[1]

The *Journal de Trévoux* was founded in 1701, printed, and published successively in Trévoux (1701–1731), Lyon (1732–1733), and finally Paris (1734–1767) by the fathers of the Parisian college of Louis-le-Grand, the most famous of the Jesuit schools in France.[2] The *Journal* was born primarily as a reaction to the learned journals published by Protestant emigrants after the revocation of the Edict of Nantes (1685) by Louis XIV, and it followed the model of the *Journal de savants*, the official publication of the French Academy. Like the *Journal de savants* the Jesuits' journal was a literary periodical published mainly for the French lettered classes, consisting of excerpts, summaries, and commentaries of books recently published.[3]

Not only Jesuits were allowed to write in the *Journal*. Eminent authors like Leibniz or Voltaire, who themselves suffered the criticisms of the Jesuit intellectuals of the *Journal*, published articles in the periodical. However, as has been observed, since most of the articles and reviews are unsigned, it may be assumed that the greatest part of the material published was written by the editorial staff and other Jesuit authors.[4] Among the founders and most notable

---

1 On the history of the learned journals in early modern Europe see Basker 2003; Habel 2007.
2 On the history of the *Journal de Trévoux* see Desautels 1956; Dumas 1936; O'Keefe 1974: 8ff.
3 On the relation between the *Journal de savants* and the *Journal de Trévoux*, see Erhard & Roger 1965; O'Keefe 1956 and 1974.
4 *Cf.* O'Keefe 1956: 54; 1974: 10.

Jesuit contributors of the *Journal* were Jean-Antoine du Cerceau, François Xavier de Charlevoix, Guillaume François Berthier, René-Joseph Tournemine, and Louis-Bertrand Castel. The last two are of importance in the following pages since both of them published in the *Mémoires* reviews of Leibniz's *Theodicy*, the second of which is the main subject of this chapter.

The *Journal* issued reviews of the most important works on philosophy, theology, and science that were published in France, but also of those that went against the judgment of the French Catholic censorship and were published in England, Holland or Switzerland and entered the country illegally. While relatively inclusive or pluralist regarding the works presented to the public, the Jesuits did denounce devotedly those books and themes they considered dangerous to the Christian faith. The most notorious among them are those that in one way or another seemed to support any kind of rationalism, atheism, and more particularly, deism, which with its emphasis on natural religion and lay morality posed, in the opinion of the orthodoxy, the most serious threat to traditional religious and moral principles in the early modern period. Thus, some of the favorite and recurrent targets of the Jesuits' criticism were the works of what they called 'Spinozism', Bayle's fideistic-skeptic-(anti) rationalism of the *Dictionnaire* (1697, 1702), Alexander Pope's *Essay on Man* (1733–1734), and Voltaire's *Lettres philosophiques* (1734). Other renowned philosophers like Descartes or Malebranche were also reviewed and criticized in the journal,[5] and also, and quite attentively, the works of the so-called French *philosophes* (Montesquieu, Voltaire, Diderot, Rousseau), including of course the *Encyclopédie* (1751–1772), reviewed first positively, then quite harshly, as the attacks of the *philosophes* against the religious establishment became more spirited.[6]

Leibniz too, of course, was a matter of interest for the French Jesuits.[7] As mentioned before, the *Theodicy* was reviewed on at least two different occasions in the *Journal*: in 1713 and 1737. The first review was most probably written by the Jesuit theologian and philosopher René-Joseph de Tournemine (1661–1739), one of the founders of the *Mémoires* and a correspondent of Leibniz.[8]

---

5 On the critical reception of Descartes's and Malebranche's thought in the *Journal de Trévoux* see Allard 1985.
6 On the conflicts between the editors of the *Journal* and the French *philosophes* see Desautels 1956; O'Keefe 1974: 134ff.
7 On the development of the attitude of the *Mémoires* towards Leibnizian thought throughout the first half of the eighteenth century see Barber 1955: 100.
8 The correspondence between Leibniz and Tournemine, devoted mainly to discussing topics related with Leibniz's "New System of the Nature of Substances" (1695), is included in NS, chapter 10: 246–51.

Tournemine's review is a very brief summary and description of the *Theodicy*. Apart from some marginal critical comments about Leibniz's religious opinions (Tournemine, 1183–4), the soundness of some of his metaphysical views (like the theory of pre-established harmony, particularly regarding freedom) (1188–9), and the effectiveness of his arguments against Bayle's skepticism (1195), Tournemine's opinion of the *Theodicy* and Leibniz's intellectual stance is by and large positive. The disposition of his review is well resumed in the following lines:

> Leibniz's analyses of Bayle's reasoning will no doubt be pleasing to the connoisseurs, as they show with complete evidence the superiority of a righteous spirit [Leibniz] over a subtle spirit [Bayle].
> TOURNEMINE, 1181

In 1737 the *Journal de Trévoux* published a second review of the *Theodicy*, more exactly of the second French edition of the book, which appeared in Amsterdam in 1734.[9] The author of the review is thought to have been the Jesuit mathematician and relatively renowned physicist Louis-Bertrand Castel (1688–1757),[10] co-editor of the *Mémoires* between 1720 and 1745, radical opponent of Newton's views on science, and member of, among other learned academies, the Royal Society of London since 1730.

Unlike Tournemine's text, Castel's review is considerably longer (while the first amounted to no more than 20 pages, the second review is almost 140 pages long), quite digressive, and more detailed regarding the examination of the nature and the main tenets of philosophical optimism, as well as the elements in Leibniz's intellectual attitude that, in the opinion of the author, gave rise to the system of the best possible world. Further, as we will see in the following pages, Castel's work is definitely more critical of Leibnizian optimism than Tournemine's was. Indeed, despite the respectful and even flattering words that Castel uses to describe the person and the intellectual accomplishments of Leibniz, Castel's opinions about the *Theodicy* are anything but positive.

The 1737 review of the *Theodicy* is interesting for us for three reasons. First, it gives an account of the position towards Leibnizian rationalism of the very important and influential intellectual milieu that the Jesuits created in the

---

9 *Essais de Théodicée sur la bonté de Dieu, la liberté de l'homme et l'origine du mal. Nouvelle Edition, augmentée de l'Histoire de la Vie et des ouvrages de l'Auteur, par M. L. de Neufville*, Amsterdam: François Changuion, 1734.
10 *Cf.* Fonnesu 1994: 132ff.; 2006: 755.

eighteenth century. Of course, Castel's views concerning the *Theodicy* and Leibnizian philosophy in general should not be thought to represent in any way an 'official' Jesuit or Catholic position towards Leibniz. However, given that the *Journal de Trévoux* was the official publication of the French Jesuits, we seem to be justified in believing that the arguments and allegations that Castel puts forward were, at least to some extent, familiar among the learned Jesuit circles of the first half of the eighteenth century.

Secondly, it is in Castel's review that the word 'optimism', which survives in everyday language to this day,[11] was coined for the first time in the history of ideas and characterized in that rather ingenuous, cheerful, and roseate manner that it is still associated with today. It would become immensely popular in the following years as a mocking nickname against Leibniz's thought[12] – or something that was considered to be Leibniz's thought.

And thirdly, one of the aspects that appear to me of particular interest in Castel's review is Castel's pretension of establishing the 'real sources' of the system of the best world. These sources are not theoretical; they could perhaps be called of *subjective* nature on the part of Leibniz. They are indeed, according to Castel, on the one hand, an exaggerated rationalist longing, on the other the attitude – for Castel representative of a great portion of the intellectual world of his times – of emphasizing and even exaggerating the positive character of the world, of considering that our world is fundamentally good, and even more important, that the evils that the world might contain are only evils in a relative manner.

In the next pages I will examine the main arguments against Leibnizian optimism contained in Castel's review. In the first section of the chapter, I examine Castel's claim that optimism emerges from a somewhat subjective source: the combination of a rationalist and cheerful posture. This is, in my opinion, the most stimulating and problematic aspect of his review. In the second section, I will focus on Castel's criticisms of particular theses of Leibnizian optimism. Finally, in the third section, I will examine problems and open questions related to Castel's claims about the idiosyncratic or subjective foundations of optimism in more detail.

---

11   On the intellectual history of the term 'optimism' see Günther 1994.
12   One need only think about the prize-contest of the Prussian Academy of Sciences in 1755, examined in Chapter 5; Voltaire's derisive *Candide ou l'optimisme* of 1759; or Arthur Schopenhauer's furious attacks of Leibniz in the first half of the nineteenth century – all of them referring more or less scornfully to 'optimism'.

1   The Happy Rationalist

As already mentioned, Castel's review begins as a commentary of the second edition of the *Theodicy* (1734), edited with a bio-bibliographical introduction by a certain L. de Neufville – who was none other than the French writer and extremely prolific *encyclopédiste* Louis de Jaucourt (1704–1779).[13] Castel expresses initially a very positive opinion about Leibniz's intellectual deeds. Very soon, however, he comes to talk about a feature of Leibniz's personality that will be stressed in quite a few passages of the review and that would seem to transform the initial apparently eulogistic depiction into an almost mocking description of the philosopher: Leibniz's tendency or aspiration of outshining in all fields of knowledge and, more important, his desire of conciliating all branches of science. Castel writes:

> Born in Germany, this illustrious sage lived among all circles and in all nations of Europe, and trained his genius in one way or another in philosophy and geometry, which are in some manner the same field; he lived and worked in all fields, in all disciplines, in jurisprudence, in history, in chemistry, in medicine, in theology itself, and in metaphysics. Politician, physicist, naturalist, genealogist, anatomist, botanist, astronomer, alchemist, casuist, grammarian, and probably also Lutheran, Calvinist, Socinian, even Catholic, if this is possible. Leibniz was everything, he knew everything, wrote about everything, and wanted chiefly to conciliate everything.

> [*Né en Allemagne, cet illustre sçavant a vécu dans tous les cercles & chez toutes les nations de l'Europe & son génie né en quelque sorte ou formé dans la philosophie & dans la geométrie, qui sont à peu-prés une même région, a vécu, a travaillé dans toutes les régions, dans toutes les parties des sciences, dans la Jurisprudence, dans l'Histoire, dans la Chymie, dans la Médecine, dans la Theologie même & dans la Métaphysique. Politique, Physicien, Naturaliste, Généalogiste, Anatomiste, Botaniste, Astronôme, Alchymiste, Casuiste, Grammairien & peut être Luthérien, Calviniste, Socinien, Catholique même, s'il es possible, M. Leibnitz étoit tout, sçavoit tout, écrivoit de tout, voulant principalement concilier tout.*]
>   CASTEL, 7–8

---

13   *Cf.* Lorenz: 1997: 78.

Leibniz, the polymath, the *Universalgelehrter* of whom we speak today, is for Castel something less solemn: a know-it-all. This characterization would be a simple curiosity, if it were not for the fact that Castel's description of Leibniz's thirst for knowledge and his conciliatory personality is connected to two aspects of Leibniz's character which, according to Castel, lie at the basis of the system of optimism.

These are, on the one hand, what could be called an ultra-rationalist attitude on the part of Leibniz, expressed in few words as the desire of explaining everything, i.e. of *giving a reason* for everything that happens. On the other, an ultra-positive (or as we would say today – at risk of falling into some sort of *petitio principii* – an ultra-*optimist*) mind-set towards the character of creation: the idea that the world is fundamentally and absolutely good. Both charges against Leibniz run through the whole review and serve Castel as an explanation of the origin of the main theses of optimism, as well as of its failures.

1.1 "Nothing More Than a Physicist": Leibnizian Optimism as Hyperbolic Rationalism

Castel's first indictment is simple: Leibniz was too much of a rationalist and the philosophical system of optimism results, at least in part, from this exaggerated rationalism. Castel writes:

> The *Theodicy* is not precisely a book that one could call orthodox; indeed, we believe to have discovered several errors that we would like to explain. But the book is not full of that skeptical venom that infects all of Bayle's writings. M. Leibniz's mistakes seem to us to result from a too philosophical, too argumentative [*raisonneur*] spirit that wants to subject everything to the light of its reason; from a spirit too accustomed to erect systems and which applies itself to matters of faith with the same easiness as it applies itself to matters of nature and physics.
>
> [*La Théodicée n'est point un livre qu'on puisse dire orthodoxe; nous avons crû y découvrir au contraire bien des erreurs que nous allons exposer. Mais elle n'est pas non plus pleine de ce venin sceptique qui infecte tous les écrits de M. Bayle. Les erreurs de M. Leibnitz nous paroissent partir de l'esprit, d'un esprit trop philosophe, trop raisonneur, qui veut soumettre trop toutes choses à la lumière de sa raison; d'un esprit trop accoutumé à faire des systèmes, & qui s'évapore avec la même facilité dans les matières de la foy que dans celles de la nature & de la physique.*]
>
> CASTEL, 203

The "too philosophical", "too argumentative" spirit that Castel detects at the basis of optimism consists, as he explains, in wanting to subject everything, even matters of faith, to the light of reason. For Castel this means something very specific, namely – following the example or the method of geometry and the science of nature – to want to *give a reason* for everything that is or occurs, not only in the world but also (and this is clearly the most problematical aspect of the rationalist approach that Castel condemns) in God. According to Castel, modern physics is "too geometric, too mechanical, too Spinozist" and thus "incompatible with freedom, either divine or human". It wants "to give a reason for everything" and ignores dangerously that one cannot explain freedom [*Nous parlons de la physique moderne: elle est trop géométrique, trop mécanique, trop spinosiste, trop incompatible avec la liberté soit divine soit humaine. On y veut trop rendre raison de tout. On ne rend point raison de la liberté.*] (Castel, 215). Leibniz, who for Castel was fundamentally a scientific mind, follows rather blindly the pretensions of physics and overlooks both the fact that we do not always have a satisfactory explanation for everything that occurs in the world, and – as Castel seems to believe, although he never gives us a clear description of his own theology – the fact that God's actions *cannot* be enlightened:

> However, the greatest principle for Leibniz is that nothing can exist on the part of God himself and on the part of his will, which is most free, *without a sufficient reason* […]. But all these philosophers do not want to hear; they are incapable of reaching the most immediate and purely corporal causes of phenomena, and they want to give a metaphysical reason for the most sublime operations of divinity; and, in want of real reasons that they ignore, they will even prescribe God their own laws.
>
> [*Le grand principe cependant de M. Leibnitz est que rien ne doit exister de la part de Dieu même, & de la part de sa volonté la plus libre sans une raison suffisante* […]. *Mais tous ces philosophes ne veulent point y entendre; & ne pouvant atteindre à la cause la plus immédiate & purement corporelle de presqu'aucun phénomène, ils veulent rendre raison métaphysique des opérations les plus sublimes de la divinité; & au défaut des véritables raisons qu'ils ignorent de fait & de droit, ils vont jusqu'a lui en prescrire, & à lui prescrire, en propres termes, des loix de leur façon.*]
>
> CASTEL, 215–6

When he writes "their own laws" Castel is of course thinking about parameters like the Principle of Sufficient Reason. We saw in Chapter 1 that for Leibniz the Principle is a law to which everything, including God's behavior (given that

God is fundamentally a rational being), is subjected. (As we will see in the following chapter, the Principle is also an important troublemaker for critics of optimism like Christian August Crusius). The claim that laws like the Principle of Sufficient Reason are valid regarding moral and divine issues seems out of place to Castel and to result from a kind of overexcited rationalism that wants to apply universally the ways of the physicist or geometrician. Castel stresses this view in several passages and claims for example that Leibniz, although certainly versed in theology, ethics, and metaphysics, was "strictly speaking nothing more than a physicist and a geometrician" (Castel, 215). Further, regarding the meddling of rationalism in theological matters, Castel writes straightforwardly:

Bad physics makes of people bad theologians.

[*Une mauvaisse physique rend, à coup sûr, les gens mauvais théologiens.*]
CASTEL, 217

At least two consequences follow from "bad physics". First, the idea that God was obliged to create the world he created and could have not done otherwise, i.e. the denial of divine freedom understood as the complete indeterminacy of the will. And second the view – which results from the combination of the idea that everything happens for a reason and the doctrine that everything God does is good, and which in Castel's understanding is central to optimism – that evil is not really evil at all.[14] I will examine both claims in the next sections of this chapter.

Before explaining the second Leibnizian character trait that, together with an exaggerated rationalism, supposedly gives rise to the system of the best, I would like to take a brief look at Castel's opinion about Leibniz's religion. As I

---

14   "Leibniz cannot conceive that God can make us enter paradise through a way different to suffering; as if in this very moment infants would not enter into it immediately after baptism without doing anything and without having suffered. For him it is inconceivable that we can have roses without thorns [...]. Should we believe that evil is by nature more capable than good to produce good? By nature, good produces good, evil produces evil." [*M. Leibnitz au moins ne conçoit pas que Dieu ait pû nous faire entrer dans son paradis par une autre voye que par celle des souffrances; comme si aujourd'hui même bien des enfants n'y entroient pas tout de suite après le Baptême, sans avoir rien, ou comme rien souffert? Il ne conçoit pas que nous puissions avoir des roses sans épines; comme si une infinité d'autres fleurs tout aussi belles, tout aussi suaves auxquelles il auroit pû se borner, ne nous disoient pas qu'absolument Dieu poivoit nous combler de toutes sortes de biens aucun mélange de maux? Croira-t-on que le mal soit de sa nature plus compétent que le bien, pour produire le bien? De soi le bien produit le bien, le mal produit le mal.*] (Castel, 217–8).

believe, this will give more details about the kind of rationalist-conciliatory attitude that, according to Castel, lies behind optimism, and his ideas regarding the noxious consequences of that rationalism.

According to Castel Leibniz, following his conciliatory spirit, also defended a kind of dilettante-religion. Leibniz was born a Lutheran and never seemed to have expressed any sort of abjuration of his confession. And still, his desire of conciliation made him maintain open and intense contact to ideas and members of other confessions:

> Polite, human, moderate toward everybody, he was in no way malicious: he spoke with the utmost respect about the Pope, the bishops, the Fathers, the clerics. He dealt with everybody. He maintained contact with several Jesuits [...] He looked into all human ideas, all beliefs, all religions, both righteous and excessive [...]
>
> [*Poli, humain, modéré envers tout le monde, il n'etoit point médisant: il parloit du Pape, des Evêques, des Pères, des Ecclésiastiques avec beaucoup de respect. Il vivoit avec tout le monde. Il étoit en commerce des Lettres & de Littérature avec plusieurs Jésuites* [...] *Il trouvoit dans toutes les pensées des hommes, dans tous les Livres, dans toutes les créances, dans toutes les religions du bon & des excès* [...]]
>
> CASTEL, 34

But this openness of mind implies something more. As was the case with the claims about Leibniz's intellectual interests, here also Castel has more than only laudatory words for Leibniz's attitude towards religion. There Castel accused Leibniz of wanting to be every kind of scientist, without being, at the end, anything at all (or "nothing more than a physicist and a geometrician"). Here he returns to Leibniz's appeasing character and maintains, not without irony, that in the *Theodicy* Leibniz wanted to conciliate everything: "the Socinians with the Lutherans, the Lutherans with the Calvinists, the Calvinists with the Catholics, the Molinists with the Predeterminants, the Predeterminants with the Jansenists" [*Dans sa Théodicée il veut tout concilier, les Sociniens avec les Luthériens, les Luthériens avec les Calvinistes, les Calvinistes avec les Catholiques, les Molinistes avec les Prédéterminants, les Prédéterminants avec les Jansénistes.*] (Castel, 34).

According to Castel, this conciliatory intention was born from a certain "righteousness" or "rectitude of reason" [*droiture de raison*] on Leibniz's part. With this, Castel seems to want to return to the idea of Leibniz's exaggerated and omnipresent rationalist temperament. Now, as Castel promptly explains: reason and religion do not necessarily follow the same aims, not necessarily respond to the same interests. In fact, reason may seem to be at odds with religion. Leibniz certainly judged religion "on behalf of a certain righteousness of reason". But as Castel goes on to emphasize, "reason does not attend to faith and one can, with all this reason, be neither Catholic nor Protestant, namely have no religion at all" [*Il jugeoit de tout cela par une certaine droiture de raison. Mais la raison n'atteint pas à la foi & on peut avec toute cette raison n'être ni Catholique ni Protestant, & n'avoir en un mot aucune religion.*] (Castel, 34). And thus, it does not come as a surprise that Castel finishes his portrait of Leibniz's religion with a poorly concealed and indeed rather eloquent accusation:

> At the end of his days and upon his return from Vienna – where the Jesuits had hoped to win him to the true religion – this mockery crossed through all Germany [...]: *Leibniz glaubt nitz* [sic], that is: *Leibniz believes nothing at all.*
>
> [*Aussi sur la fin de ses jours & à son retour de Vienne, où les Jésuites avoient espéré de le gagner à la vraie religion, ce quolibet populaire courut toute l'Allemagne* [...]: Leibniz glaubt nitz; *c'est-à-dire:* Leibniz ne croit rien.]
> CASTEL, 34–5

To be sure, Castel never explains his own understanding of the relationship between faith and reason, or for that matter *any* of his own theological beliefs. Neither does he explain which are exactly the problems that he recognizes in 'Leibniz's religion' (apart, of course, from the fact that Leibniz defends a rationalist-conciliatory approach that Castel considers perilous and possibly foolish). Since his comments on Bayle are also, to say the least, disdainful, one could guess that concerning the question of the rationality of faith, Castel would perhaps defend a somewhat intermediate position between Bayle's anti-rationalism/skepticism/fideism (faith and reason cannot be conciliated, only the blind following of faith can 'solve' the paradoxes that reason poses concerning the mysteries of religion, etc.) and Leibniz's conciliatory rationalism (well expressed in "On the Conformity of Faith with Reason", the openly anti-Baylean dissertation that precedes the text of the *Theodicy*). At any rate, interesting for us here is to note that Castel's criticism of Leibniz's approach to religious questions follows from the same idea that an ultra-rationalist spirit implies very dangerous philosophical and theological consequences.

1.2 *"Everything Is Good, Everything Is Better, Everything Is Very Good"*

One of the main purposes of the *Theodicy* is to answer to the philosophical and theological difficulties related to Pierre Bayle's reintroduction of the problem of evil into the intellectual debate at the end of the seventeenth century. Also, to propose a rationalist solution to Bayle's skepticism regarding the ability of reason to examine questions of faith, and particularly his view of the mutually exclusive or contradictory relation between reason and faith. Bayle's name is, thus, a constant throughout the treatise and much of Leibniz's philosophical efforts in the *Theodicy* are directed towards refuting Bayle's arguments and paradoxes. Castel exploits this duel by referring in a number of places to the contrast between Bayle's and Leibniz's positions, apparently in order to stress his comments and criticisms of the Leibnizian account. Thus, as we saw previously, the exposition of the idea that an extreme rationalist-conciliatory temperament on the part of Leibniz underlies philosophical optimism includes the mentioning of Bayle's skepticism as a contrasting attitude to that of Leibniz.

Castel's second claim concerning the origin of optimism – the system of the best follows from an exaggeratedly positive view of the world – also seems to feed upon the motif of the almost mythical battle between Leibniz, the ultra-rationalist, and Bayle, the skeptical heretic. In this case, however, not the theoretical (or pseudo-theoretical) aspect of both positions is referred to by Castel, but the opinions of both philosophers regarding the evils and, so to speak, the moral quality of the world.

Describing the intellectual attitude that optimism supposedly stands for, Castel writes:

> To Bayle and to all those who criticize Providence regarding the physical and moral disorders [...], the new Conciliator, full of humanity, answers that there is no evil nor anything to criticize; that everything is good or at least that it exists for a greater good [...]; that God has done his best, that not only God could have not made and known better, that he could have not done and known otherwise [...]

> [À M. Bayle & à tous ceux qui critiquent la Providence sur les désordres physiques & moraux [...], le nouveau Conciliateur plein d'humanité, répondoit qu'il n'y avoit pas de mal, ni de quoi critiquer; que tout étoit bien ou pour le bien au moins, & pour un plus grand bien [...], qui Dieu avoit fait de son mieux, que non-seulement il n'avoit pû ni sçû faire mieux, qu'il n'avoit pû ni sçû faire autrement [...]]
>
> CASTEL, 207–8

Several problematic claims are included in this passage. Apart from the new sarcastic reference to the Leibnizian character ("the new Conciliator") Castel maintains that for Leibniz, strictly speaking, there is no evil in the world, since for optimism everything is either good or promotes the good. Further, he returns to a point of criticism that was mentioned before and will be examined in more detail in the next section: the idea that optimism implies that God could have not done otherwise.

Here I shall focus on the idea that optimism claims that "everything is good". For Castel it would seem that such a thesis does not result from a theoretical approach to the nature of creation, but from a somewhat intellectual *posture* that seems, in circular manner, to both motivate the system of philosophical optimism *and* to be encouraged by that system. Castel – in the haughty manner in which he likes to refer to optimism – describes this positive posture towards creation as a new "fashion" or a "trend" (*nouvelle mode*) that has come to mark the character of the century, as opposed to the gloomier attitude towards the world held by thinkers of the seventeenth century.

> This is one of the keys of the *Theodicy*. Leibniz, with a really inventive genius, has opened a new way and has introduced the new fashion of the philosophy of '*bel esprit*' [...]. The fashion of criticizing Providence is over. Its critics are exhausted and are openly impious and libertine. The new fresh fashion is to applaud Providence and to say of all things: 'it's good' [...]
>
> [*C'est une clef encore de la Théodicée. M. Leibnitz, avec un genie véritablement inventif, a ouvert une carriere nouvelle & introduit une nouvelle mode de Philosophie bel esprit. [...]. Ce n'est plus la mode de critiquer la Providence. Ces Critiques son trops usées & trop ouvertement impies & libertines. Le grand air est d'applaudir à la Providence & de dire à toutes choses tant mieux [...]*]
>
> CASTEL, 219–20

Whereas "sublime misanthropes" of the previous century like Pascal or Bayle himself exaggerated the amount of evil in the world and believed firmly that "everything is infected, everything corrupt", according to Castel, a new sect of "*beaux esprits*" tirelessly praises God and his works in the current century. These joyous, cheerful, satisfied spirits proclaim: "Everything is good, everything is better, everything is very good" [*Tout est bien, tout est mieux, tout est très-bien*] and argue gaily that evil is not really an evil, since "it is the necessary cause of the good, necessary in God himself, who does not only know how to extract the good from the bad, but knows and can only extract it therefrom; and this not only in spite of his wisdom, but more precisely: because of his wisdom" [*Le mal n'est pas un mal, puisque'il est la cause necessaire du bien, necessaire à Dieu même, qui non-seulement sçait, tirer le bien du mal, mais ne le sçait, ou ne le peut tirer que de là; non-seulement encore malgré sa sagesse, mais précisement à cause même de sa sagesse.*] (Castel, 221).

This smiling clique, as every creed, has a high priest. For Castel, the pontiff of the optimist religion of reason is, of course, Leibniz. The German philosopher has been followed by others – Castel talks about "P. in England" and "V. in France", obviously referring to Alexander Pope and Voltaire – that in a kind of mission and driven by some optimistic enthusiasm have dedicated themselves, in prose and rhyme, to preach "[…] that there is no evil, that everything in nature is good, that the ruling kingdom is that of the beautiful nature, that nature is such as nature had to be, that nature could have not been otherwise […]" [[…] *qu'il n'a pas de mal, que la nature est bien, que le système regnant es celui de la belle nature, qu'elle est telle qu'elle a dû être, qu'elle ne pouvoit être autrement* […]] (Castel, 222).[15] The connection between Leibniz and Voltaire and Pope (especially the latter) is a commonplace among the eighteenth-century critics of optimism.[16] Castel's reference is perhaps one of the first in the history of that motif,[17] which will find (one of) its climax(es) in the prize-question of the Prussian Academy of Sciences of 1753 ("*An examination of the system of Pope as it is contained in the dictum: 'Everything is good'* […], *compared to the system of optimism or the choice of the best*"), to be examined in Chapter 5 of this work.

For Castel, then, optimism follows from an excited rationalism – i.e. the wish or the pretension to give (rational) reasons for everything that is and occurs – mixed with the rather subjective drive of exaggerating the good in the world.

---

15 The usual reference to the 'optimist' works of both authors is Pope's famous poetic treatise *Essay on Man* (1733–1734) and Voltaire's "On Mr. Pascal's *Pensées*" (twenty-fifth letter of the *Philosophical Letters* of 1734), as well as his poem "Le mondain" (1736).

16 On the relationship between Leibniz and both authors see Barber 1955: 107–22 and 174–243; Brooks 1964; Hellwig 2008: 17ff.; Moore 1917; Rogers 1948; Weinrich 1986.

17 Another notable initial station of the history of the Leibniz-Pope connection in France is the *Examen de l'Essai de M. Pope, sur l'Homme*, published in the same year as Castel's review by the Swiss theologian and philosopher Jean Pierre Crousaz (1663–1750), who censures the 'optimist' theses of Pope's *Essay on Man* and compares them critically to the Leibnizian system of the best. On this debate see Barber 1955: 116ff; Hellwig 2008: 123ff.; Rogers 1948, as well as Chapter 5.

This drive of "applauding Providence" and considering that everything is good is the exact opposite, and perhaps the timely reaction, to Bayle's exceptionally negative depiction of the world. But precisely for that reason it would seem that, for Castel, philosophical optimism is no less extreme, excessive, and at the end gratuitous, than Bayle's heterodox approach.

Castel uses a simile to depict the idle contrast between Bayle and Leibniz that, in my opinion, describes his point well. He writes that regarding their views about the character of the world, "these two strange men, unique men each one in his own kind", are like the doctors of Molière,[18] the one of them saying of everything "so much the better", the other one "so much the worse" [*Ces deux hommes rares, uniques mêmes, chacun dans leur espèce, étoient vis-à-vis l'un de l'autre comme ces médecins qui consultent chez Molière & dont à toutes choses, l'un dit tant mieux & l'autre tant pis.*] (Castel, 206–7). As I believe, this claim is of some importance, since it underlines the fact that, for Castel, philosophical or 'metaphysical' optimism follows from a subjective view of the world's quality; a view as justified or gratuitous, as right or erroneous, as Bayle's pessimism. At the end, Castel would seem to think, in the debate between "it's bad" and "it's good", we are left in the presence of two as learned and genial as tyrannical preachers, each one of them deaf-defending an opinion that is exactly that: an *opinion*, apparently irrefutable by any kind of argument. It is in this polemic context that Castel coins the term 'optimism', which will become the trademark for referring, now mockingly (it is clearly Castel's intention,[19] and in the eighteenth century that intention seems to be the rule), now more or less neutrally, to Leibniz's system of the best:

> It is clear that the one who says 'so much the better' is Leibniz. Indeed, this is his word and his solution to all difficulties. He calls it the *rule of the best* or [...] the system of the best [*le système de l'Optimum*] or *optimism*.
>
> [*On devine bien que le tant mieux est de M. Leibnitz. Réellement c'est son mot & sa solution à toutes les difficultés en termes de l'art, il l'appelle la raison du meilleur ou plus savamment encore & théologiquement autant que géométriquement, le système de l'Optimum, ou l'optimisme.*]
>
> CASTEL, 206–7

---

18   See for example Molière's *Le Médecin malgré lui* (1666).
19   *Cf.* Hübener 1978: 238: "The completely negative and critical-intentioned technical term '*optimisme*' is the answer of a voluntarist theology to the aesthetic attitude of a superficial, overhasty applause of the Providence".

Playing with an anachronism we could then say that for Castel, optimism (i.e. Leibniz's metaphysical system of the best of all possible worlds) results from an exacerbated rationalism and from optimism (i.e. Leibniz's somewhat subjective opinion that this world is, basically, great). Its ultimate message for humanity, in spite of all the theoretical and argumentative machinery that the *Theodicy* exposes, is that, at the end of the day, "everything is good".

Castel's account is problematic, or at least provokes questions both about Castel's claims as well as about the philosophical strength of Leibniz's system of optimism. On the one hand, it is not clear why, as Castel would seem to want to insinuate, the theoretical and argumentative machinery of the *Theodicy* should really be a façade, behind which almost nothing more than an idiosyncratic wild love for the world operates. On the other hand, the claim that Leibnizian optimism maintains that "everything is good" certainly did have a rather successful history in the eighteenth century, influenced as it was by the problematic idea of the supposed intimate relation between Leibniz's *Theodicy* and Pope's *Essay on Man* (and more specifically, Pope's motto "Whatever is, is right", which, as I will explain later on, was translated and interpreted as meaning "everything is good"). From Castel's review to the above mentioned prize-contest of the Prussian Academy and Voltaire's *Candide*, Leibniz was depicted throughout the first half of the eighteenth century as claiming that everything is good and denying naively, or at least minimizing the evils of the world.[20] But does Leibniz really maintain, in some way or another, that "*everything is good*"? In which way does optimism, if it really does, deny or minimize the evils in the world? These questions will be examined in the last section of this chapter.

2   God's Freedom and Evil in the Best of All Worlds: Some New Names for Usual Criticisms of Optimism

Castel's criticisms of particular aspects and theses of philosophical optimism are quite general, never deepening into a specific problem, neither offering a thorough examination, nor arguments that could render his criticisms truly effective. Nevertheless, for two reasons his criticisms are interesting for us. On the one hand, regarding Castel's view of optimism, they stress the motives for which Castel believes that the rationalist-optimist 'attitude' that in his opinion gives rise to optimism is problematic or noxious. On the other hand, regarding the critical reception of optimism in the first half of the eighteenth century, Castel's complaints – both because of their nature, as well as because

---

20   *Cf.* Hellwig 2008.

they received far more publicity than, for example, the criticisms by Budde and Knoerr examined in the last chapter – seem to be representative of the difficulties of digesting philosophical optimism some of Leibniz's contemporaries had.

Castel's critique can be divided roughly into two groups: first, criticisms concerning the complete necessity supposedly introduced into the world and the actions of rational beings by optimism; and second, criticisms directed against the idea that this world is the best of all possible worlds.

2.1 *"Nothing More Than a Spiritual Spinozism": Optimism, Necessitarianism, and the Problem of Divine Freedom*

One of the clearest statements in Castel's review concerning his disdainful opinion of optimism is the following:

> Optimism [...] is nothing more than a disguised materialism, a spiritual Spinozism [...] The regularity and systematic unity of the curve, through which our author described the march and the behavior of every particular human being, and without doubt of all human beings and the rest of beings, probably without the exception of God himself, was a brilliant geometric idea, but no more than a branch of pre-established harmony and pure Spinozism.

> [*L'optimisme [...] n'est qu'un matérialisme déguisé, un spinosisme spirituel [...]. La régularité & l'unité systématique de courbure, par laquelle l'auteur exprimoit la marche & toute la conduite de chaque homme, & sans doute de touts les hommes & de tous les êtres, sans en excepter peut être Dieu même, étoit une idée géométrique des plus brillantes, mais une branche de l'harmonie préétablie & un spinosisme tout pur.*]
>   CASTEL, 208–9

Behind the furious rhetoric of Castel's tirade there lies a simple idea: the regularity that Leibniz introduces into the behavior of rational beings (God included) transforms the free actions of those beings into elements of a necessitarian system (that is, following Charles Sanders Peirce's definition, a system in which an actions of the will is "the necessary effect of the antecedent causes" and "subject to the general mechanical law of cause and effect" [Peirce 1891]). Optimism is a "disguised materialism" because it maintains, in Castel's opinion, that the rules and laws usually applied to nature are also valid regarding the actions of rational beings. And it is therefore also a "spiritual Spinozism", because Leibniz apparently subjects spirits to the same necessity, to which Spinoza subjects everything that happens in nature. (In this vocabulary Castel shows himself as a rather up-to-date critic of Leibniz, following the very usual eighteenth-century fashion of labeling as 'Spinozism' any idea that in some manner seemed to deny the contingence of natural and 'spiritual' occurrences.[21])

The main lines of Castel's reproach against Leibniz have been mentioned already in the previous section: Leibniz, an excessive rationalist, wanted to explain the behavior of rational beings through the same methods and the same hypotheses with which a geometrician works, i.e. by supposing that everything can be explained through reasons, or, more exactly, that there is a reason for everything, which determines why things happen in a particular manner and not otherwise, etc. Certainly Castel is not *that* explicit and does not even mention Leibniz's understanding of the Principle of Sufficient Reason (well, Castel does not even mention the Principle), but it is clear that this is the kind of argument he has in mind when he denounces optimism as a "spiritual Spinozism".

Castel does seem to be more explicit when referring to the danger that optimism poses to divine freedom. He writes, for example:

> In particular, optimism presents God as an automaton. By subjecting him to the Law of the Best, [Leibniz] deprives God of freedom of choice and of every kind of freedom.
>
> [*L'optimisme en particulier, règle Dieu comme un automate. En l'assujettissant à la Loi de meilleur, il ne lui laisse ni la liberté du choix ni aucune espèce de liberté.*]
> CASTEL, 209–10

In Castel's view, the Rule or Principle of the Best holds that everything created by God is the best possible. The genealogy of the principle is simple: for Leibniz, on the one hand, God's actions are also subjected to the Principle of Sufficient Reason. On the other, God is an infinitely good being, whose reason for acting is always the good. From this follows naturally, at least in a Leibnizian context, that everything God does is the best possible.[22]

---

21   Spinoza writes in the *Ethics*: "[A]ll things in nature proceed from a sort of necessity and with the utmost perfection" (E, I, Appendix, 2). In *A Spinoza Reader: The Ethics and Other Works* (ed. and trans. Edwin Curley), Princeton: Princeton U.P., 1994. On the history and the use of the concept of "Spinozism" to denounce in the eighteenth century the idea that there is no contingence in the world nor in the actions of rational beings, see Gawlick 2007; Israel 2002.

22   On the Principle of Perfection or of the Best see Chapter 1, 2, 2.3.

In Castel's opinion, to maintain that God responds to any principle or rule of action is equivalent to saying that God is a machine incapable of really *choosing*. If God is bound to principles of action, he cannot just act in *any* way he wants, since he has to follow the parameters established by those principles.[23] For the particular case of the subjection to the Principle of the Best, God has no real freedom of choice, since he can only choose one alternative: the best. As Castel writes:

> Leibniz, as good geometrician, postulates first his axioms: 1) *God is the first cause of all things*; 2) *The divine understanding is the source of essences*; 3) *The divine will is the source of existences*, etc. Let us examine attentively the system that results therefrom. *This supreme wisdom* – he says – *united to an infinite goodness, cannot but have chosen the best* [T, §8/GP VI 107]. Now the term 'to choose' is here excessive; a necessary choice is no choice at all.
>
> [*M. Leibnitz en bon géomètre pose d'abord ses axiomes, 1°* Que Dieu est la première raison des choses. *2°* Que l'entendement divin est la source des essences. *3°* Que la volonté est l'origine des existences, *etc. Rendons nous attentifs, voici le système qui en résulte.* Cette suprême sagesse, *dit-il*, jointe à une infinie bonté, n'a pû manquer de choisir le meilleur. *Le terme* choisir *est ici abusif; un choix nécessaire, n'est point un choix.*]
>
> CASTEL, 448

As I said before the review does not give us any distinct idea as to what exactly are Castel's views with regard to divine action, nor what he considers divine freedom to be. However, it seems clear to me that he defends some kind of indifference or arbitrariness-theory,[24] according to which God's actions, in order to be free, must result from undetermined acts of the will, that is from arbitrary decisions that do not follow laws like the Principle of the Best (or, for that matter, the Principle of Sufficient Reason). Whether this suffices to classify Castel as a voluntarist (as we did for the case of the particular Cartesian voluntarism of Budde and Knoerr in the preceding chapter and as we shall do for the case of Crusius in the next chapter) is not clear, since Castel does not develop any theory of the divine will in his review. Be that as it may, it is obvious that for Castel

---

23 On this respect see for example, in Chapter 2 Budde and Knoerr's criticism of the Leibnizian theory of uncreated eternal truths.

24 Fonnesu (1994: 134) talks about "arbitrarism" or "arbitrarianism" [*Arbitrarismus*].

to maintain, on the one hand, that God can *only* do the best and, on the other, that he is nevertheless (or – as Leibniz thinks – *therefore*) free, is unacceptable.

For Leibniz himself, as we have seen previously, this issue is rather more simple. As we know, for him the talk about a will (divine or human) that is completely undetermined is nonsense. First, rational beings always have a reason to act, since otherwise they would be incapable of choosing.[25] That reason of action is the representation of the good, provided by the understanding. This means that rational beings *are* determined in their actions. But, as I have mentioned before, for Leibniz to be determined by the representation of the good is exactly what it means to be free.[26]

Leibniz admits that there is a necessity in the actions of rational beings. This necessity, however, is not the same one that the events of mathematics or the physical world have, i.e. absolute or physical necessity, but what he calls *moral* necessity. In his account, moral necessity does not contradict freedom of choice, since it consists in the determination of actions by final causes or, specifically, by the purpose of obtaining the best, and, for Leibniz this purposiveness, in accordance with the best, is completely compatible with freedom.[27]

For Castel the matter is also simple, only in a very different way: for him *necessity is necessity*. For him, once one has accepted that God acts according to rational principles, that God chooses only the best, etc., the denial of freedom has already taken place:

> The necessity that our author draws from the divine wisdom is for him no more than a *moral* necessity. But isn't this necessity just as metaphysical as that of Spinoza? It is at least just as absolute as that one. Indeed, God is absolutely wise at all times, in every aspect, in all his actions. *It is a happy necessity* – Leibniz says – *which obliges the wise to do good* [T, §§175, 191, 344, 374/GP VI 218–9, 230, 318–9, 338]. The necessity which obliges God to do good and prevents him from doing evil is a very absolute and very natural necessity, and Leibniz calls it improperly *moral necessity*, only because it concerns the morality of actions. This is an abuse of the terms: God is free only to choose the best.
>
> [*La nécessité que notre auteur tire de la sagesse divine, il ne l'appelle que morale. Mais n'est-elle pas tout aussi métaphysique que celle de Spinoza? Elle est au moins aussi absolue. Car Dieu est absolument sage en toutes*

---

25   See for example T, §§35, 46ff., 303/GP VI 122–3, 128ff., 296–7.
26   T, §§236, 288/GP VI 258–9, 288. Also LC, L.V.7/GP VII 390.
27   On the distinction between absolute (or logical, or metaphysical) and moral (or hypothetical) necessity see Chapter 1, 3, 3.2.

> *tems, en tout lieu & dans toutes ses opérations. C'est une heureuse nécessité, dit M. Leibnitz, qui oblige le sage de bien faire. La nécessité qui oblige Dieu de bien faire & qui l'empêche de mal faire, est une nécessité très-absolue & très-naturelle; & M. Leibnitz l'appelle improprement nécessité morale, uniquement parce qu'elle regarde la moralité des actions. C'est abuser des termes: Dieu n'est libre que dans le choix des biens.]*
>
> CASTEL, 964–5

In the next chapters, when examining August Christian Crusius's and Adolf Friedrich Reinhard's criticisms of the Leibnizian theory of divine agency, we will observe a similar reaction as Castel's rejection of Leibniz's doctrine of moral necessity. Castel seems to ignore or misunderstand the concept of moral necessity. In fact, he does not even explain *how* he understands that concept. This is certainly problematic since, as I will explain in the next chapter, Leibniz does seem to think that it is possible to be bound by moral necessity and nevertheless be free. (Leibniz's explanation might be itself problematic, but it is still an explanation, and Castel overlooks it completely.)

As I suspect, even if Castel would have taken Leibniz's moral necessity into account, things would not necessarily be different: no matter how moral necessity be explained by Leibniz (or anybody else), for critics like Castel, the mere talk of a will that is determined by any sort of principles of reason or by the motive of the good, etc., contains the denial of divine freedom. For them, the problem is not *what kind* of necessity determined divine actions. The problem is *that* God's will is determined.

2.2   *Against the Best World*

Castel's second group of criticisms of optimism refers to the concept of the best possible world. Leibniz's identification of our created world with the best possible world is for Castel unacceptable. A first set of criticism is expressed by Castel in the following words:

> Only God is *a best* ["*un* optimum"]. He is also simple, indivisible, unique. We want to admit that all his works have to be not only better than those of human beings and every created being but absolutely good and very good, *bona, valde bona*, as the Scripture tells us that they indeed come out of his hands. But to demand that they should be necessarily the best that he could do would mean that we want to say that they are his equal […]
>
> [*Dieu seul es un* optimum. *Aussi est-il simple, indivisible, unique. Nous voulons bien convenir que tous ses ouvrages doivent être, non seulement meilleurs que ceux des hommes & de tout Être créé, mais absolument bons &*

> *forts bons*, bona, valde bona *comme l'Écriture nous apprend qu'ils étoient en effet au sortir de ses mains. Mais d'exiger qu'ils soient nécessairement les meilleurs qu'il puisse faire lui – même c'est vouloir, si l'on y prend garde, qu'ils lui soient égaux* [...]]]
>
> CASTEL, 210–1

Two different ideas are included in this passage. First, the view that "only God is 'a best'" and therefore to describe the world as 'the best' is incongruous and even heretical. Second, the view that this world is certainly good, but not the best that God could have made, since that supposition would deny God's freedom and his omnipotence. At least with regard to the first issue, Castel seems to be operating on the basis of either a crass misunderstanding or a mischievous depiction of what Leibniz actually thinks. Indeed, Leibniz never says that the world created by God is *the optimum per se*, i.e. Leibniz never claims that the world is *the best* entity in absolute terms. The world, for him, is 'just' the *best alternative among infinite possible worlds*. To say something different would be absurd, since it would mean that God created something identical to himself (*the* best). However, this is what Castel seems to be saying,[28] committing thus a rather serious interpretation error or simply misrepresenting Leibniz.

More interesting is Castel's second claim: optimism implies that God can create only the best and nothing else, thus limiting God's freedom of choice (since, as we saw before, for Castel, to be able to do only the best – to have only one alternative – means the contrary of being truly free). As we have seen, for a voluntarist or for anybody who, like Castel, defends some kind of theory of the indifference or arbitrariness of divine actions, this certainly seems to be a problem. From this perspective, Leibniz's idea of a will motivated by the representation or of the good, bound to act within the limits established by the Principle of the Best, is simply intolerable, and optimism necessarily incorrect.

Apart from these somewhat theoretical criticisms of the idea that our world is the best possible, Castel returns in his review to a very important issue already examined in the last chapter: the apparent contradiction between the reality of sin, with all its consequences for the character of human beings and the world, and the doctrine of the best. Castel argues:

> After all this, how could a man of intelligence, how could a Christian who has all the views, all the insights that Christianity and the most metaphysical, most reasonable theology can give, could have thought that a world in which there is evil and sin could be the best world that God could create? Sin alone is a great evil that all the perfection of a world

---

28   *Cf.* Fonnesu 1994: 134; Hübener 1978: 237.

infinitely superior to this one could not balance, and which has required nothing less than the coming and death of the Son himself in order to make this world, by a sort of [new] creation of a supernatural order, worthy of its creator [...]

[*Après cela comment un homme d'esprit, comment un Chrétien qui a toutes les vues au moins, toutes les lumières que peut donner le Christianisme & la Théologie même la plus métaphysique, la plus raisonnée, a t'il pû penser qu'un monde où il y a du mal & du péché, soit le meilleur monde que Dieu puisse faire. Le péché seul est un si grand mal, que toute la perfection d'un monde infiniment supérieur à celui ci, ne pourroit encore balancer & qu'il n'a falu rien moins que l'avènement & la mort du Fils même de Dieu, pour rendre, par une espèce de création, d'un ordre surnaturel, ce monde digne de son Créateur.*]
   CASTEL, 214

For Castel, as I mentioned earlier, Leibniz's thesis of the best world results from a flawed, too-rationalist, "bad" theology. This mistaken theology leads to the denial of divine freedom, since it maintains that God can create only the best. But it also leads to theological or dogmatic difficulties, since it seems to overlook the fact that there *is* sin and evil in our world and that for this reason the world simply *cannot* be the best possible world.

Castel's objection follows the same reasoning as Budde and Knoerr's criticism of the Leibnizian identification of our actual world with the best possible world, examined in the previous chapter. The Judeo-Christian doctrine of the Fall of Man, or at least a particular reading of that doctrine, implies that primordial sin modified and corrupted the world essentially, whereby the world *ante lapsum* and the world *post lapsum* are, so to speak, two different worlds (i.e. two different, opposing states of the world). For critics like Budde and Knoerr and Castel – critics that could be called, as I noted earlier, 'pessimists' in a rather anachronistic manner – the question concerning the character of the world is not a difficult question: the world *is* corrupt, or has been corrupted essentially by sin, and only the intervention of God himself through his son Jesus Christ can in some way balance the moral corruption of creation. For Castel, as for Budde and Knoerr, Leibniz's optimism ignores these facts, making the world rather more 'positive' than it is or, as I mentioned earlier, turning it into a world that is in no need of redemption,[29] since it maintains that ours is already the best possible world.

---

29 See Chapter 2, 3.

3   Final Comments and Open Questions

In the first section of this chapter I examined Castel's claims about the sources of philosophical optimism. For him, optimism results mainly from the blend of two aspects of Leibniz's intellectual personality: an exaggerated conciliatory rationalism – the desire of "giving a reason for everything" – and an exaggerated cheerfulness regarding the character of God's actions and the created world.

As I mentioned there, through this explanation, Castel wants to stress the idea that philosophical optimism comes from an essentially subjective source. Castel repeatedly compares Leibniz to Bayle: whereas Bayle's paradoxes are the outcome of "skeptical venom", Leibniz's certainties follow from a "too philosophical" spirit. In a similar manner, whereas Bayle's gloomy opinions concerning the character of the world manifest the desire of criticizing Providence, Leibniz's optimism expresses the disposition of "applauding Providence" following the "trend" of presenting an exaggerated positive view of the world. Both stances, however, seem to be equally based on rather subjective motives.

Further, Castel depicts philosophical optimism as maintaining that "everything is good". This depiction, as I said before, appears repeatedly in other criticisms of optimism in the eighteenth century, like Jean Pierre Crousaz's *Examen de l'Essai de M. Pope, sur l'Homme* (1737), the prize-question of the Prussian Academy of Sciences in 1753–1755, or Voltaire's *Candide ou l'optimisme* in 1759. For Castel, as for those other critics, optimism denies that the evils of the world are evil at all, but the vehicle of good, and minimizes or simply ignores the reality of sin and its very serious consequences.

Is Castel justified in his portrayal of optimism as a philosophical construct based on a rather subjective disposition? How *theoretically* consistent or robust is Leibniz's optimism? On the other hand, does Leibniz really maintain that "everything is good" or something similar, as Castel suggests? Has philosophical optimism necessarily to be read as arguing for the absolute goodness of the world, or even for what could be called a radical empirical optimism that denies the weight of world-evils completely? In the following sections, I will examine these questions in some detail.

3.1   *The Theoretical Consistence of Optimism and the Faith in Reason*

Leibnizian optimism is a theoretical construct. A philosophical system, one would say, or rather, a particular aspect of a system of philosophy.[30] In this sense, there is of course a theoretical justification of optimism. That means: philosophical optimism, as was explained in Chapter 1, follows from certain

---

30   *Cf.* Rutherford 1995.

theoretical philosophical and theological presuppositions. The most important among them are, as we saw there, the belief in the essential rationality of God, that is his following of a particular set of rational principles that are universally valid and independent of God's willing; the idea of God's infinite goodness, omnipotence, and omniscience, etc. As I have noted in several passages of this work, among the fundamental assumptions of optimism, a special *concept of God* plays a central role. I described the Leibnizian view of the divine nature as an 'intellectualist' concept that maintains basically that "God acts for good reasons" – meaning that God's willing is always subordinated to the representations of the good provided by his understanding (Nadler 2011a: 525–6).

The theoretical consistency of optimism is explained by Wilhelm Schmidt-Biggemann in the following words:

> The justification of the complete project [of Leibniz's philosophical optimism in the *Theodicy*] is relatively simple: a philosophical concept of God is presupposed. This God of the philosophers has in every case the predicates 'good', 'all knowing', and 'omnipotent'. When the omniscient, good, and omnipotent God creates a world, he creates [...] the best of all possible worlds. For Leibniz, this concept of the best of all possible worlds responds also to the Principle of Sufficient Reason, which can be formulated easily: *nihil sine ratione* [...] Optimism works only under these metaphysical assumptions. Thus one justifies metaphysically and *a priori* that the world must be the best; experience plays in this conception only a secondary role.
>
> CARO 2010: 26

As I believe, this last sentence is of importance to understand what it means to say that philosophical optimism is, above all, a theoretical system. Indeed, according to this view of things optimism is first and foremost the logical consequence of a set of theoretical presuppositions about God and the rationality of his actions. Leibniz wants to make that clear already in the very first paragraphs of the *Theodicy*, where he writes: "Now this supreme wisdom, united to a goodness that is no less infinite, cannot but have chosen the best. [...] [I]f there were not the best (*optimum*) among all possible worlds, God would not have produced any" (T, §8/GP VI 107). The thesis of the best world is not an examination, and therefore neither a description, of the empirical world (such description, Leibniz seems to believe, would require an infinite understanding, since it implies the comparison of infinite possibles). The world *exists*. Given the aforementioned theoretical assumptions about God's rationality, his infinite goodness, wisdom, power, etc., this world *must* be the best. As Leibniz writes, regarding the superiority of the created world one "must judge with me *ab effectu*, since God has chosen this world as it is." (T, §10/GP VI 108).[31]

The good of the world, the mark of its 'bestness' is for Leibniz (as we will see in the second part of this section) certainly *also* an empirical good. However, first of all, it is an intellectual or 'rationalist good' that results from the fundamental rationality of the creator and his creation. As Donald Rutherford appropriately writes:

> [A] principal measure of the world's perfection for Leibniz is its 'rational order', or the degree to which reason [...] has been realized within the constitution of created things. It follows on this reading that the perfection God finds in the world is, at the most fundamental level, an intellectual good [...] Given this, it should already be clear that Leibniz's optimism is very different form that of Pangloss [Voltaire's simple-minded optimist of *Candide*]. The ground of Leibniz's belief in the doctrine of the best of all possible worlds is a thoroughgoing faith in the governing power of reason: reason as it directs the creative will of God, reason as it is subsequently realized in the intelligible order of the created world, and reason as it helps human minds discern and appreciate that order.
>
> RUTHERFORD 1995: 2

Now, as I noted in the previous chapter, the rationalist concept of God that underlies Leibnizian optimism was definitely not the only concept of God defended by early modern philosophers. Philosophers like Descartes, Arnauld or Budde and Knoerr uphold a concept of God that contradicts most of Leibniz's assumptions regarding God's nature and his essential rationality, and that I called a 'voluntarist' view of the divine nature. According to this concept, God transcends rationality: his will does not follow the guidance of reasons provided by the understanding, i.e. strictly speaking God does not follow *rational reasons*.[32] As I also mentioned previously that the question which of these two concepts of God, the rationalist or the voluntarist, is more consistent with God's nature seems to be unsolvable. Indeed, how can we really know which concept of God applies better to God?

---

31   See also Barber 1955: 87–8: "Bayle's approach [to the problem of evil] is essentially empirical [...]. Leibniz, on the other hand, never really abandons *a priori* argument. He bases his knowledge of God's nature on *a priori* rational considerations, not on any canonical authority, and once God's infinite goodness and wisdom have thus been established, all else also follows deductively".

32   *Cf.* Nadler 2011a and 2011b.

If we cannot really *know* whether God is rational according to external criteria or rational according to criteria that he himself lays down, then to say that God is essentially rational, that his works can be explained resorting to rational methods, categories, principles, etc. implies a sort of *bet* for rationality. The assumption of the fundamental rationality of God and the world would therefore seem to be precisely that: an assumption. In this sense, Rutherford is right when he says that "the ground of Leibniz's belief in the doctrine of the best of all possible worlds is a thoroughgoing faith in the governing power of reason". Once we assume that God is a rational being, good, omnipotent, etc., optimism seems to follow rather naturally (at least apparently). But, as the voluntarist philosophers show, we do not *have* to assume that God is essentially rational. That God is rational seems indeed to be a thesis based, at least to some extent, on the "faith in the governing power of reason". Schmidt-Biggemann expresses a similar awareness in the following words:

> *That means that Leibniz assumes the rationality of both God and his creation ...* – Yes. For the case of Leibniz and the whole rationalist project of explaining the reality and evil there is at the beginning something like a *decision for rationality*. Now this process is certainly paradoxical, because if one decides to choose rationality, then this decision is in itself not rational. [...]
>
> CARO 2010: 27[33]

As I have tried to explain, this does not mean that optimism is necessarily inconsistent, for *within* the decision for rationality one can indeed show that optimism, as a theoretical construct, seems to be theoretically consistent. In a certain 'meta-theoretical' sense, however, there does seem to be an important assumption at the basis of rationalist optimism: the assumption of the rationality of all that exists. Leibniz *assumes* that God is rational, that one can give an explanation for everything that happens, that the will of rational beings acts upon reasons, etc.[34] But does this necessarily mean that it is impossible

---

[33] Also Barber is quite radical in this respect: "[A]ll his [Leibniz's] explanations lead back inevitably to an incomprehensible absolute, and his optimism is little different from the soldier's faith in his commander, or the nervous man's whistling in the dark. None of these is ultimately rational, even if it appears to be in some degree [...]" (Barber 1955: 89).

[34] Of course, Leibniz himself would deny the presence of any subjective element in his thought: the world is there; God is there; if we are to make some sense, any sense, of the world, we have to assume that God, who is good, etc., had good reasons for creating the world, etc. As he says, we must judge "*ab effectu*, since God has chosen this world as it is" (T, §10/GP VI 108). But precisely the idea *that* we have to make sense of God's actions

to confront philosophical optimism and its counter-optimist antagonists, to weigh and compare their advantages? I am not sure that this is the case. This important question will be examined at the end of this work.[35]

3.2   Is Everything Good?

As I mentioned earlier, the idea that Leibnizian optimism maintains that "everything is good" comes most probably from the common eighteenth-century habit of linking Leibniz's thought to Alexander Pope's *Essay on Man*. Ironically enough, Pope does *not* write that maxim in the *Essay*. However, his famous dictum "Whatever is, is right"[36] was very soon translated and interpreted as meaning that everything is good. Thus, the very first French translation of the *Essay* by the diplomat Étienne de Silhouette, published one year before Castel's review,[37] translates Pope' "Whatever is, is right" as "*Tout ce qui est, est bien*", and a second translation published one year later by the French ecclesiastic Jean-François Du Resnel du Bellay[38] reads: "*Tout est bien dans toute la nature...*"[39]

Of course, the important question for us is whether Leibniz explicitly writes in the *Theodicy* that "everything is good". Does he? No, he does not. And does he write something in the *Theodicy* that could at least be interpreted as meaning, in some way, that everything is good? Yes and no.

---

and of the world clearly belongs itself to an assumption of rationality. Now one can ask: Is rationality necessarily the best assumption, the best bet in philosophy? The answer, of course, also depends on what kind of explanation one chooses. According to Nadler: "Maybe it is a bet, but it is certainly a good one to make. There is, of course, no guarantee that the world is rationally organized. But the advancements of science do strongly suggest that it is. Our attempts to rationally understand nature over the millennia are increasingly successful and have led to greater improvements in life (reduced mortality rates, better health over lifetimes, managing and predicting natural events, etc.). I'm not sure there is any alternative to rationalism other than a woeful quietism or fatalism about things. But that would be of no help to anyone" (Caro 2011).

35 *Cf.* Chapter 6, 3.
36 The maxim, a continuous motive of the Essay, is stated by Pope al least five times throughout the poem. For example: All Nature is but Art, unknown to thee; / All chance, direction, which thou canst not see / All discord, harmony not understood, / All partial evil, universal good; / And, spite of pride, in erring reason's spite, / One truth is clear, whatever is, is right. (*Essay*, Epistle I: 51f.)
37 *Essai sur l'homme, par M. Pope*, Lausanne-Geneva: Bousquet, 1736.
38 *Les principes de la morale et du goût, en deux poëmes, traduits d l'anglois de M. Pope, par M. Du Resnel*, Paris: Briasson, 1937.
39 On both translations and their interpretation of Pope's words, see Hellwig 2008: 118ff. As Hellwig shows (2008: 187ff.) in Germany, the translations of the *Essay* follow the French practice. Beginning in 1740 German translators translate: "[A]*lles das, was ist, ist gut*", "*Die Welt ist gut!*", "*Was ist, ist gut!*", etc.

Castel's claim that optimism maintains that everything is good may be understood in two ways. On the one hand, as meaning not that the world contains any evils at all, but that evils are the vehicle and the source of greater goods. ("[T]hat everything is good or at least that it [evil] exists for a greater good" [Castel, 207].) On the other, as meaning something like: the world is a wonderful place and a kingdom of happiness – more in the spirit of the French version "*Tout est bien*". ("[T]hat there is no evil, that everything is nature is good, that the ruling kingdom is that of the beautiful nature" [Castel, 222].) This second kind of interpretation seems to be what Donald Rutherford has in mind when he writes that Leibniz's thought was commonly depicted in the eighteenth century as "the brand of simple-minded optimism that is satirized so effectively in Voltaire's *Candide*: Whatever happens, whatever evils may visit our lives, we may always take comfort in the thought that this is the best of all possible worlds" (Rutherford 1995: 1).

With regard to the first interpretation there are good reasons to think that Leibniz indeed thought that good comes out of evil. As I mentioned in Chapter 1, in the *Theodicy* Leibniz argues, for example, that evil only occurs as a concomitant factor of greater goods, i.e. as an accompanying phenomenon that contributes to the general good: "Thus the evil, or the mixture of goods and evils wherein the evil prevails, happens only *by concomitance*, because it is connected with greater goods that are outside this mixture" (T, §119/GP VI 170). God certainly does not will moral evil or sin, but he permits it, Leibniz explains, because this corresponds better to his own perfect and infinite good nature:

> It is in this sense that God permits sin: for he would fail in what he owes to himself, in what he owes to his wisdom, his goodness, his perfection, if he followed not the grand result of all his tendencies to good, and if he chose not that which is absolutely the best, notwithstanding the evil of guilt, which is involved therein by the supreme necessity of the eternal verities.
>
> T, §25/GP VI 117

With this Leibniz is apparently referring to the traditional Augustinian explanation of moral evil as the consequence of freedom of choice, which is in itself a major good. As for physical evil, as we have seen earlier, it is defined by Leibniz – according also to the traditional explanation – as a consequence of sin. Now, physical evil as a penalty for sin is not only a just but, moreover, a convenient consequence, since it also stimulates the good by making possible the improvement of rational beings:

> [O]ne may say of physical evil, that God wills it often as a penalty owing to guilt, and often also as a means to an end, that is, to prevent greater evils or to obtain greater good. The penalty serves also for amendment and example.
>
> T, §23/GP VI 116

Further, evil permits us to recognize and *taste* the good: "Evil often serves to make us savor good the more; sometimes too it contributes to a greater perfection in him who suffers it [...]" (T, §23/GP VI 116).

It is not clear whether Leibniz would accept or not the idea that evils are a *necessary* condition of the good in the world, as Castel argues that optimists do.[40] As I tend to believe, he would not. Evil certainly belongs to the rational structure of the created world and promotes through its presence the general order, harmony, etc., of creation. For this reason, Leibniz argues, God has permitted evil to enter the world. However, to say that without evil there could have not been any good in the world would seem to be an exaggeration. Yet, I do admit that the issue of the necessity of evil is a challenging problem for the interpretation of Leibnizian optimism (or, for that matter, of traditional Christian theodicy in general).

In any case, Castel's claim that according to optimism "everything is good" does seem to be justified in a particular manner – as meaning that there *are* evils in the world, but they promote the good. In fact, as we have seen, the idea that good can come out of evil is explicitly maintained by Leibniz and is a central aspect of his idea of what it means that we live in the best of all possible worlds.

What about the second possible sense of Castel's "everything is good", the idea that in this world "Everything is good, everything is better, everything is very good"? As I said before, with those and other words Castel seems to want to depict Leibnizian optimism as maintaining that God's creation is some wonderful place, in some way absolutely good. Does this correspond to Leibniz's story?

---

40 Interestingly enough, some modern commentators also explain Leibnizian optimism as maintaining the necessity of evil for the existence of good. For example Arthur Lovejoy: "It is, of course, true that the optimistic writers were eager to show that good comes out of evil; but what it was indispensable for them to establish was that it could come in no other way" (Lovejoy 1936: 211). And Odo Marquard: "There is also a stronger form of the concept of compensation: only *through* evil does the good arise, and it would not arise without it. This is (as I would like to call it) the *bonum-through-malum-idea* [...]. This figure also comes from Leibniz's *Theodicy* (Marquard 1981: 45).

Taken for itself, Leibniz's slogan that this 'the best of all possible worlds'[41] could be interpreted in a neutral manner, as maintaining neither that the world is good nor bad but simply the best that God could create or wanted to create. Just as Pope's "Whatever is, is right" can be interpreted in a dispassionate manner, i.e. as meaning simply that everything in the world is *just as it has to be*, Leibniz's theorem of the best world seems to admit of a similar neutral reading.

However, as we saw in the previous chapter, Leibniz does consider, against Bayle's empirical pessimism, that the world is good also in an empirical manner and that there is definitely more good than evil in the world.[42] Now this does not imply that everything in the world will eventually turn out for the best for all of us. In the end, there will be unmitigated suffering and evils for which we will not be, so to speak, compensated. This means: for Leibniz the goodness of the world cannot be interpreted as a universal value that guarantees the happiness of all creatures – and definitely not of all *rational* creatures. In this point, I think, Castel's sarcastic criticism is all but justified.

Indeed, as commentators like Lovejoy have adequately explained, for Leibniz neither moral goodness, nor pleasure, is that what makes the world the best among all possibles: "Virtue and happiness both, of course, have their places in the scale of values; but if it were the highest place, it is inconceivable that God would have made the kind of world he has made" (Lovejoy 1936: 224–5). Leibniz is clear in this respect in several passages of the *Theodicy*. Human happiness, at least understood as physical pleasure, is certainly important for God, but it was not his main criterion for the election of our world:

> [T]he moral or physical good and evil of rational creatures does not infinitely exceed the good and evil which is simply metaphysical, namely that which lies in the perfection of the other creatures [...] No substance is absolutely contemptible or absolutely precious before God. [...] It is certain that God sets greater store by a man than a lion; nevertheless it can hardly be said with certainty that God prefers a single man in all respects to the whole of lion-kind.
>
> T, §118/GP VI 168

The felicity of all rational creatures is one of the aims he has in view; but it is not his whole aim, nor even his final aim. Therefore it happens that

---

41   *Cf.* T, §§8ff., 52, 117, 119, 124, 130, 167f./GP VI 107f., 131, 167f., 169, 178, 182.
42   *Cf.* T, §§13, 148/GP VI 109, 198.

> the unhappiness of some of these creatures may come about *by concomitance*, and as a result of other greater goods.
>
> T, §119/GP VI 169–70

It is false, Leibniz maintains, that the contentment of rational creatures is the sole aim of God. The order of the universe demands that the spirits adjust to "matter, movement, and its laws" (T, §120/GP VI 172–3); to other non-rational creatures that God, by virtue of his desire of creating a world as rich as possible, decided to create; in short: to the connection of particular things in the whole system of the world. These elements, together with the fact that God wanted to give freedom of choice to rational beings, makes the emergence of evil a rather natural phenomenon in the best of all possible worlds.

> Virtue is the noblest quality of created things, but it is not the only good quality of creatures. There are innumerable others which attract the inclination of God: from all these inclinations there results the most possible good, and it turns out that if there were only virtue, if there were only rational creatures, there would be less good. [...] And besides, wisdom must vary. To multiply one and the same thing only would be superfluity and poverty too. [...] Nature had need of animals, plants, inanimate bodies; there are in these creatures, devoid of reason, marvels which serve for exercise of the reason. What would an intelligent creature do if there were no unintelligent things? [...] Therefore, since God's wisdom must have a world of bodies, a world of substances capable of perception and incapable of reason; since, in short, it was necessary to choose from all the things possible what produced the best effect together, and since vice entered in by this door, God would not have been altogether good, altogether wise if he had excluded it.
>
> T, §124/GP VI 179

Does this mean that human happiness and delight are not relevant variables in the formula of the best of all possible worlds? Not necessarily. Human happiness *is* of course a central element in Leibnizian optimism – however, not understood in hedonistic terms, as physical pleasure or the joy that could possibly result from the absence of moral evil and suffering. In Leibniz's best of all possible worlds everything is connected and this universal harmony – as we saw in Chapter 1 when examining the concept of the best possible world[43] and as we will see in the next chapter – is what defines the superiority of our world.

---

43   *Cf.* Chapter 1, 1, 1.1.

And it is precisely from this harmony, or more specifically, from the *contemplation* of this harmony, that the happiness of rational beings arises. Thus, in a certain way, the happiness of rational creatures *is* God's purpose in creating this world. Yet this happiness has to be understood in strong rationalist terms. As Donald Rutherford explains, it has to be understood as the "lasting state of pleasure sustained through the exercise of reason". Pleasure, in turn, is according to Leibniz "the perception of perfection". Without any doubt, as Rutherford further comments, Leibniz's view entails a "very special interpretation of what human happiness involves" (Rutherford 1995: 51–4).

Castel's assessment that optimism maintains that "everything is good" must therefore be either discarded completely or understood in a very special, *Leibnizian* manner. The world is the best of all possible worlds and in a certain sense everything *is* good, because everything is as it has to be. This does not entail, however, that *every* rational creature will know only joy and be spared from suffering. Rather, as Steven Nadler comments, the last word of optimism would seem to be in fact a word distant from the cheerfulness that Castel denounces:

> Leibniz's view – which is basically a standard kind of theodicy – is that the problem of evil is resolved if you take a broader perspective on things. 'Consider the whole' might be a good way of summarizing this approach. For Leibniz, this means considering the world as a whole and recognizing that it is the best of all possible worlds (something that can be seen *a priori*, through philosophical reasoning) and thus understanding that what makes it the best of all possible worlds is every single event within it. Thus, even the so-called 'evils' contribute to the overall best-ness of the world. [...] Not very comforting, however, for those who do, in fact, have to suffer evils. [...] 'Resignation' might be a better term to capture what he is saying.
> CARO 2011

CHAPTER 4

Banning the Best World, God's (Supposed) Freedom, and the Principle of Sufficient Reason: Christian August Crusius's Criticism of Optimism (1745)

Christian August Crusius is an unfamiliar name in conventional accounts of the history of modern philosophy. Yet he was a leading character of the early German *Aufklärung*, both because of his role as a relevant influence on Kant's pre-critical thought, and due to the fact that he was one of the most fervent opponents of Leibnizian and Wolffian rationalist metaphysics in the eighteenth century.

Crusius was born in 1715 near Halle and Leipzig in eastern Germany as the son of a Lutheran pastor. He studied philosophy and theology in the University of Leipzig, became professor of Philosophy at that University in 1750 and five years later professor of Theology. He died in Leipzig in 1775. His main philosophical works are the *Dissertatio philosophica de usu et limitibus principii rationis determinantis, vulgo sufficientis* (*Philosophical Dissertation Concerning the Use and Limits of the Principle of Determinant or Sufficient Reason*) (1743), a critical examination of the Principle of Sufficient Reason; the *Anweisung, vernünftig zu leben* (*Guide to Rational Living*) (1744), his system of ethics; the *Entwurf der nothwendigen Vernunftwahrheiten, wiefern sie den zufälligen entgegengesetzt werden* (*Outline of the Necessary Truths of Reason, as Opposed to Contingent Truths*) (1745), his main treatise on metaphysics;[1] the *Weg zur Gewissheit und Zuverlässigkeit der menschlichen Erkenntniss* (*Path to the Certainty and Reliability of Human Knowledge*) (1747), a system of logic; and the *Anleitung, über natürliche Begebenheiten ordentlich und vorsichtig nachzudenken* (*Instruction on How to Reflect Correctly and Cautiously on Natural Events*) (1749), his physics.[2]

---

1 An English translation of parts of this work can be found in Watkins 2009.
2 Until this day, the best general exposition of Crusius's life and work is Tonelli 1969. On Crusius's influence of Kant, see Campo 1953; Ciafardone 1982; Heimsoeth 1926; Heinrich 1963; Kanzian 1993; Marquardt 1885; Tonelli 1966; Treash 1989. On his metaphysics and his criticism of Leibniz-Wolffianism see Carbonicini 1986, 1987, 1989, and 1991: 195–217; Krieger 1993; Röd 1984: 261ff.; Roldán 1990; Seitz 1899; Wundt 1945: 230–54.

During his studies in Leipzig Crusius was strongly influenced by the teachings of Adolph Friedrich Hoffmann (1703–1741). Hoffmann had studied under Andreas Rüdiger (1673–1731), who in turn was an important follower of Christian Thomasius (1655–1728), himself a renowned detractor of Wolff's rationalist philosophy. As is known, Christian Wolff (1679–1754) was instrumental for the popularization of Leibnizian thought in the eighteenth century (even though the exact relationship between the philosophies of both rationalist thinkers remains controversial and the traditional picture of Wolff as a simple divulgator of Leibniz's philosophy has been shown to be superficial).[3]

It is within the Thomasian tradition that Crusius's philosophy should be thought of. The advocates of this tradition upheld the limited character of human knowledge and with it the impossibility of knowing and explaining entirely the non-empirical nature of reality. They rejected the use of the mathematical method in metaphysics, the Leibnizian theory of pre-established harmony, the doctrine of the universal validity of the Principle of Sufficient Reason, as well as the intellectualistic account of moral agency that Leibniz and Wolff seem to promote. Against this intellectualism, in order to establish a theory of the absolute, undetermined freedom of the will, the Thomasian philosophers propounded the complete independency and priority of the will with respect to the understanding. For this reason, they have been traditionally described as maintaining a radical voluntarism, according to the terminology explained in Chapter 1.[4]

Accordingly, Crusius opposes Leibniz and Wolff on almost every major issue of their teachings. Yet, it should be noted that the most significant aspect of Crusius's attack on traditional rationalism is, in fact, his rejection of characteristic motives of *Leibniz's* thought, the knowledge of which came most probably directly from the works by Leibniz that could be known in Crusius's day: the *Theodicy*, the correspondence with Samuel Clarke, and the *Monadology* in the German translation of 1720. Those characteristic Leibnizian motives rejected by Crusius are: the general theory of monads, the hypothesis of pre-established harmony, the Principle of Sufficient Reason, and the doctrine of the divine choice the best of all possible worlds. Wolff's own philosophical and mathematical views seem to have been of secondary interest to Crusius, who locates – much according with the spirit of his times – Wolff's principal merit in the "reproduction and propagation" of Leibniz's philosophy (*De usu*, §10/36).

Already in 1743, the year he published the treatise against the Principle of Sufficient Reason, Crusius was convinced that the Leibnizian principles

---

3   *Cf.* Hettche 2019; Wilson 1995.
4   *Cf.* Röd 1984: 258; Tonelli 1969: xvi–xxii; Wundt 1945: 254ff.

were "the immediate antithesis of the kind of sound philosophy that is based on common sense"[5] – a view that is one of Crusius's working theses against Leibniz's metaphysics. The others are: Leibniz's most important teachings are based on erroneous proofs and prejudices, as well as on obscure concepts and falsely interpreted experimental data; Leibnizian metaphysics renew antique fatalistic, deterministic, and skeptical explanations of nature; and most importantly, they lead to the denial of divine and human freedom of choice.

In this last point Crusius follows the other major figures of the Thomasian tradition, whose denunciation of Leibnizian philosophy is motivated primarily by moral concerns (Leibniz's philosophy destroys the freedom of will of both God and humans, and with it all morality and religion, by subjecting that freedom to universal rational principles). Yet, as conventional as Crusius's motives might have been, there is something distinctive and very significant to the type of opposition to traditional rationalism practiced by Crusius: its philosophical character.

As Sonia Carboncini has explained, both the expressions that Crusius uses to describe Leibnizian and Wolffian philosophy – "fatalistic", "deterministic", "skeptical", or even "Spinozistic" – as well as his chief motivations against it – Leibnizian rationalism contradicts the Christian dogma, it destroys religion and morals, etc. – were a quite emblematic ingredient of the polemical treatises against Leibniz and Wolff of the first decades of the eighteenth century. However, it is first with Crusius, at least in the Thomasian tradition, that Leibnizian and Wolffian metaphysics is confronted philosophically in a systematic and comprehensive manner. Indeed, Crusius interests were not merely polemic: he articulated conventional arguments against classical rationalism with the purpose of building a system of philosophy that could be a real alternative to Leibnizian metaphysics.[6]

In this chapter, I will focus on Crusius's dismissal of philosophical optimism. As I believe, Crusius' criticism, while being directed against a specific aspect of Leibniz's thought, illustrates both the moral drive, as well as the essentially philosophical spirit of Crusius' approach. The problem of philosophical optimism is examined by Crusius in the Cosmology section (§§385–389) of the *Entwurf der nothwendigen Wahrheiten*. There he argues that the system of the best is conceptually flawed, logically unsound, and renders freedom and morality impossible. These claims will be expounded in the first part of the chapter.

The idea that optimism destroys freedom and morality is connected directly with Crusius' negative opinion concerning the nature and role the Principle of

---

5 Quoted in Carboncini 1986: 112ff.
6 *Cf.* Carboncini 1986; Tonelli 1969: XVIIIff.

Sufficient Reason has according to Leibniz. Although Crusius' critique of the Principle is not addressed explicitly in the *Entwurf*, I consider this critique to be fundamental to his philosophical attack on optimism. The second part of the chapter will, therefore, be devoted to its examination.

In the final section, I will comment critically on two specific problems of Crusius' account: his rejection of the concept of the best possible world and his claim that the Principle of Sufficient Reason introduces absolute necessity into the world.

1 Conceptual Flaws and the Moral Danger of Optimism

Crusius criticizes the doctrine of the best world from three angles: 1) the concept of the best possible world is unacceptable; 2) the main argument for optimism is faulty; 3) optimism is morally hazardous: if it is true, there is no divine freedom.

1.1 *Against the Best of All Possible Worlds*

What does it mean that God created the best possible world? What is 'the best' among all possible worlds? For Crusius, to say that our world is the best possible alternative can mean one of two things: either that our world "contains all possible perfections" that any created world can contain, or, supposing that God created the world for the "sake of achieving some specific purposes", that the world is the only one among all possible worlds that permits the achievement of such specific purposes (*Entwurf*, §385/742[7]). For Crusius both alternative definitions are unviable: in its first meaning, the concept of a best world is "impossible"; according to the second, it is "unprovable" [*Unsere Entscheidung ist, dass seine beste Welt in der ersten Bedeutung unmöglich, in der anderen aber unerweislich sei*] (§385/743). This essential unviability of the concept of the best of all possible worlds depends fundamentally on Crusius's conception of an almighty and, above all, absolutely free God.

Regarding the first assumption – a world containing all possible perfections is impossible – Crusius argues that every possible world, by definition, must be limited. God has certainly the capacity of producing an infinite quantity of creatures, ends, and means of achieving those ends. However, "what is actually created is always necessarily finite" [*dasjenige, was wirklich erschaffen wird,*

---

[7] Citations from Crusius's works will be referenced as Title, Paragraph/Page number, according to the edition of *Die philosophischen Hauptwerke* (ed. Giorgio Tonelli *et al.*), 4 vols., Hildesheim-New York: Georg Olms, 1964–1987.

ist allezeit notwendig endlich] (§386/743-4). The perfection of created beings must, therefore, be finite as well: it is impossible for any created or possible world to contain all possible perfections. Furthermore, God must limit the features of the world he creates, given the necessarily restricted nature of creatures. This means that this world could have been different. Thus, our world cannot be the best of all possible worlds (and for that matter, no world can be *the* best possible world). God, in virtue of his power and freedom, "could have always included still more things in it – a world which is absolutely the best is not possible" [*Daraus aber folget, dass er allezeit noch mehr hätte hinzutun können, und dass also keine Welt möglich sei, welche schlechterdings die beste ware*] (§386/744).

Crusius takes into account two possible objections to this view: (i) the world *is* infinite, therefore it can contain infinite perfection; (ii) even though the quantity of possible creatures is infinite, the quantity of possible good combinations among them is finite; accordingly there *can be* a world – our world – which contains the best of all possible combinations. Crusius rejects (i) without much argument: the notion of an infinite world is incongruous and, as a matter of fact, blasphemous, since creatures are finite by definition and infinite perfection is only predicable of God. As for (ii) he argues that due to our ignorance of things divine, just as it is impossible to postulate with absolute certainty an infinite number of potential combinations, it cannot be proven that such combinations are indeed finite. Also, to postulate a finitude of possible combinations restricts, again, divine omnipotence and goes against the concept of his infinity. In fact, there are good reasons to think that the number of possible combinations is actually *infinite*, given God's wholly unrestricted freedom and his capacity of producing and choosing "always more creatures under a bigger quantity of determinations" [*Der Grund liegt in der göttliche Freiheit, vermöge welcher er noch immer mehrere Geschöpfe machen und unter einer großen Menge möglichen Determinationen* [...] *wählen kann*] (§386/745).

Regarding the second assumption – one cannot prove that our world contains the best means of achieving a certain specific end – Crusius maintains that God is never obliged to choose one specific way of doing things: he can always achieve a particular end through different means. Besides this, God can produce an infinite number of similar creatures of every type. Again, this means that God could well have decided to create a different world to attain the same particular ends he pursued. For God, it is indifferent which among all possible types of creatures he produces in order to achieve his purposes; "even if two things are not completely similar, they can both be appropriate regarding the achievement of the same particular ends" [*Es wird also seinem Zwecke gleich gelten, welches unter so vielen möglichen er zur Beförderung desselben zur Wirklichkeit bringt. Ferner wenn auch zwei Dinge an sich nicht ganz ähnlich sind: so können sie doch in Absicht auf die gesetzten Zwecke gleichgültig sein [...]]* (§387/746). Even if one supposes that God *had* to produce a world in order to fulfill some hypothetical aim or aims, he still wouldn't have been obliged to create our world. Given Crusius's notion of God, the concept of a world which is the best in virtue of its 'instrumentality' is, thus, unverifiable.

1.2 The Fallacy of Optimism

After arguing for the unviability of the concept of the best among all possible worlds, in the second stage of his critique, Crusius examines the argument by which the optimist allegedly wants to demonstrate the fact that our world is the best of all possible worlds. In Chapter 1 we saw that optimism results from certain principles of reason and other assumptions (God's infinite goodness and the existence of the world, for example), which lead to the conclusion that the world is (or must be) the best possible. Crusius offers a similar explanation. According to him, the basic 'argument' for optimism reads somewhat like this:

- He who knows and wants the best, also does the best.
- In virtue of his omniscience, God is capable of knowing the best; in virtue of his omnipotence, he is capable of doing the best; in virtue of his wisdom, he is capable of wanting the best.
- God created this world.
  Therefore, this is the best of all possible worlds

Wer das beste wisse und wolle, und auch machen könne, der tut das beste. Da nun Gott, als er eine Welt erschaffen wollen, das Beste vermöge seiner Allwissenheit bewusst, vermöge seiner Allmacht gekonnt und vermöge seiner Weisheit gewollt habe: so habe er notwendig die beste Welt erschaffen
   §388/748-9[8]

For Crusius such a demonstration is invalid. It is "already assumed that one world among all possible worlds must be the best". Therefore, the argument "proves nothing at all". [*Dieser Schluss beweiset deswegen nichts, weil darinnen schon voraus gesetzt wird, dass irgendeine unter allen möglichen Welten die beste sei*] (§388/748-9).

The step from the premise 'God created the world' to the conclusion 'This is the best of all possible worlds' is interpreted by Crusius as implying the idea that God created our world *because* he identified it as the best among infinite

---

[8] See for example T, §8/GP VI 107; §226/GP VI 252f.

possible worlds. (The details of this supposition become clear when we think about the role that the Principle of Sufficient Reason plays within the argument for optimism. Crusius' account of that role will be examined in the forthcoming section.) That is why he can consider that the argument "proves nothing at all": God created this world, therefore the world is the best of possible worlds. But why did God create precisely *this* world and none other (or simply nothing at all)? Well – thus the optimist's reply in Crusius's account – because there is, among all possible worlds, one which is the best possible, which God identified as such and consequently created. Now, since Crusius has formerly alleged that the concept of a best of all possible worlds is bogus, the whole argument must also be flawed.

But one could ask, if the argument for optimism really includes the assumption of the superiority of the world? Does it really have to include it in order to work as an inference? One could say, for example, that the fact of the superiority of the world is, so to speak, *contained* in the concept of God as an infinitely good and powerful being: everything created by God is the best possible (or the so-called Principle of the Best[9]). In such a case, the argument would be no inference, but rather the product of the analysis of the concept of God:[10]

- God created the world. (Fact)
- God creates only the best possible. (Principle of the Best)
  Therefore the world is the best possible.

Every question concerning the premises of the inference, as well as the charge of inconsistency, would then be out of place.

Crusius, of course, does not have to accept this alternative interpretation of the argument. Once again, since there is no best world in the realm of the possible, our created world cannot be the best possible world. More than some kind of logical invalidity, the interesting point in this seems to be that, for Crusius, the concept of God does *not* imply the necessary superiority of the created world. That is, as surprising as it may seem, Crusius's God is not subjected to the Principle of the Best. As he writes in the *Entwurf*, a world created by God is only "very good" (§389/753) – but not necessarily *the best*.

---

9   On the Principle of the Best (or Principle of Perfection) see Chapter 1, 2, 2.3. As we saw there, Leibniz states for example: "God is supremely perfect, from which it follows that in producing the universe he chose the best possible design [...]" (PNG, §10/GP VI 603). *Cf.* the appendix to the *Theodicy* "Summary of the Controversy, Reduced to Formal Arguments", VIII/GP VI 385–7 and DM, §§1ff./GP IV 427ff. See also Look 2020; Rescher 1979: 33ff.

10 On optimism as a "doctrine without [any possible] demonstration" see Rateau 2008: 510ff.

Crusius is even more explicit regarding what he thinks about the form of the optimist's argument. For him, the system of optimism is certainly connected with, and dependent on, the idea of an infinitely good God, but also, and more importantly, it incorporates a theoretical assumption essential to the Leibnizian rationalist mindset: the presupposition of the unrestricted validity of the Principle of Sufficient Reason.

Crusius's critical view of the way in which – in his opinion – the Principle of Sufficient Reason was understood by rationalist philosophers, is a central aspect of his campaign against Leibnizian metaphysics and it will accompany us throughout the rest of this chapter. For the time being, I will consider only the role played by the Principle in Crusius's criticism in the *Entwurf* of what he considers to be the main argument for optimism. There he writes:

> The real reason why one arrived at the principle of the best world and why one defends that principle is partly the obscurity of the ideas that many have of God's wisdom and the goodness and perfection of things, partly the falsely called Principle of Sufficient Reason.
>
> [*Die wahre Ursache, wodurch man auf den Satz von der besten Welt gekommen ist, und warum man ihn verteidigt, ist teils die Dunkelheit der Begriffe, welche viele von der Weisheit Gottes und von der Güte und Vollkommenheit der Dinge haben; teils aber der fälschlich so genannte Satz vom zureichenden Grunde.*]
>
> §388/747–8

The Leibnizian Principle of Sufficient Reason states that nothing happens without a sufficient reason why it should be so rather than otherwise.[11] According to Crusius, the doctrine of optimism follows automatically from the combination of that Principle and the concept of a powerful and good God.[12] Optimists maintain that by virtue of the Principle, God "must have had a determinant reason to choose among all possible worlds precisely this one and none other", that is: God does not act arbitrarily. Given the principle according to which God always creates the best, this "determinant reason" must

---

11   *Cf.* Leibniz, T, §44/GP VI 127; M, §32/GP VI 612 and Chapter 1, 2, 2.1. In the following paragraph, I explain Crusius's understanding of the Principle in more detail and examine his rejection of the traditional account of the Principle of Sufficient or, as he prefers to call it, of 'Determinant' Reason.

12   Of course, this is not only Crusius's opinion, as we saw in Chapter 1: as Catherine Wilson observes, this view – or some slightly modified version of it – can be considered the "standard interpretation" concerning the origin of optimism (Wilson 1983: 767).

have been "the overwhelming goodness of the world that he actually created" (*Entwurf*, §388/748). According to this reading, the proposition 'God created the world' is itself already a consequence of the combination of the Principle of Sufficient Reason with the Principle of the Best ('God must have a reason for creating the world and he only creates what is best') *and* the assumption that 'There is a world among all possible worlds which is the best':[13]

A)
- God must have a reason for creating the world. (Principle of Sufficient Reason)
- God creates only what is best (Principle of the Best)
- There is a world among all possible worlds which is the best. (Optimist's assumption)

Therefore God created the world.

B)
- God created the world.
- God creates only the best possible. (Principle of the Best)

Therefore the world is the best possible.

Strictly speaking, from a logical point of view the optimist's argument is not invalid, since what it presupposes, in order to prove that our world is the best possible world, is that *there is* a best among all possible worlds (not that *our* world is the best). However, since Crusius has argued that the concept of the best of all possible worlds is unacceptable, his claim that the 'argument for optimism' proves nothing at all seems to be justified – that is, I emphasize, given Crusius's own rejection of the concept of the best possible world.

To sum up: Crusius intends to show that both the conceptual and argumentative foundations of metaphysical optimism are faulty. The concept of 'the best of all possible worlds' is unacceptable on all fronts. On that account, the argument used for demonstrating the truth of optimism proves to be illegitimate as well.

Now, although Crusius is devoted mainly to showing that optimism is inconsistent in the *Entwurf*, it should be evident by this point that metaphysical optimism, with its organic dependence on the Principle of Sufficient Reason, also entails rather problematical consequences regarding divine freedom.

---

13   *Cf.* T, §8/GP VI 107: "[I]t may be said likewise in respect of perfect wisdom, which is no less orderly than mathematics, that if there were not the best (*optimum*) among all possible worlds, God would not have produced any".

Before turning to Crusius's criticism of the Principle, let us conclude the present analysis of the *Entwurf* by taking a brief look at Crusius's opinion about the practical difficulties that follow from the system of the best world, and at his own voluntarist approach to the topic of divine freedom.

1.3 Optimism, the End of Freedom, and Crusius's Voluntarist Response

> Leibniz's doctrine of the best world eliminates divine and human freedom.
>
> [*Die Leibnizische Meinung von der besten Welt hebet die göttliche und menschliche Freiheit auf.*]
> §388/750

Crusius, as I pointed out at the beginning of the chapter, considers Leibnizian metaphysics to be a deterministic and, moreover, a fatalistic or, rather, necessitarian philosophy. He is not less vehement about the deadly threat that the doctrine of the best world poses to freedom.

The triple assumption presupposed by optimism – God cannot fail to choose the best; there exists a best world among all possible worlds; the Principle of Sufficient Reason has unrestricted validity – gives rise to a state of affairs in which God, once having identified that best world among all possible worlds, was compelled, on the one hand, to *create* (being incapable of deciding to produce no world at all); and on the other, to create *one* specific world: the best (not being able to decide to create an alternative world). This means according to optimism, that God could not have created anything he wanted, which amounts to denying divine freedom for Crusius. If divine freedom should mean anything at all, Crusius maintains, it should mean absolutely unrestricted and undetermined freedom of choice. God – even if one option existed, which was the best – must be able to decide to create an alternative world (or nothing at all). This is clearly at odds with the Leibnizian theory.

As we already know, for Leibniz, to say that the divine and human will is completely undetermined is absurd. There is always a reason for action. Without such a reason the will would simply be incapable of making any choice at all.[14]

---

14   As I explained in Chapter 1, complete indeterminacy of the will is called by Leibniz "indifference of equipoise" (liberty of indifference) and it is rejected by him with ardor. For example: "It is not to be imagined, however, that our freedom consists in an indetermination or an indifference of equipoise, as if one must needs be inclined equally to the side of yes and of no and in the direction of different courses, when there are several of them to take. This equipoise in all directions is impossible: for if we were equally inclined

Free substances, he explains, are "inclined" ("without being compelled") by the "motive of good", perceived by the understanding (T, §288/GP VI 288). But does this not mean that the motive of the best necessitates God to act in one specific manner (i.e. the best manner)? It does, but this necessity, Leibniz explains, is not an absolute or physical necessity, but merely a *moral* one, which does not contradict freedom. Indeed, precisely *that* is what it means for Leibniz to be free: to be bound by the representation of good. As he writes to Samuel Clarke: "For when a wise being, and especially God, who has supreme wisdom, chooses what is best, he is not the less free upon that account: on the contrary, it is the most perfect liberty, not to be hindered from acting in the best manner." (LC, L.V.7/GP VII, 390).[15]

Crusius discards these views as untenable. Freedom, he claims, cannot merely be defined as the ability to choose only the best. If one accepts Leibniz's attempt of "modifying the concept of freedom", then it is not even possible to talk about a *choice* in the case of divine actions, for "what kind of choice is that where only one action is possible?". God's freedom does not lie in the fact that he can recognize and want the best, but in his ability of "acting or not, in this or that manner" (*Entwurf*, §388/752–3). Contrary to the Leibnizian account, Crusius advocates the primacy and independence of the will regarding all choices. God's will is never subjected, never "inclined" by reasons which are in some way independent from the will itself – the representation of the good, the existence of a best among all possible worlds, etc. Certainly, the will – Crusius explains in the *Anweisung, vernünftig zu leben* (1744) – is "the power of a mind to act according to its representations". However, it is always the "efficient cause" of actions, the representations are only "the model" (*Anweisung*, §2/4–5). Representations are not the *reason* for choosing, since they cannot move the will to action (the understanding only works within the realm of ideas, "it can never produce or make real that what it thinks about"; §7/9–10). It is the will that makes it possible to go beyond mere thought. While the will certainly moves on the basis of representations, it nevertheless always moves itself to

---

towards the courses A, B and C, we could not be equally inclined towards A and towards not A. This equipoise is also absolutely contrary to experience, and in scrutinizing oneself one will find that there has always been some cause or reason inclining us towards the course taken, although very often we be not aware of that which prompts us: just in the same way one is hardly aware why, on issuing from a door, one has placed the right foot before the left or the left before the right." (T, §35/GP VI 122–3). *Cf.* T, §§46ff./GP VI 128ff.; §303/GP VI 296–7.

15 See also T, §236/GP VI 258–9.

action and responds to no other reason that itself, being thus "neither externally nor internally compelled" (§38/44).[16]

The Leibnizian theory of freedom pretends to defend God's perfection by subjecting him to the moral obligation of the motive of good. However, by doing this, Crusius explains, optimism deprives God of the greatest perfection of all: freedom. For this reason, Crusius writes, "unless the supporters of the best world amend and improve Leibniz's belief, we will have to reject it, because through it divine freedom is completely abolished" [*Wenn die Verteidiger der besten Welt die Leibnizsche Meinung davon nicht etwa selbst ändern und verbessern, wie sie gemeiniglich tun: so muss man dieselbe auch schon deswegen verwerfen, weil dadurch die göttliche Freiheit völlig aufgehoben und unter dem Vorwande, als ob man die Vollkommenheit Gottes verteidigen wollte, ihm die größte Vollkommenheit abgesprochen wird.*] (*Entwurf*, §388/750).

2   On the Use and Limits of the Principle of Sufficient Reason

Two works by Crusius are devoted exclusively to the Principle of Sufficient Reason: the *Dissertatio philosophica de usu et limitibus principii rationis determinantis, vulgo sufficientis* (1743; henceforth: *De usu*) and the *Epistola ad Hardenberg de summis rationis principiis, speciatim de principio rationis determinantis* (*Letter to Hardenberg Regarding the Principles of Reason, Especially*

---

16   Also in the *Entwurf* is Crusius straightforward regarding his voluntarism. The will, he explains, is in every soul the "dominant power, by virtue of which all the rest of faculties exist as means". All the other faculties of the soul must be "completely or in some sense" subordinated to it, and they are "directed or employed" by the will. The understanding also exists on account of the will: "The direction and the use of the powers of the understanding are subordinated to the will, as the experience confirms it. Certainly all volition presupposes thought. But the use of the understanding depends on the will in the following manner: when by some cause there already exist ideas on the basis of which the will can act, then the understanding can be moved to cogitate over those ideas and [...] make them more clear, complete and copious. [...] The longer this work is pursued [...], the greater will knowledge be extended. [...] In this way, the state of the understanding will be improved or deteriorated by the will" [*Der Wille ist in einem jedweden Geiste die herrschende Kraft, um welcher willen alle andere als Mittel da sind, welcher auch alle andere ganz oder gewisser Massen dergestalt unterworfen warden müssen, dass sie von ihr gerichtet und angewendet warden können. Insonderheit aber soll in den freien Geistern die Freiheit die herrschende Kraft sein [...]. Denn die freien Taten sind der göttliche Hauptzweck in der Welt. [...]*] (*Entwurf*, §454/885–90).

the Principle of Determinant Reason) (1752), which reissues the main claims of the former work.[17] The present examination will focus on *De usu*.[18]

Crusius begins by stating a formulation of that Principle that follows from the traditional definitions given by Leibniz and Wolff:

> Everything that occurs or is true has a sufficient reason for occurring or behaving in this manner and not otherwise.
>
> [*Alles, was geschieht oder wahr ist, hat einen zureichenden Grund, warum das, welches geschieht, oder derselbe Satz sich vielmehr so und nicht anders verhält*]
>
> *De usu*, §1/2[19]

Two things can be established from this summary definition. First, *everything has a reason*. Second, a reason is what permits us to understand why something is, or specifically, why something *exists or happens in this and no other way*. Obvious as they may be, these two ideas – *everything* and *in this and no other way* – represent the menace posed by the Principle for Crusius.

In the passages to come, I will present Crusius's considerations regarding the definition and the meaning of the Principle of Sufficient Reason; his proposal for renaming it and the reasons he adduces for maintaining that it cannot be

---

17 For more details concerning the appearance and reception of both works, see Carboncini 1987: XI–XVI and 1991: 195ff.

18 In the following exposition I will refer to the German translation of *De usu*: *Ausführliche Abhandlung von dem rechten Gebrauche und der Einschränkung des sogenannten Satzes vom zureichenden, oder besser, determinierenden Grunde* (transl. Christian Friedrich Krause), Leipzig: Langenheim, 1744.

19 Crusius's refers explicitly to Leibniz's definitions in the *Theodicy* ("[T]he other principle is that of the *determinant reason* [*principe* [...] *de la raison déterminante*]: it states that nothing ever comes to pass without there being a cause or at least a reason determining it, that is, something to give an *a priori* reason why it is existent rather than non-existent, and in this wise rather than in any other" [T, §44/GP VI 127]) and the *Monadology* ("The other is the *principle of sufficient reason* [*de la raison suffisante*], by virtue of which we consider that no fact could be found to be genuine or existent, and no assertion true, without there being a sufficient reason why it is thus and not otherwise" [M, §32/GP VI 612]), as well as to Wolff's reformulation in the *Philosophia prima sive ontologia methodo scientifica pertractata qua omnis cognitionis humanae principia continentur*, also called *Latin Ontology* ("Nihil est sine ratione sufficiente, cur potius sit, quam non sit" ["Nothing is without a reason for being, rather than not being"] [§70]). *Cf.* also Wolff *Vernünftige Gedanken von Gott, der Welt und der Seele des Menschen, auch allen Dingen überhaupt*, also called *Deutsche Metaphysik* (*German Metaphysics*), §§29–30.

admitted without restrictions. Finally, I will introduce his proposal for a new formulation of the Principle.

In the preceding section, I quoted a passage from the *Entwurf* in which Crusius maintains that the system of the best is based upon the obscurity of the ideas many have of God and his creatures, as well as the "falsely called Principle of Sufficient Reason" (*Entwurf*, §388/748). There, I reviewed Crusius's claims concerning the intimate and problematical relationship between optimism and the Principle. I did not examine, however, why Crusius talks about the "falsely called" Principle of Sufficient Reason. His reasons for considering such a designation to be inadequate are explained early on in *De usu*.

According to common understanding, Crusius claims, a sufficient reason accounts for the existence or occurrence of something. It does not, however, *determine* that something is to be or to occur in *the* particular way in which it actually happens. In the specific case of the creation of the world, for instance, God's action of creating it certainly had a sufficient reason, namely "the omnipotence and the resolutions of the divine will". Creation, however, could have taken place in "another part of space, in another point of eternity" (*De usu*, §2/8). That is, God's actions respond – as everything else does – to a sufficient cause and can be explained through it. Yet this does not mean that God could not have done otherwise. His omnipotence and the resolutions of his will could have been the cause of a completely different way of acting – a sufficient reason does not determine God's actions to occur in one particular manner.[20]

This contradicts what the Principle, in the 'Leibnizian sense', establishes, namely that there is a reason why *everything* is or occurs in *one* specific way. Therefore, Crusius suggests, the Principle should not be called of 'Sufficient' but rather of '*Determinant*' Reason, "since to determine means to admit of only one possibility why a thing, given these circumstances, should be as it

---

20   This reasoning, Crusius acknowledges, is drawn from the correspondence between Leibniz and Samuel Clarke of the years 1715 and 1716. Clarke accepts that it is true that nothing is without a sufficient reason. However, "this sufficient reason is oft-times no other than the mere will of God". Therefore, the creation of this "particular system of matter" could have occurred otherwise since, according to Clarke's (and Crusius's) view, it had no other reason but God's will. Indeed, God does not act with a "predetermining cause". To think otherwise would "take away all power of choosing, and [would] introduce fatality" (LC, C.II.1/GP VII 359–60). Clarke later adds that in God's decisions the "mere will, without any thing external to influence it, is alone that sufficient reason" (LC, C.III.2/GP VII, 367). Against Clarke's voluntarism Leibniz defends his strict rationalist approach. Thus he writes: "In things absolutely indifferent, there is no choice; and consequently no election, nor will; since choice must be founded on some reason, or principle. A mere will without any motive is a fiction [...]" (LC, L.IV.1–2/GP VII, 371–2).

is" (§3/9). This redefinition constitutes Crusius's first step away from Leibniz (who, as I commented in Chapter 1, seems to have handled 'sufficient' and 'determinant reason' as synonyms).

The second step is rather more drastic. It consists in the rejection of the Principle in its traditional form and the proposal of a new, restricted version. The need of restricting the Principle (or, for Crusius, the occasion of not having to accept it in its traditional form) rests on three reasons:

1) The Principle introduces an "unlimited necessity of all things" (§5). This unrestrained necessity gives rise to the introduction of *fatum* or destiny (§7) and the complete abolition of free will of choice and morality (§8).

In the preceding section, we saw why the Leibnizian teachings collide with Crusius's view of freedom. Crusius now explains specifically how those teachings introduce a total necessity in all affairs that occur in the world. Crusius refers to the distinction between absolute and hypothetical necessity, which I examined in some detail in Chapter 1, 3, 3.2. As I also mentioned previously, the distinction between absolute and hypothetical necessity is used by Leibniz to explain how it is possible that given the general validity of the Principle of Sufficient/Determinant Reason, it is still possible to talk about the contingency of the actions of free rational beings. Moral actions, Leibniz explains, certainly occur for a reason and are therefore necessary. They are, however, only *hypothetically* (i.e. not absolutely) necessary and, thus, contingent.

Crusius explains the distinction between both types of necessity as follows: something is absolutely necessary, if it follows directly from necessary conditions and its opposite cannot be thought of. On the contrary, something is hypothetically necessary, if it follows from a condition that is not necessary in itself and its opposite can be thought of (§5/17–8). Such a distinction, Crusius argues, is "merely verbal". If one accepts the Principle of Determinant Reason, everything that occurs has a determinant reason. This is true "for the reason of a reason, and for the third and the thousandth determinant reason of the previous reasons". This means that the first feature of hypothetical necessity according to Crusius – to follow from something which is not necessary – is unattainable: nothing can follow from something which is not necessary. For everything that occurs in the world, there is "a whole series of previous things", which is itself necessary (§5/20).

What about the second feature, the possibility of thinking the opposite of an action? Concerning the creation of the world, for example, it is indeed possible to imagine that God could have created another order of things. However, Crusius responds, this does not reduces the necessity of the action. It does not matter that the opposite, "separately and for itself", can be thought of – "given the reigning conditions, the reality, with which it should be associated, is still unthinkable" (§6/22). It is certainly possible to think or imagine another order of things. Yet, given the conditions that determined God to create this world, according to optimism, no other order could have come into reality.

Thus, Crusius concludes, the distinction between absolute and hypothetical necessity is not a real distinction of nature, but simply of degree. Therefore, it could be replaced with the distinction between *direct* and *indirect* necessity. In the first case, the opposite of a thing cannot be thought by virtue of the thing itself; in the second, the opposite which cannot be though of rests rather in the "connection of things, which determines truly and necessary" (§6/23). In both cases, nevertheless, there is unrestricted necessity.

2) The Principle of Determinant Reason cannot be proven. And all existing proofs are erroneous (§§10–15).

Leibniz explains in one of his letters to Clarke that he does not consider it necessary or possible to undertake any *a priori* proof of the Principle.[21] Nevertheless, Wolff did intend to offer proofs of the Principle. Those proofs rely on two strategies. On the one hand, Wolff starts from the assumption that 'nothing comes from nothing' and tries to deduce from it the truth of the Principle.[22] On the other, he attempts to show that if the Principle of Determinant Reason is not valid, then the Principle of Contradiction must be invalid as well.[23]

Those strategies, Crusius argues, are completely flawed. The first one is circular, presupposing in the proposition 'nothing comes from nothing' the truth of what is to be demonstrated, i.e. that there cannot be or occur anything without a determinant reason (§§11–13). The second one is unacceptable precisely because it is build upon the Principle of Contradiction, which is "a completely identical proposition" that pertains "only to one thing, in only one manner, and in one instant". Therefore, it cannot be used to prove the connection between two entities, in this case between effect and cause (§14).[24]

3) The Principle of Determinant Reason goes against our awareness of our own freedom of choice.

According to Crusius, the subjective experience that rational beings have of the way in which their own decisions take place contradicts the conditions of the Principle regarding the strict determination of all things and occurrences. Internal experience, he writes, "shows us the various possibilities of acting

---

21 Cf. LC, L.V.125–30/GP VII, 419–20.
22 Cf. *Latin Ontology*, §70 and *Deutsche Metaphysik*, §30.
23 Cf. *Deutsche Metaphysik*, §31.
24 For a more detailed exposition, followed by a harsh criticism, of Wolff's arguments for the Principle of Sufficient/Determinant Reason, see Kahl-Furthmann 1976.

that appear to us, which must be carried out according to a sufficient reason that differs greatly from the one in the Leibnizian vocabulary" (§15/219 [of the Latin edition[25]]).

The Principle of Determinant Reason is morally destructive, it cannot be proven, and it contradicts subjective experience. There is, therefore, no reason why it should be accepted in its traditional, unrestricted form. If the Principle should be somehow valid (and it must be, since its total rejection would dispute "the wise order and connection of causes and effects" – something Crusius still seems to be willing to acknowledge), it can only be in a restricted form that agrees with our (i.e. with Crusius's) views about the nature of freedom of the will, as well as with our psychology. The restricted form that Crusius proposes reads as follows:

> Everything, with the exception of first free actions [*actio prima libera/ erste freie Aktion*], is produced by [or follows from] a sufficient cause in such a way that under the same circumstances it could not have occurred otherwise.
>
> [*Alles, was keine erste freie Aktion ist, das wird, wenn es entsteht, von einer wirkenden Ursache also hervorgebracht, dass es bei eben den Umständen nicht anders würde haben entstehen oder gar außenbleiben können*]
> De usu, §26/72[26]

---

25 Curiously enough, this passage is not reproduced in the German translation of *De usu*.
26 Cf. *Entwurf*, §84/150 ("The genuine Principle of Determinant Reason [states that] everything, with the exception of the fundamental actions of freedom, has in its origin a determinant reason, i.e. a reason by virtue of which things cannot fail to emerge, nor be or occur elsewise.)" [[*D*]*er wahre Satz vom determinierenden Grunde* [...]: *alles, was nicht eine Grundtätigkeit der Freiheit ist, das hat, wenn es entsteht, einen determinierenden Grund, das ist, einen solchen, bei dessen Setzung es nicht unterbleiben, auch nicht anders sein oder geschehen kann*]) and §380/724–5 ("Therefore, it is true that everything, except what is immediately a marvel or a free action of creatures, has its determinant reason in the preceding condition of the world. Furthermore, everything whose determination is not influenced by free actions must occur in a world and can neither be prevented from happening nor occur otherwise – unless God introduces some change by miracle. On the contrary, free actions and everything which depends upon them occur in a world in a way that could have been otherwise. This does not diminish the perfection of the world, but is rather absolutely essential to its perfection [...] [*Demnach ist nur so viel wahr, dass alles dasjenige, was nicht unmittelbar entweder ein Wunderwerk, oder eine freie Tätigkeit der Geschöpfe ist, in dem vorhergehenden Zustande der Welt seinen determinierenden Grund hat. Und ferner, dass alles dasjenige, in dessen Bestimmung die freien Tätigkeiten keinen Einfluss haben können, in einer Welt erfolgen müsse, und nicht außenbleiben, oder anders erfolgen könne, wenn nicht Gott wundertätig eine Veränderung macht. Hingegen die freien*

As was to be expected, in its restricted version the Principle is valid regarding all empirical/physical, as well as logical/mathematical matters, but not regarding the voluntary actions of God and rational creatures.

What does this exactly mean for voluntary actions? Does it mean that it is ultimately contradictory to talk about 'reasons for free actions'? Not at all, and with this in mind Crusius explains the distinction between sufficient and determinant reasons.

Everything that occurs in the world follows from a *sufficient cause* ("a cause in which nothing is missing which should be necessary for the production of an effect" [*De usu*, §44/120–1]). Physical events occur by virtue of sufficient causes that determine them to occur or behave in one specific way, excluding the possibility of alternative courses of events. This kind of cause from which an effect follows necessarily is a determinant reason (also "physical reason" [§§16–7/58ff.]). For their part, free actions also occur by virtue of a sufficient cause (which is the freedom of the will), but this cause does not determine the action to happen in only one possible way (§45/121ff.). It is merely a sufficient (or "moral") reason: one that, while explaining why an action occurs as it does, does not exclude different courses of action, i.e. does not determine the action to occur in only one way. Crusius explains:

> A free substance when it acts freely is equipped with sufficient forces, but these forces are equally sufficient to allow the omission of the action, since the substance acts freely. What the substance undertakes does not exceed its forces; such forces are therefore sufficient. Nevertheless, other courses of action were possible as well, for which the forces would not have been less sufficient in the same moment. I leave, but I can also sit down. I sit, but I could also leave. I am capable of both courses of action and I am in no need of a new determinant reason, but I determine myself.

> [*Denn eine freie Substanz, wenn sie frei wirket, ist mit zureichenden Kräften zur Aktion versehen, die aber auch zur Unterlassung derselben nicht weniger zureichend sind, in wieferne nehmlich die Substanz frei agiert. Das, was sie unternimmt, übersteigt ihre Kräfte nicht, und mithin sind sie eben darzu zureichend gewesen; aber es waren noch viel andere Aktionen möglich, zu deren Unternehmung dieselben Kräfte zu eben der Zeit nicht weniger zureichend waren. Ich gehe, aber ich kann mich auch niedersetzen. Ich sitze,*

Taten, und was davon abhängt, erfolgen in einer Welt dergestalt, dass sie auch anders hätten geschehen können. Und dies vermindert die Vollkommenheit der Welt nicht, sondern es ist der Vollkommenheit der Welt schlechterdings wesentlich [...]]).

> *aber ich kann auch gehen. Beides steht in meinem Vermögen, und ich bedarf nicht eines neuen determinierenden Grundes, sondern ich determiniere mich selbst*]
>
> De usu, §45/122–4

Thus, the divine and the human will are for Crusius independent from the Principle of Determinant Reason in its traditional, Leibnizian form. The kind of voluntarism that Crusius upholds implies the rejection of any account of causality that maintains that volition is bound to the same kind of causal principle that governs the rest of events that occur in the worlds.

Let us return to optimism. As we saw previously, the doctrine of the best of all possible worlds follows organically from Leibnizian metaphysics, to which the hypothesis of the universal application of the Principle of Determinant Reason seems to be fundamental.

For Crusius, given the threefold assumption of divine goodness or the Principle of the Best, the optimist's postulation of the existence of a best among all possible worlds, and the theory of universal determinacy that seems to follow from the Principle of Determinant Reason – given these three assumptions, God was obliged to create the one single world that he identified as the superior. The attack on the Principle of Determinant Reason is, thus, an essential complement of the rejection of the concept of the best of all possible worlds, as examined in the first section. Indeed, as Crusius would surely claim, only if the concept of the best of possible worlds *and* the doctrine of the universal validity of the Principle are rejected, is it possible to ensure God's absolute and undetermined freedom of will.

3   Final Comments and Open Questions

Clearly, Crusius' anti-Leibnizian account of the independence of the divine will has certain problems. These concern, on the one hand, moral aspects of voluntarism, for example: If God is not determined by anything to act, not even necessarily by the representation of the good, what prevents him from doing evil? On the other, theoretical aspects: According to voluntarists, how does the will actually function? What gives 'direction' to the will? If the will is not 'guided' by the representations of the good, then how does it decide? How does it come to action, to 'movement'?[27] Problems of this sort are examined by Leibniz in innumerable passages of his work. The *Theodicy* alone is full of such

---

27   On this respect see, for example, Schneewind 1996.

criticisms of Descartes', Pufendorfs' or Hobbes' supposedly voluntarist views, as well as of Pierre Bayle's arguments against the Leibnizian view of the determinacy of the will.

The basic problems regarding the philosophical consistence of voluntarism will be addressed again in Chapters 5 and 6. Here I will focus on two different problems concerning Crusius's criticism of philosophical optimism directly: his dismissal of the two possible definitions of the concept of the best possible world, and his reasons against the Principle of Sufficient/ Determinant Reason, particularly his understanding of the Leibnizian theory of absolute and hypothetical necessity.

3.1 *The Perfection of the Best of All Possible Worlds*

At the beginning of his criticism of optimism in the *Entwurf*, Crusius presents and subsequently rejects two ways of defining the superiority of the created world: our world either contains all possible perfections that any created world can contain, or it is the only one among all possible worlds that permits the achievement of some divine purpose. From a Leibnizian perspective, it is not clear why these two possible definitions should be unfeasible, as Crusius maintains. Indeed, it seems to be perfectly adequate to understand the concept of the best possible world in ways that show, against Crusius's view, that such a concept is, at least, plausible. Furthermore, Crusius' understanding of what the perfection of the best possible world means does not even seem to correspond to Leibniz's account.

Few topics are so controversial among Leibniz's scholars as the question what the philosopher actually meant when he said our world was the best possible. As I explained in Chapter 1, in recent years a substantial aspect of this discussion has revolved around the question whether Leibniz thought that God chose our world because through it he could obtain the best possible balance between simplicity of laws and variety or richness of phenomena,[28] or because our world has the greatest quantity of perfection or, as Leibniz also writes, of essence or reality.[29] The first thesis has been advocated notably by Nicholas

---

28 For example DM, §6/GP IV 43: "But God chose the most perfect order, that is, the order that is at once simplest in general rules and richest in phenomena – as would be a geometrical line whose construction was easy yet whose properties and effects were very admirable and very far-reaching". Also T, §§204–205, §208/GP VI 238, 241.

29 "[P]erfection is just the amount of essence. This makes it obvious that of the infinite combinations of possibilities and possible series, the one that exists is the one through which the most essence or possibility is brought into existence" (UOT/GP VII 303). Also: "[W]hat I have said implies not only that the world is physically (or, if you prefer, metaphysically) most perfect, i.e. the series of things that has been produced is the one that brings the

Rescher[30] and has been sometimes called an 'optimization thesis'. The second thesis, defended principally by Donald Rutherford against Rescher, has been called by Rutherford a 'maximization thesis'.[31]

As Rescher and Rutherford have shown, each one for his own part, both alternatives of conceiving Leibniz's best possible world are, at least, *plausible*. Further, as I explained before, Rutherford seeks to argue that both options are not necessarily contradictory. According to Rutherford's account of maximization, the best possible world does not have to be either the world with the highest degree of perfection (or essence, or reality) *or* the most appropriate way of obtaining some desired purpose (in this case, the best balance between simplicity of laws and richness of phenomena). For Leibniz it would seem to be *both*. Thus, being the best possible world means that our world contains the greatest quantity of essence *and* the most appropriate means of obtaining the best equation between simplicity of laws and variety of phenomena.[32]

It follows from what we saw in Chapter 1 that the additional problem of what exactly perfection means, and whether it is possible that the world, as a limited creation, could nonetheless have "all possible perfections" – a possibility ruled out by Crusius – also seems to be solvable *in Leibnizian terms*. Crusius seems to defend a quantitative, static notion of perfection: perfection is something that, so to speak, 'fills' some other thing. When he argues that God could have included more things in the world, and, therefore, our world is not the most perfect possible, it becomes clear that Crusius believes that more perfection can be 'added' to something, in this case to a possible world, if that world has more creatures, means, and ends, that is, if the world is, in a certain manner, 'bigger'. Against this, the Leibnizian notion of perfection seems to be more refined. If one follows Rutherford's account, Leibniz advocated a more dynamic conception of perfection: a potential for happiness. And as we have seen, this

---

greatest amount of reality into existence, but also that the world is morally most perfect, because moral perfection is really physical perfection with respect to minds" (UOT/GP VII 306).

30 *Cf.* Rescher 1979: 28ff. and 1981: 4ff.
31 *Cf.* Rutherford 1995a: 22ff.
32 Rutherford writes for example: "Leibniz does not regard variety and order as competing factors in the design of a world. Instead, he holds that a maximization of perfection presupposes God's choice of the optimal world order: an order that enables the coexistence of the greatest possible variety of beings within the confines of a single world" (Rutherford 1995a: 26). *Cf.* Rutherford 1995b: 394; M, §§53–55/GP VI 615–6; PNG, §10/GP VI 603.

view is compatible with other Leibnizian claims about perfection as essence or reality, as well as harmony and balance between variety and simplicity.[33]

Considering the dangers Crusius believes the concept of the best of all possible worlds leads to, his interest in criticizing the concept is comprehensible. However, the effectiveness of the critique can be questioned. As Rescher and particularly Rutherford show, the concept of best or most perfect world can be made meaningful in ways different and more complex than Crusius' understanding of it.

3.2 The Arguments Against the Principle of Sufficient/Determinant Reason

As we saw in the second part of this chapter, Crusius adduces three main reasons why, in his opinion, the Leibnizian Principle of Sufficient/Determinant Reason cannot be accepted and therefore can, or should, be restricted: first, the Principle introduces an unlimited necessity of all things; second, it cannot be proven; third, it collides with our internal experience of freedom. All three reasons are questionable.

From the Leibnizian perspective, the two last arguments are unsustainable. On the one hand, as Leibniz claims (and Crusius endorses) the Principle requires no proof to be accepted. Its truth is presupposed by every possible reasoning and it is impossible to produce a counter-example to it.[34] As for the talk about internal experience, Leibniz considers that such a way of arguing is powerless. In the *Theodicy* he discards Descartes' reference to "intense inward sensation" as a proof of the independence of our actions:

> Hence it is that the reason M. Descartes has advanced to prove the independence of our free actions, by what he terms an intense inward sensation, has no force. We cannot properly speaking be sensible of our independence, and we are not aware always of the causes, often imperceptible, whereon our resolution depends. It is as though the magnetic needle took pleasure in turning towards the north: for it would think that it was turning independently of any other cause, not being aware of the imperceptible movements of the magnetic matter.
>
> T, §50/GP VI 130

---

33 On the exact nature of Rutherford's interpretation of the concept of the best world, see Chapter 1, 1, 1.1.

34 *Cf.* LC, L.V.125–30/GP VII, 419–20.

Not being able to perceive distinctly the causes that determine our choices does not mean that there are no such causes.[35] Proofs, or in Crusius' case, counterproofs based on some internal awareness of the complete independence of our choices, prove nothing at all.

More interesting (and problematic) is Crusius' first argument concerning the introduction of an "unlimited necessity" through the acceptance of the principle of Sufficient/Determinant Reason, and especially his rejection of the Leibnizian distinction between absolute and hypothetical necessity. As we saw in the preceding paragraph of this chapter, that distinction – by which Leibniz explains how the contingency of moral actions is possible despite the universal validity of the Principle of Sufficient/Determinant Reason – is for Crusius "merely verbal". For him, hypothetical necessity means that something follows from a condition which is itself not necessary. However, given the universal validity of the Principle, everything must have a determinant reason. Therefore, at the end of the day, nothing can follow from something which is not, at some point, absolutely necessary.

But does Crusius do justice to Leibniz's concept of 'hypothetical necessity'? At least in what regards the Leibnizian depiction of both sorts of necessity, he doesn't seem to. As I explained previously,[36] for Leibniz the hypothetical character of the necessity of moral actions lies in the fact that those actions are not determined by efficient or moving causes, but by final causes, i.e. by aims or purposes, which is for Leibniz the best (or what the rational being considers to be the best). Final causes, as determining causes of actions, certainly introduce a kind of necessity into actions. This necessity, however, is not physical, but moral. Or rather, as Leibniz also puts it, moral actions are certainly determined, but are never absolutely necessary:[37] when the agent decides how to act, he is determined by the representation of what is best for him (i.e. his decisions always have a reason). He nevertheless *decides* and, therefore, acts freely. In this way, it is possible for Leibniz, within a system inexorably governed by the Principle of Sufficient/Determinant Reason, to make necessity and freedom compatible.

Crusius's understanding of hypothetical necessity seems to miss the point. The non-necessary conditions, from which, according to him, something hypothetically necessarily follows, are nothing more than good old efficient causes,

---

35 *Cf.* NE, II.21.13/GP V 164, as well as the appendix on William King's *De origine mali* (1702) at the end of the *Theodicy*, where Leibniz argues against King's use of the argument of internal experience in favor of voluntarism: T, "Observations on the Book Concerning *The Origin of Evil*", §3/GP VI 401–3.
36 *Cf.* Chapter 1, 3, 3.2.
37 *Cf.* NE, II.21.13/GP V 164.

not the final causes that determine moral actions in Leibniz's account. It is not a surprise, then, that Crusius considers the distinction between absolute and hypothetical a purely verbal distinction. Now, as was the case with other critiques of optimism examined in the previous chapters, the following supposition also seems to apply to Crusius' case: for the examined critics the big problem is not the definition of one or the other concept of Leibnizian metaphysics. The problem is the system itself, and particularly the belief in the essential rationality of God, which, for Leibniz's censors, amounts to the negation of divine freedom. For the present case, it seems reasonable to say that no matter how Leibniz would have defined the concept of hypothetical necessity, Crusius would have probably judged the definition as being completely false, that is: as completely noxious, given the validity of other major tenets of Leibnizian thought – first among them the belief in the universal applicability of the Principle of Sufficient Reason.

CHAPTER 5

The Prize-Contest on Optimism of the Prussian Academy of Sciences: Adolf Friedrich Reinhard's *Examen de l'optimisme* (1755)

The contest of the Prussian Academy of Sciences in Berlin for the year 1755 – immediately before Voltaire's attacks on optimism following the Lisbon Earthquake – was without doubt the most widely debated affair concerning the doctrine of the best of all possible worlds in the eighteenth century. In 1753 the Academy published a notice demanding an examination of the system of Pope as it is contained in the dictum: 'Everything is good' [*Tout est bien*]. The examination should: (1) specify the true sense of that proposition, according to the hypothesis of the author; (2) compare the author's hypothesis with the system of optimism or the choice of the best, in order to establish as accurately as possible their particular similarities and identify the differences between them; (3) adduce the most important reasons for either establishing or rejecting the system.[1]

As I mentioned before, Alexander Pope's (1688–1744) hypothesis "*Tout est bien*" is a somewhat prejudiced interpretation of the original English maxim "Whatever is, is right". This dictum was a central motive of the extensive poem *Essay on Man*, which was written between 1733 and 1734 and gained great attention in Europe in the first half of the century. For its part, "optimism or the choice of the best" may be understood as referring to Leibniz's system of philosophical optimism as expounded in the *Theodicy*. As I explained previously, the identification of Leibniz's thought with the 'doctrines' contained in Pope's *Essay on Man* was a common practice by mid-eighteenth century (in spite of being also a very problematic inclination).[2]

That an European Academy of Sciences could propose that the philosophy of optimism be judged in relation to the ideas of a poet who, though a master of literature no doubt, did not consider himself a philosopher,[3] seems rather odd. Indeed, many contemporaries held the opinion that the question the Academy

---

1 My account of the history of the Prussian Academy and its prize contests is based for the most part on Buschmann 1987 and 1989b, Harnack 1900; Hartkopf 1990.
2 *Cf.* Chapter 3, 3, 3.2.
3 *Cf.* Lessing & Mendelssohn, *Pope ein Metaphysiker!*, 445: the authors refer to a letter from Alexander Pope to Jonathan Swift of September 15, 1734, in which Pope denies all interest in being "thought a Divine, a Philosopher, and what not" (Pope, *Letters*: 258).

had proposed was biased against Leibniz. To make things worse, the prize was awarded in 1755 to an unknown philosophy aficionado and public servant called Adolf Friedrich Reinhard (1726–1783) for his essay entitled *Le système de Mr Pope sur la perfection de monde, comparé à celui de Mr de Leibnitz, avec un examen de l'optimisme* (*The System of Mr. Pope Concerning the Perfection of the World, Compared With That of Leibniz, With an Examination of Optimism*). Reinhard's work is a vehement critique of optimism but, as we will see in the following pages, also a problematic, even superficial one. It is, therefore, not surprising that the Academy's decision was as disputed as the prize-question itself. A brief look into the history and nature of the Academy may help to understand better the motives behind both the polemic prize-question and the problematic awarding of the prize to Reinhard.

The Royal Prussian Academy of Sciences in Berlin was established on July 11, 1700 during the reign of the Prince-Elector Friedrich III of Brandenburg (as from 1701 King Friedrich I of Prussia), following the visionary plans and the counsel of none other than Gottfried Wilhelm Leibniz, who was also the first president of the Academy. In the most general terms, Leibniz's vision when suggesting to Friedrich I, through the mediation of the King's wife Sophie Charlotte, the creation of a Society of Sciences was that of promoting the common welfare and the welfare of Germany (in this case of Prussia), and the reunification of the Catholic and the Evangelic Churches through knowledge. Further, following the example of the English Royal Society (founded in 1662) and the French Académie des sciences (1666), the Academy should be in charge of the organization of scientific work and the gathering of all intellectual productive forces under one institution. Its more specific purposes, as King Friedrich I established in his founding letter of July 11, 1700 to Leibniz, where the "contemplation of God's wonders in Nature", the "annotation and exercise of inventions, works of art, businesses, and doctrines, useful studies, sciences, and arts", as well as the care and "conservation of the German language in its decent purity".[4] (Ironically, as it is well known, with the later rise of Friedrich II to the throne of Prussia, French became the official language of the Academy.)

After Leibniz's death and some hard years under the reign of Friedrich Wilhelm I (1713–1740), who was not exactly fond of the institution and made no effort to hide it (for example, he constantly abused the Academy's finances for military purposes and appointed one of its presidents as a court jester), the Academy underwent vital restructuring upon the ascent of Friedrich II, Voltaire's 'Philosopher King', to the Prussian throne in 1740. Among the innovations introduced by Friedrich were the annual essay contests that the different

---

4   *Cf.* Harnack 1900: 93f.

departments of the Academy (Physics, Mathematics, Astronomy, Philology/ Literature, and Philosophy) began holding in 1746. The significance of the competitions for the history of European Enlightenment is evident, judging from the names of some of the contestants during the eighteenth century: D'Alembert, Lessing, Condillac, Abbt, Mendelssohn, Kant, Herder, Michaelis, and Garve.

The first philosophical contests showed a strong tendency to put under examination different Leibnizian doctrines. Also, they showed a strong tendency to approach those doctrines *censoriously*. Thus, the first philosophical competition (1747) concerned the theory of the monads. The second (1751) demanded the critical examination of the notion of Leibnizian determinism. The contest for 1755 just seemed to confirm this penchant. There are at least two reasons for the interest in Leibniz's thought and for a possible anti-Leibnizian leaning of the Academy. First, of course, the weight of Leibnizian thought in mid-eighteenth-century Prussia.[5] Secondly, and perhaps more importantly, the passionate philosophical atmosphere within the Academy itself. From 1746, the year in which Friedrich II appointed the French mathematician Pierre Louis Maupertuis (1698–1759) as president of the rehabilitated Academy, there were two well-outlined intellectual parties clashing within the institution: the Newtonians vs. the Leibnizians. Maupertuis, together with the Swiss mathematician Leonhard Euler (1707–1783) and other Academy members, was on the side of English natural philosophy, while the Academy's secretary, the Wolffian Johann Heinrich Samuel Formey (1711–1797), and Johann Georg Sulzer (1720–1779), another Swiss mathematician, led the faction that struggled to defend Leibniz's rationalist legacy.[6]

Discussing the first philosophical contest on Leibniz's doctrine of monads, Adolf von Harnack claims in his history of the Academy that the decision of awarding the prize to the essay presented by J.H.G Justi, an opponent of the Leibnizian theory, was definitely not an impartial decision:

> Euler himself later accepted that another contender, a qualified supporter of Leibniz, had been done wrong and that Justi should have shared the prize with him. But the bitterness of the Newtonians allowed of no conciliating decision: they argued for the victory of the exact sciences over a speculation that they considered a fantasy.
>
> HARNACK 1900: 403[7]

---

5 On this respect see for example Buschmann 1989a.
6 On the Newtonian critique of rationalist philosophy in the Prussian Academy see Ahnert 2004; Calinger 1969; Shank 2008; Terral 2002.
7 *Cf.* Buschmann 1989b: 183–6.

The predominance of the Newtonians may also explain the eccentricity of the Academy's prize question on optimism. The terms of the contest had been discussed heatedly among the members of the Academy. After its announcement in 1753 the grievances of Leibniz's followers became uncontainable; they felt provoked and complained that the contest was yet another attempt to defame Leibniz. Two important critical reactions to the Academy's request were published by leading figures of the German *Aufklärung*. Johann Christoph Gottsched (1700–1766), critic, translator, professor for Philosophy in Leipzig, and devoted supporter of Leibniz-Wolffianism (he had famously reedited the works of Leibniz in 1746 and had himself written an apology of philosophical optimism some years before[8]), published in 1753 the short pamphlet *De optimismi macula diserte nuper Alexandro Popio anglo, tacite autem G. G. Leibnitio, perperam licet, inusta*, which criticized severely the terms of the contest of the Academy. And Gotthold Ephraim Lessing (1729–1781) and Moses Mendelssohn (1729–1786), perhaps the most renowned representatives of the Berlin Enlightenment, published in 1755 the satirical piece *Pope ein Metaphysiker!* (*Pope a Metaphysician!*), which underlined the complete dissimilarity between the interests, the methods, and the subject-matter of philosophers and poets, denouncing the Academy's attempts to mock Leibnizian philosophy.[9]

The extent of the attention aroused by the Academy's calling can also be judged from the number of essays sent to the contest: at least 18 works,[10] among them one which openly defended the Leibnizian optimist cause. I refer to this because it is, at least incidentally, of some interest for understanding the internal workings of the Academy. The mathematician Sulzer assured the author of the pro-Leibnizian piece, Martin Künzli, that he would surely be elected as winner of the competition, due to the fact that the Leibnizians controlled the philosophical department. However, as Harnack recounts, the Newtonians managed to assert themselves: despite the criticisms and complaints, and later to the surprise and rage of Leibniz's friends within and outside the Academy, the prize went to Reinhard's counter-optimistic treatise.

I will now examine Adolf Friedrich Reinhard's *Examen de l'optimisme*. As I believe, more than due to its particular criticisms of optimism (which, as we will see in the forthcoming pages, are to a great extent a restatement of Christian August Crusius's arguments examined in the preceding chapter), Reinhard's *Examen* is significant because, on the one hand, from all the critical texts I have examined so far, Reinhard's essay is the only one that states clearly

---

8   *Beweis, dass diese Welt unter allen die beste sei* (*Demonstration That This World is the Best Among All Possible*, 1742).
9   On this work see Altmann 1969: 184–208.
10 *Cf.* Buschmann 1989b: 199, who rectifies Harnack's reference to only eight essays.

what its author considers optimism to be. On the other, in spite of its problems and possible shallowness, the *Examen* became a very influential and discussed text in the first years of the second half of the eighteenth century.

In the first section of the chapter, I take a closer look at Reinhard's notion of optimism. In the second section, I examine his version of Crusius' double criticism of the doctrine of God's choice of the best or most perfect world. In the final section, I offer some concluding remarks concerning the problems contained in Reinhard's answer to Leibnizian rationalism, which can be described as a voluntarist answer, as well as concerning the philosophical character of the *Examen*, its originality, and its significance for the present examination of early criticisms of optimism.

1 Reinhard's Picture of Optimism

Adolf Friedrich Reinhard, *Kammersekretär* of the duchy of Mecklenburg-Strelitz, studied Law and Theology in Thorn and Halle but according to his biographer, became "neither a theologian nor a lawyer, but fancied himself rather as a philosopher".[11] Reinhard was an enthusiastic follower and translator of Crusius'. The *Examen*, as I claimed before, is more or less an amended application of Crusius' arguments against optimism to the prize-question of the Academy.

Reinhard begins by reminding the reader that an examination of Pope's *Essay* and the thesis "*Tout est bien*" has in fact already been carried out by "Mr. de Crousaz, a grand philosopher", who reproaches Pope "his fatalism, the ruin of all morals, an infinity of contradictions, of inconsistencies, of unjust and absurd expressions; and, above all, the crime of having adopted the system of Leibniz [...]" (*Examen*, 4). This reference is to the debate between the Swiss theologian and critic of Leibniz and Wolff Jean Pierre de Crousaz (1663–1750), already mentioned in Chapter 3, and the English bishop William Warburton (1698–1779) concerning the philosophical and theological soundness of the 'system' contained in the *Essay on Man* and its relation to Leibniz's thought. Crousaz argued[12] that Pope's *Essay* reproduced the Leibnizian doctrine of the best of possible worlds, which lead inevitably to the noxious upshots listed by Reinhard. While sharing Crousaz's views regarding the dangerous character of

---

11   On Reinhard's life and works see Krause 1889.
12   *Examen de l'Essai de M. Pope sur l'Homme* (1737).

Leibniz's teachings, Warburton[13] thought that it was possible to defend Pope of Crousaz's charges by denying the Leibniz-Pope connection.[14]

According to Warburton, Reinhard explains, there is a major difference between the systems of Pope and Leibniz. Following Plato, Pope is supposed to have advocated a kind of optimism that ensured God's absolute freedom in the most complete sense "that is, the liberty of indifference [*l'indifférence de l'equilibre*]",[15] by admitting the existence of several possible worlds with the same degree of perfection. Leibniz, on the contrary, "rejects this kind of liberty and does not admit any volition which is not determined by the motive of the one and only best" (7) ... For Reinhard whether Warburton is right or not regarding Pope is not really important.[16] For him, as to the dogma of the best of possible worlds and its corollaries, the systems of Pope and Leibniz are identical. And as a good disciple of Crusius, Reinhard believes that the system of the best denies divine liberty. That is enough to reject both Leibniz's *and* Pope's optimism in one sweep.

My main interest in this section is to understand what optimism is according to Reinhard. Reinhard summarizes his picture of optimism with the following words:

> What Pope teaches here is nothing more than Leibnitz's optimism [...]. No difference, same spirit, same ideas, same system. This is the best of all possible worlds. This combination, this arrangement, this admirable

---

13 *A Vindication of Mr. Pope's Essay on Man* (1739).

14 On the Crousaz-Warburton controversy see Barber 1955: 116–9, Hellwig 2008: 123ff.; Rogers 1948. There was still another important reply to Crousaz, that of the Swiss diplomat and philosopher Emer de Vattel (1714–1767), the *Défense du système Leibnitien contre les objections et les imputations de Mr. De Crousaz, contenues dans l'Examen de l'Essay sur l'homme de Mr. Pope* (1741). Vattel writes that although "everyone talks about the Leibnizian philosophy [...]", the majority of its censors "only know it through the various writings for or against it, which are published in the magazines" (Preface). He thus undertakes a text-oriented defense of so-called Leibniz-Wolffianism, specifically regarding the charges of fatalism brought against it by Crousaz. On Vattel see Barber 1955: 119–21.

15 That is, the idea – which Leibniz calls 'indifference of *equipoise*' and criticizes harshly – that God is not determined in his actions by one compelling reason, but is wholly undetermined in his willing. *Cf.* Chapter 1, 3, 3.1.

16 As I mentioned before, the motive of the connection between Leibnizian philosophical optimism and Pope's *Essay* was commonplace among the learned circles in the mid-eighteenth century. The Leibniz-Pope connection has been denied resolutely in the twentieth century: "From any point of view, the assumption that Pope was necessarily indebted to the *Theodicy* is untenable" (Moore 1917: 101); and Barber: "The views which Pope advanced in his *Essay* [...] have something in common with those of Leibniz's *Théodicée* [...]. These affinities, however, disappear upon a closer investigation" (1955: 109–11).

chain of all parts that compose the universe is the most perfect possible; if one would change the smallest thing, the world would cease to be the most perfect [...]. Even evils are part of the most perfect system; they are the means or the necessary conditions of infinite goods [...]. For this same reason, every individual who belongs to the composition of the universe could not have received more or less perfection than it actually does without disturbing the order of the best of all possible worlds. [...] This is optimism; this is the system of Pope and Leibniz.

[*Ce que Pope enseigne ici, n'est point autre chose que l'optimisme de Leibnitz* [...]. *Point de différence, même esprit, mêmes idées, même système. Ce monde – ci est le meilleur de tous les possibles. Cette combinaison, cet arrangement, cet enchaînement admirable de toutes les parties qui composent cet univers, est le plus parfait qui soit possible; de sorte que, si l'on y vouloit changer même la moindre chose, le monde ne seroit plus aussi parfait* [...] *Les maux mêmes donc font partie de ce système le plus parfait. Ce sont, ou des moyens, ou des conditions indispensables d'une infinité de biens* [...] *Par la même raison chaque individu, qui entre dans la composition de cet univers, ne sauroit avoir ni plus ni moins de perfection qu'il n'a actuellement, sans déranger l'ordre essentiel du Monde le plus parfait.* [...] *Voilà l'optimisme; voila le système de Pope & de Leibnitz.*]
  Examen, 8

Our world is an "admirable chain" of elements that constitute together the best possible order; evil belongs to the general composition of "the most perfect system" as a necessary constituent; every creature has its place in this perfectly designed system: these seem to be principal motives of optimism, according to Reinhard. Let us take a more detailed look at them.

 The doctrine of the best possible world, Reinhard argues, is inseparable from the "dogma of the *universal connection* of all the parts that compose the world" (*Examen*, 8; my emphasis). According to that dogma, even the smallest thing in the universe is a constituent element of the system of the world and is linked to each of the other parts that compose the whole. Thus, every particular thing in the universe "has an influence upon the determination of the state of every other part" and the slightest modification in the correlation of the elements implies a modification of the whole.[17] From this Reinhard infers

---

17 The dogma of the universal connection has been called notoriously by Arthur Lovejoy the idea of the 'Great Chain of Being'. That idea, as he writes, is "the conception of the plan and structure of the world which, through the Middle Ages and down to the late

that Leibniz teaches the *necessity of the world*, which manifests itself in the impossibility of modifying one particular feature of the actual world without changing the complete order, and, thus, the very essence of the world. This applies to the whole system of the universe as well as to particular substances: no essential determination of an existent being can be modified without producing a new and essentially different being:

> To ask why did God not grant more perfection to a particular being is equivalent to asking why he did not, among the infinite number of beings eternally present to his intellect, choose to create some other particular being.
>
> [*Demander, pourquoi Dieu n'a pas donné plus de perfections à un être? c'est demander, pourquoi Dieu dans ce nombre infini d'essences, présentes éternellement à son intellect, n'a pas choisi toute une autre au lieu de celle – ci, pour lui donner l'existence?*]
> *Examen*, 10

As it has been said Reinhard, following the teachings of Crusius, focuses his criticism of Leibnizian optimism on the rejection, on the one hand, of the dogma of the existence of a best world and, on the other, of Leibniz's theory of divine agency. His concern is, thus, the same as that of the authors examined in the previous chapters: the traditional conviction that optimism limits or rather eradicates God's freedom of choice. Although Reinhard only develops arguments against the two mentioned particular aspects of optimist metaphysics, he naturally disagrees with the optimists on other issues. Thus, for example, the anxiety regarding the supposed denial of freedom by optimism also encourages him to reject the dogma of the universal connection. His argument, which appears at the end of the *Examen*, is quite succinct, it goes like this: It is impossible to prove the reality of the "general chain" that supposedly connects

---

eighteenth century many philosophers, most men of science, and, indeed most educated men were to accept without question – the conception of the universe as a 'Great Chain of Being', composed of an immense or […] infinite, number of links ranging in hierarchical order from the meagerest kind of existents […] through 'every possible' grade up to the *ens perfectissimum*" (Lovejoy 1936: 59). Leibniz is also affiliated to this conception. For example, as he writes in the *Theodicy*: "For it must be known that all things are *connected* in each one of the possible worlds: the universe, whatever it may be, is all of one piece, like an ocean: the least movement extends its effect there to any distance whatsoever, even though this effect become less perceptible in proportion to the distance" (T, §9/GP VI 107).

all things in the universe (*Examen*, 46). For that reason, optimism must be erroneous.

The rejection of the dogma of the universal connection of the parts that compose the world obviously derives from Reinhard's desire to wipe away all theoretical or metaphysical principles that, in his opinion, unavoidably lead to necessitarianism. Considering this, Reinhard's motivation, at least in principle, is reasonable. The problem is that his arguments against those principles very often suffer from the same disorder as his criticism of the dogma of the universal connection: they are no arguments at all. The rejection of the idea of a universal connection is no doubt a further radical step against the kind of rationalist metaphysics that underlie optimism, far more radical than Crusius's limiting of the Principle of Sufficient Reason, which we examined previously.[18] But, of course, Reinhard offers no explanation at all of what the world would look like without universal connection. Which is the relationship between the creatures and objects that compose the world if there is no 'great chain' that connects them? Reinhard remains silent – and, thus, adopts the same attitude that he will assume when criticizing other Leibnizian dogmas: rejecting a particular theory without much explanation and ignoring the problems or contradictory consequences that such rejection entails. In the next section, we will see more of this routine.

But let us return to Reinhard's depiction of optimism. Regarding the optimistic approach to the problem of evil, Reinhard explains that metaphysical evil consists in the finite character of created beings, from which all imperfections in the world derive, i.e. so-called physical evil and moral evil (*Examen*, 14). In Reinhard's terminology the last source of evil is the "collision" between the different rules of perfection within creatures; this collision follows unavoidably from the finite character of creatures. This means two things: first, God, obliged as he is by the requirement of creating the best possible world, must "necessarily allow exceptions" (particular evils), since – given the nature of created beings – the rules of perfection are bound to conflict with each other (at least at a particular level). These "exceptions" guarantee the minimizing of general imperfection and the resulting of "the greatest possible perfection in the whole". And second, optimism is coupled with a theory of the *necessity of evil* in general. Evils are either "the means or the indispensable conditions of the greatest possible goods. From this combination of evils and goods arises the greatest possible perfection of the universe, which would not have been obtained in the same degree through any other means" [*Tous les maux donc qui arrivent dans ce monde, sont, ou des suites nécessaires, ou des moyens, ou*

---

18   *Cf.* Chapter 4.

des conditions indispensables des biens les plus grands qui soient possibles. De cette combinaison des maux & de biens nait la plus grande perfection possible de l'univers, qui n'auroit pu être obtenuë dans la même degré d'aucune autre maniere.] (*Examen*, 15). Since the God of the rationalists is subjected to certain rules of order and perfection, God permits evil, on the one hand, to avoid the breach of the rules of perfection set for the world; on the other, to make "greater goods" possible.

Reinhard seems to misinterpret Leibniz in at least one point regarding the question of the source of evil. As I believe, Leibniz would very probably disagree with Reinhard's definition of evil as resulting from an inevitable 'collision' of rules, as an *exception* made by God in order to minimize "the general imperfection". Evil, for Leibniz, is not really an exception, an accident, or something in the like. As we have seen in Chapter 1, evil results for Leibniz from the essential imperfection of creatures, or what he calls 'metaphysical evil'. Yet, evil is no real mishap, a logistic accident, but a constitutive brick of the harmonious building of creation, one more element of a universal harmony that we could easily grasp if we could only assume God's perspective of the world as a whole (i.e. Catherine Wilson's "aspect of the world which is not directly available to perception" [Wilson 1983: 767], referred in the same chapter). Thus Reinhard seems to misrepresent Leibniz by maintaining that evil is an exception made by God.

It is also with reference to the motive of the necessity of evil that Reinhard interprets the optimistic account of moral evil. Moral evil is a necessary outcome of God's fashion of creating and of the nature of creatures. The "nature and essence" of man determine that he have "confused ideas, sensual appetites, passions"; without them he would not be capable of doing good nor acting. According to Reinhard, evildoing is for Leibniz (and Pope) a "natural consequence" of these very same "appetitive and cognitive faculties of the soul" (19). Moral evil, thus, comes from the same source as moral goodness. For this reason, if God would want to render human evil impossible he would have either to take away from us "the faculty of doing one thing or another", or to "infringe constantly the laws of spiritual nature" that he himself has established for his creatures. Hence, *moral evil is necessary*, since it derives from the combination of the freedom of rational creatures, their essence (their finite nature), and the laws of creation. And again, as it was the case with metaphysical evil, moral evil is certainly an imperfection, but only, if seen from the perspective of particularity. With regard to the whole, it indeed serves to increase the perfection.

From the fact that moral evil derives both from the misuse of freedom by rational beings and from the fact that God created the world in accordance with general laws of perfection, Reinhard deduces that, in the end, for the optimists freedom can be nothing but the *capacity of acting in accordance with laws*: Moral misdeeds and physical evils are the deviation from a rule. Still, they all are a consequence of the ordered structure of creation, of which freedom is just one more element. Thus, Reinhard writes: "Is it not evident that [Pope] subjects the human will to a necessity of nature?" [*N'est-il pas évident qu'il assujettit la volonté humaine à une nécessité de la nature?*] (20).[19]

But for Reinhard, the necessity of the actions of rational beings is not just an obscure suggestion in Pope's poem. In his opinion, it is contained in Leibniz's own teachings, namely in the concept of 'hypothetical necessity' (and this seems to be one of the few times that Reinhard uses an expression actually related to Leibnizian vocabulary). As it was the case with Castel's review of the *Theodicy* in the *Journal the Trévoux* (Chapter 3) and Crusius' critique of optimism (Chapter 4) for Reinhard *necessity is necessity*, no matter how we or better, Leibniz, may try to elude it. Leibniz subjects the will to a "hypothetical necessity". Reinhard asks: "But isn't it obvious that our author [...] fully agrees with Mr. De Leibnitz on this issue? And what is this but a necessity of nature, just as indispensable as the necessity contained in the actions of the bodies and the machines?" [*Mais n'est il pas évident encore, que notre auteur [...] est parfaitement d'accord avec Mr. De Leibnitz sur ce chapitre? Qu'est ce que la nécessité hypothetique à laquelle ce dernier soumet la volonté, sinon une nécessité de la nature aussi indispensable que celle qui est dans les actions des corps & des machines?*] (20). As we will see in the following section, Reinhard's criticism of the doctrine of hypothetical necessity is rather harmless, as there is more to that theory than Reinhard seems to be willing to admit.

2 Against Optimism

According to Reinhard, optimism relies on two principles, against which he directs his criticisms. In the previous chapters, we have already mentioned and examined the centrality of these assumptions within the metaphysics of optimism. First: "Among all possible worlds there is one which is the most perfect

---

[19] It is not from examining Leibniz's but Pope's words that Reinhard 'verifies' his problematic definition of freedom. For example, the verse in Pope's *Essay*: "What makes all physical or moral ill? / There deviates nature, and here wanders will. / God sends not ill; if rightly understood, / Or partial ill is universal good, / Or change admits, or nature lets it fall, / Short, and but rare, 'till man improv'd it all. / We just as wisely might of heav'n complain / That righteous Abel was destroy'd by Cain, / As that the virtuous son is ill at ease, / When his lewd father gave the dire disease. / Think we, like some weak prince, th' eternal cause / Prone for his fav'rites to reverse his laws?" (*Essay*, Epistle I: 109–118).

of all". (If there were several equally perfect worlds there would be no reason at all for God to prefer the actual world to the other possible worlds.) And second: "Due to the supreme perfection of his will, God could have not chosen a different, less perfect world" [*Parmi les mondes possibles il y en a un qui est le plus parfait de tous. Car, s'il y en avoit plusieurs également parfaits, il n'y auroit aucune raison qui eû déterminé la volonté divine à choisir le monde actuel préférablement à tous les autres possibles. 2) Ce monde est celui que Dieu a choisi comme le plus parfait de tous les possibles & par la souveraine perfection de sa volonté il n'a pû en choisir un autre moins parfait.*] (*Examen*, 29). Reinhard's criticism of both principles clearly follows Crusius' reasoning. Against the first principle, Reinhard carries out an analysis of the concept of perfection and criticizes the idea that there can be a supreme perfection. Regarding the second principle, after rejecting the idea that God is in some way obliged to create the world, Reinhard focuses on condemning the Leibnizian theory of causation and the deterministic theory of divine action that in his opinion underlies optimism, offering a voluntarist alternative to Leibniz's account of divine freedom.

2.1   Is the Most Perfect of All Possible Worlds Possible?

Reinhard's critical examination of this question rests on his analysis of the concept of 'perfection'. Since this analysis seems to be a somewhat sophisticated version of Crusius' criticism of the concept of the best world, I will describe Reinhard's account of perfection only briefly. Perfection is defined by Reinhard as "the amount of reality" contained in a thing (*Examen*, 23).[20] This amount is determined either by the degree in which that thing or that being accomplishes a certain end or by the number and variety of ends that it is capable of attaining. The end or purpose (*"le but"*) of a given perfection is the point of incidence in which all its realities meet. Each one of the purposes towards

---

20   As we saw in Chapter 1, 1, 1.1, Leibniz also considers that the best/most perfect world is the world that "brings the greatest amount of reality into existence" (UOT/GP VII 306). In this sense, Leibniz would indeed agree with Reinhard's very first definition of perfection. However, as we will see next, this appears to be the only important thing that Leibniz's and Reinhard's conceptions of perfection have in common. In fact, it would seem that it is his own *definition* of perfection which allows Reinhard to contradict the notion of a best world. While for Leibniz, the reality of the world is defined by its degree of harmony and intelligibility and its subsequent capability of producing (rational) happiness, and, thus, related to its objective superiority over other possible worlds, for Reinhard (as well as for Crusius) that reality seems to relate mainly to the degree in which the world permits God to attain certain ends. Given that Reinhard advocates a concept of God which is radically opposed to Leibniz's and which we know well from the past chapters, it comes as no surprise that he rejects the idea that this world, or any world, can be the best possible.

which a given perfection is directed is called "a rule of perfection". If a thing is determined by a rational being to attain one specific purpose, this purpose will be called "main rule of perfection" or "main purpose". The other ends, which are subordinated to the main purpose, are the "secondary purposes". Therefore, with regard to each thing there is a certain proportion among the importance of its different rules or purposes. This proportion is always established by the rational being which determines the main purpose of a thing (24–5).

A central aspect of Reinhard's notion of perfection is the concept of 'collision', which describes the disagreement between the different rules of perfection of one thing. In such cases, the rational being which establishes the purpose or purposes of a thing (or which carries out an action for some specific purpose) must "make an exception" – or rather, one would say, making a *compromise* – regarding the rules of perfection. That is, he must give preference to the fulfillment of one rule over another and "admit the emergence of a flaw" (25) in order to attain his desired purpose. In these cases, the rational being will prefer the accomplishment of the main purpose and will make an exception of one or several of the secondary rules. (There are as well some cases in which the rational being decides to make an exception of the *main* rule, if the flaw ensuing from the application of the main rule is larger than the one ensuing from the application of secondary rules.)

The criterion for establishing the desirability of the application or exception of a rule is the specific relation of proportion between the quantity of perfection obtainable by applying the main and the secondary rules, and the amount of defect following from the application or exemption of those rules. Thus, for a rational being the choice of executing an action for some specific purpose depends on the calculus of the collision implied by such an action. By means of several algebraic examples Reinhard shows that, although the collision between different rules of perfection can compel rational beings to make the exception of one rule or the other, thus preferring *one* particular set of rules and ends to all the others, there are also cases in which it makes no difference to dismiss one rule or another in order to attain an specific purpose: the degree of perfection accomplished by applying one rule or another, as well as the ensuing amount of defect, will be exactly the same (25–8). It is obvious what Reinhard wants to prove through this theory of collision: an intelligent being is not always obliged to follow *one* particular arrangement of rules and ends – i.e. not always obliged to create one particular world or set of rules, ends, and creatures – to attain his purposes. Moreover,

> an intelligent being, striving for perfection in its works is able to find in the execution of the ends and the rules that it has set several ways of

acting in accordance with its purposes. Those ways have all the same perfection, and to choose one or another will be indifferent for that being".

[*Un être intelligent, qui tend à la perfection dans ses ouvrages, peut dans l'exécution des fins & des règles qu'il s'est proposées, trouver plusieurs manières d'agir également conformes à ses intentions, qui sont par conséquent d'une perfection égale & entre les quelles il lui est indifférent de choisir l'une ou l'autre.*]
  Examen, 28–9

On the basis of his hypotheses concerning perfection and collision, Reinhard develops a critique of the optimistic dogma of the "greatest perfection". This critique takes place in three stages:

(a) When we call something "a perfection" we do it always in view of some particular end or set of ends. Thus "something is perfect as long as it is that which it has to be", in accordance with a specific purpose (*Examen*, 30). This means, for example, that a tool may be as perfect in its own genre as a man can be in his; it would be absurd to want to compare their advantages, for they simply have different purposes (a hammer is the best means for hammering a nail, but only man can attain happiness through the exercise of his rationality, or something in that fashion). Hence, since different ends make different types of perfection possible, "heterogeneous perfections", as Reinhard calls them, they cannot be compared to one another. In this case, it is impossible for a perfection to be superior to others.

(b) But what if there is just *one* end or set of ends to be achieved? In that case, Reinhard argues, "there can be different, equally good ways to reach those ends" (30), as it was proved earlier by Reinhard through his theory of collision. According to him, nature, the arts, and science offer "all over proofs of the indifference of using different means to reach the same end" (31). Experience teaches that when somebody wants to build a house there are "different inventions, different plans, all equally good in view of making this residence delightful and charming" (30), each one of these plans will contain beauties that the others do not. And in the same manner, geometry shows that one can construct the same figure or prove the same theorem by several different methods. It is therefore clear "that there are infinite equivalents with regard to the main purpose, and the choice among them is completely arbitrary" (30).

(c) Nevertheless, optimism upholds that this world created by God is the best among all possible alternatives. What exactly does that mean? Regarding the specific issue of optimism, what does it mean for a world to have supreme perfection? As Reinhard explained earlier, this can mean two things:

On the one hand, perfection can mean "reality in general", in which case optimism would maintain that our world contains more reality than every other possible world (32). Now, Reinhard argues, each world is a system of finite beings and a particular set of rules. How is it possible that one world contains more reality than all the others? One world can contain realities that another does not, without necessarily containing *more* realities than the rest of possible worlds. Why should it not be possible for different worlds to contain different types of realities, the sums of which are nevertheless identical? Just as two series may be equal and still have parts that follow one another in dissimilar order, two sums might be equivalent, their parts nevertheless different from one another (32). For Reinhard, no world can contain all possible realities (this would contradict the concept of 'finiteness' implied by the concept of 'creature'). There is, therefore, no reason to maintain that two or more possible worlds cannot contain the same degree of reality/perfection.

On the other hand, the optimist can also claim that our world is the most perfect world not owing to its supreme reality, but with regard to the ends or purposes that God could achieve through its creation. This means that: (i) this world, which is a system of ends and means, contains the ends that are most worthy of the divine perfection; (ii) those ends are reached through the most perfect means; (iii) such ends are fulfilled in the highest possible degree (33). Reinhard rules out these ideas by returning to his past arguments. Against (i) he maintains: God's ends are either undetermined or determined. If the first, then there is no reason why they could not be determined in different ways, that is, why undetermined ends should not be obtainable through different systems (different worlds). If, on the contrary, God's ends are determined, then, as we have seen, it is still possible to achieve one and the same purpose in several different ways. Regarding (ii): since the best of all possible worlds is not possible, then there also are no 'most perfect means'. But even if there could be something as 'best means' then there would also be different ways to combine and apply them, which would give origin to different equally perfect worlds. As for (iii), one can only compare the degrees of perfection of worlds which contain the same kinds of means (combined with each other in different ways). But if two or more worlds contain identical means, is it really possible to talk about fulfilling ends in a "highest degree" of perfection? Why should it not be possible for two or more worlds that contain similar kinds of means to fulfill their ends in the same degree?

From these speculations Reinhard concludes that there is nothing in the notion of perfection – neither the perfection of ends nor that of means – that could allow us to think that *one* world can be regarded as the best of all possible worlds.

There is an additional way in which the optimist may struggle to prove the pre-eminence of this world, namely by referring not to the world's but to *God's* perfection. According to this line of argument our world must be the best possible, otherwise God would have not created it.[21] Against such a presumption Reinhard argues that if we accept the fact that God has infinite perfection, we must also acknowledge that he is not under the necessity of creating finite beings to be able to execute or fulfill his perfection. Every kind of perfection in God "finds its fulfillment in itself and has no object outside him" (36). Divine perfection is independent of the existence of finite beings and does not require creation in order to achieve completion. The optimist might now argue that, if not God's perfection, at least his *goodness* requires the existence of beings for its fulfillment, since God's goodness is the inclination to act according to his creatures' welfare, and this presupposes the existence of creatures. Reinhard replies that this kind of argument is also flawed, since the goodness of God, just as his perfection, finds its fulfillment in itself ("its object is present to the divine intellect for all eternity"); that is, divine goodness does not require the existence of any object besides God in order to be good. From this, it follows that, first, from God's viewpoint the existence of creatures is not required; secondly, with regard to God's perfection *and* goodness, the actual existence or non-existence of creatures is completely indifferent. "Consequently, for God it must also be indifferent which creature among all possible comes into existence" (36). Reinhard's account seems to be problematic in this point as well. That God's perfection does not require the existence of anything apart from God himself is simple to understand. But what does it mean to say that his *goodness* does not require creatures? It would seem – at least for the Christian tradition that Reinhard appears to revere – that God's goodness, his love, can only manifest itself in relation to something else, i.e. to his creatures, whereby God wants that there should be something besides him.[22] Leibniz himself maintains that God created the world in order to share his goodness with creatures.[23] This particular issue cannot be examined here. Be that as it may, Reinhard's argument that divine goodness does not require the existence of anything apart from God remains problematic. But, in the end, as we have been able to establish various times in the past chapters, rather than having a problem with specific details of optimism, the main menace of the system of the best for Reinhard is the notion of a God guided and determined in his actions by reason(s).

---

21 See for example the well-known T, §§8, 226/GP VI 107, 252–3.
22 See for example Psalm 8:1; 19:1ff; 50:6; 89:5. *Cf. Catechism of the Catholic Church*: 68ff.
23 *Cf.* GR, 355–6 and Murray 2016.

2.2   *Once Again: Theological Voluntarism*

Indeed, for Reinhard, as was also the case in Crusius' criticism of optimism, only by assuming the complete indifference of God regarding creation is it possible to secure two essential attributes of divine will: God's freedom to act or not to act, and his freedom to act in one way or another regarding the same object (i.e. the scholastic distinction between 'liberty of contradiction' and 'liberty of contrariety'). The dogma of the best of all possible worlds threatens both aspects of divine freedom by postulating reasons for the creation of the world (such as the world's supreme perfection or God's own attributes). This is evidently Reinhard's major concern about optimism. For him, only if the existence of the world is regarded as an "arbitrary product of God's absolute freedom will", as an act of will that does not respond to *any* reason apart from itself, can God's freedom of will concerning the creation of the world be preserved. According to this view, God did not create the world, because he needed to create it in order to satisfy his perfection or his goodness, nor because he identified this world as the best among all possible options. He created the world simply because he *wanted* to. As Reinhard writes, echoing voluntarist conceptions as the ones we have encountered and examined in the preceding chapters, "the world is perfect because it is what it has to be according to God's intention" (37).

Despite the lack of systematicity of the *Examen*, it is clear that Reinhard considers at least three particular aspects of Leibniz's teachings to be responsible for the denial of divine freedom: first, the doctrine that God's choices depend on the perception of the good provided by the intellect. Secondly, Leibniz's commitment to the Principle of Sufficient or – in the terminology of Crusius – 'Determinant Reason'. And thirdly, the related concept of 'hypothetical necessity', mentioned several times in the past chapters.

Concerning the first, Reinhard explains that Leibnizian freedom "is based upon the representation of the intellect" (38). With this Reinhard means that for Leibniz, as we have seen various times throughout this work, the divine will is determined to action by the representation of the good provided by his understanding. Throughout this work, I have been calling this Leibnizian approach an *intellectualist* theory of divine agency. According to this view, God's will is determined, guided or motivated by the practical intellect. For Reinhard, as for all the critics we have examined previously, intellectualism is at odds with divine freedom. His alternative is a doctrine of the absolute independence of the divine will. According to it, divine acts of will are not only independent of what critics like Reinhard consider to be 'external' motivations (such as the existence of a best among all possible worlds; the necessity of doing good to creatures, etc.), but also, and most importantly, of any 'internal' causes (such as the representation of the good by the divine intellect, etc.). Reinhard, therefore, also seems to advocate a rather radical form of voluntarism.

Concerning the second issue, Reinhard explains that the motive by which the Leibnizian philosophy is compelled to maintain that any act of the will presupposes some reason for it is the basic stipulation of the Principle of Sufficient or Determinant Reason, according to which nothing exists or occurs without a reason.[24] Reinhard argues that Leibniz's followers apply that Principle "in spite of the counter-evidence given against the way in which Leibnizians understand it" (38). He does not consider it necessary to examine or even make clear what he means by "counter-evidence". His argument consists in writing mysteriously: "I do not need to repeat what has been said by others about this principle" (38). Reinhard is obviously thinking about the critique of Leibniz's and Wolff's handling of the Principle of Sufficient/Determinant Reason of his mentor Christian August Crusius. As we saw in the last chapter, Crusius basically proposes to restrict the validity of the Principle: a 'hard theory' of causation – based on the Principle of Determinant Reason – should apply exclusively to the natural world and to mathematical truths, whereas the Principle of Sufficient Reason, which grounds a sort of 'soft theory' that gives place to several alternatives of action when a particular antecedent is given, should only be valid in relation to the actions of God and of rational creatures. It is, nevertheless, irritating that Reinhard does not refer explicitly to Crusius at this or any point in the *Examen*.

Regarding the third point, Leibniz's theory of hypothetical necessity, as we know, is fashioned according to his commitment to the Principle of Sufficient Reason, in order to explain how it is possible that the actions of rational beings can, nevertheless, be regarded as free. For Reinhard, even though the concept of hypothetical necessity seems to be in complete accordance with the principles of "most modern philosophers", it contradicts our "most natural ideas" about the nature of freedom. As one would expect, Reinhard does not bother to examine Leibniz's theory of hypothetical necessity, which, as we saw in the previous chapters, is rather complex. Reinhard's single argument reads as follows: any kind of necessity – "no matter if absolute or hypothetical necessity" – simply contradicts the idea of freedom. The mere talk of a *reason* for action implies a drastic determinism to him, "a series of causes that goes all the way back to the first instant of the existence of the world" and denies freedom. Likewise, even to claim that God's actions are determined by his own perfection and by his own essence ("the most necessary among all beings"), as Leibnizians do, also involves a denial of divine freedom, for God's will is

---

24 *Cf.* T, §§44, 175/GP VI 127, 218–9; M, §32/GP VI 612), and Chapters 1 and 4.

subjected to something besides itself. Reinhard writes: "If God's perfections contain the determinant reason of divine volitions, then there is no freedom; each one of his actions is just as necessary as the mathematical truths" [*Si les perfections de Dieu contiennent la raison déterminante des volitions divines, il n'y a plus de liberté; toutes ses actions sont aussi nécessaires que les vérités mathématiques* [...]] (38).

Against Leibniz's theory of divine agency Reinhard propounds the doctrine of the liberty of indifference – and hypothetical necessity is never mentioned again:

> One might say to me that my observation is based on the ideas of freedom denied by most of modern philosophers. One might say that this kind of freedom, this liberty of indifference, are no more than pipe dreams that have fooled the world for a long time, and of which philosophy has fortunately been purged by Leibniz. Now, Dear Sirs, you will allow me to reply that I do nothing but develop the most natural ideas that are the foundation of all that what human beings have always considered just and good regarding ethics.
>
> [*On m'objectera peut-être, que je me fonde ici sur des idées de la liberté que la plupart des philosophes modernes rejettent. On me dira que cette liberté, cette indifférence de l'équilibre, sont des chimères, qui ont longtemps abusé le monde & dont Mr. de Leibniz est venu heureusement à bout de purger la philosophie. Que ces messieurs me permettent de leur dire à mon tour, que je ne fais ici que développer les idées les plus naturelles, qui sont la base de tout ce que le genre humain a jamais connu de juste & de bon en fait de morale.*]
> Examen, 37–8

By "liberty of indifference" Reinhard understands the kind of freedom that guarantees that God's choices are completely independent and undetermined, there being no reason why he should choose to act in the way he does in preference to any other. When deciding how to act, God always encounters a complete balance between different options, there being not one single option or reason that could determine him to act in one particular way.[25] God acts how

---

25 As I mentioned in the previous chapter, Leibniz calls this liberty of indifference also 'equipoise' and rejects it completely, since in his opinion, if God or any rational being would be equally inclined towards different courses of actions, he could not act at all. See for example: T, §§35, 46ff., 303/GP VI 122–3, 128ff., 296–7.

he acts moved only by the decrees of his will, and strictly speaking there are no reasons, for which God acts apart from God's unmotivated desires (whatever that might mean).

3 Final Comments and Open Questions

3.1 *The Paradoxes of Unlimited Freedom*

Reinhard's main motivation against Leibniz's optimism is his conviction that the system of the best denies divine freedom. In this respect, Reinhard shares the same concern as the other critics I have examined in the last chapters. His answer to Leibniz's theory of divine agency also reminds us of Budde and Knoerr's and Crusius' attitude: the rejection of the Leibnizian posture we have defined in several passages as intellectualism and the proposal of a theory according to which God's will is completely unrestricted, neither determined by any 'external', nor by any 'internal' influence, such as the intellectual representation of the good. Despite its possible specific differences, I explained that both Budde and Knoerr's, as well as Crusius' conceptions of God can be described as sorts of voluntarism, i.e. the idea that in God does not act guided or determined by (intellectual) reasons, and in his acting his will has some kind of primacy, independency over (or, like in the case of Budde and Knoerr, is identical with) his understanding. Reinhard, as I showed previously, also seems to advocate a strong form of voluntarism.

Reinhard seems to be aware of the difficulties that can ensue from a voluntarist theory and from the concept of liberty of indifference. The main problems are, first: *how* does God act if not by reasons – how does he decide if not by weighing options? And second: is God capable of doing evil?

In the *Examen*, the first question is left unanswered. As to the second question Reinhard maintains simply that unlimited divine freedom "excludes all imperfection". This unrestricted perfection implies that God cannot do evil; therefore "God cannot act against his own perfection nor against the essential perfection of things once this perfection is established" (*Examen*, 39). But then, it can be further asked, can God, in virtue of his completely unrestricted freedom, prefer something less perfect to something more perfect? To which Reinhard answers genially: it depends. The degree of perfection that a thing has depends on the ends or purposes that God has freely established for that thing. Once these purposes are established, God ascribes to each of his creatures the degree of perfection necessary to the fulfillment of those ends. In this sense, it is true that God creates different things with different degrees of perfection, but simply because he creates them in accordance with the ends he himself has established for them – *God cannot choose to act against his own purposes*.

As I see it, Reinhard's replies to the questions concerning God's absolute freedom and the possibility of him doing evil or at least choosing less than the best, show clearly the problems and difficulties a voluntarist theory of the complete indeterminacy of divine will has to deal sooner or later with (at least from the perspective of an intellectualist account). If God is free to choose *anything* at all with absolute independence of any specific parameters (like for example the uncreated eternal truths examined in Chapter 2) and every representation provided to it by divine intellect, then, at least hypothetically, he is also able to do evil or at least choose lesser goods. In order to rule out this possibility, voluntarists have to take what it would seem to be a step backwards and accept that *there is* some kind of restriction for the divine will, God's 'perfection', his 'own nature', etc. – something that, in turn, restricts the absolute indeterminacy of will. This is exactly what Reinhard does. He writes:

> From this it can be observed that God's freedom does not extend to all things. He is not free to act against his own perfection or against the fundamental perfection of things. His freedom extends only to what is indifferent; freedom can be exercised only in such cases, in which different possible ways of acting are present. Thus, freedom extends only to the arbitrary fixing of the ends; to the choice between the different, equally appropriate ways of attaining those ends; the choice between possible systems that are suitable to divine wisdom; the arbitrary determination of contingent perfections and indifferent circumstances; the arbitrary distribution of the degree of perfection that each individual must have, etc. The object of divine freedom is nothing but general good; its exercising consists of the determination of that which can occur in more than only one way. This is the genuine notion of freedom […]

> [*Cela fait voir que la liberté de Dieu ne s'étend pas sur toutes choses. Il n'a point de liberté pour agir contre sa propre perfection, essentielle des choses. La liberté ne s'étend que sur ce qui est indifférent; elle ne peut être exercée que là où il y a plusieurs manières d'agir également possibles. Ainsi la liberté ne regarde que la condition arbitraire des fins, le choix entre plusieurs moyens également propres à ces fins, le choix entre plusieurs systèmes possibles & dignes de la sagesse divine, la détermination arbitraire des perfections accidentelles, des circonstances indifférentes, la répartition arbitraire du*

dégrée de perfection que doit avoir chaque individu, etc. L'objet de la liberté divine n'est que le bien en général; son exercice ne consiste que dans la détermination de ce qui peut être de plusieurs manières. Voici la notion génuine de la liberté [...]]]
    Examen, 39–40

"God's freedom does not extend to all things", Reinhard claims. God "is not free to act against his own perfection or against the fundamental perfection of things". Is this not simply the acceptance, on the one hand, of the *restrictedness* of God's freedom, and on the other, of *parameters*, and in fact external parameters ("the fundamental perfection of things"!) that limit or 'guide' the divine freedom of will? And further, Reinhard concludes: "The object of divine freedom is nothing but general good; its exercising consists of the determination of what can occur in more than only one way. This is the genuine notion of freedom". – This does not seem to be *that* different to Leibniz's own definition of freedom when he writes, for example:

> The decrees of God are always free, even though God be always prompted thereto by reasons which lie in the intention towards good: for to be morally compelled by wisdom, to be bound by the consideration of good, is to be free.
>   T, §236/GP VI 258–9[26]

At the end of the day, the problems entailed by Reinhard's voluntarism condemn him either to fall into paradoxes or accept restrictions that would seem to draw his views near to a position not completely different from intellectualism. Reinhard's voluntarist 'solution' has a difficulty that other forms of theological voluntarism seem to share, namely the difficulty, on the one hand, of providing criteria for divine action (given that God cannot want *anything*, for then the scenario of God choosing to do evil seems possible), and on the other, of assuring that those criteria do not restrict God's supposedly unlimited and indifferent freedom of will. It is dubious that Reinhard's hazy explanations can really supply a viable alternative between necessitarianism and a radical and highly problematic voluntarism. I will return briefly to this problem in the next chapter.

---

26   *Cf.* LC, L.V.7/GP VII, 390.

3.2 The Relevance of Reinhard's *Examen* at the Beginning of the End of Optimism

Modern commentators of Reinhard's *Examen* have not been exactly tender when judging the quality and argumentative meticulousness of that work. Adolf Harnack observes that Reinhard criticized optimism "violently, but not in a particularly scientific manner, and tried to refute it through wholly insufficient means" (Harnack 1900: 405). And Fritz Mauthner, after backing up Harnack's opinion, notes in his belligerent *Wörterbuch der Philosophie* that the treatise was written in French – "or at least it was published in French; in a questionable French, that puts forward words like *praelection* ('lecture' [German: '*Vorlesung*']) and *finitude*". To which he then adds, commenting on the general affaire of the Academy's contest for 1755: "Small men deciding upon big principles" (Mauthner 1923: 478). To what extent the decision of the Academy of awarding Reinhard the prize could have been motivated by 'political' or 'factional' interests cannot be conclusively established. In any case, the reports of Harnack and Mauthner, as well as those from other commentators[27] – not to mention the *Examen* itself – leave room for doubt concerning the Academy's objectivity.

Truly, the *Examen* is no paradigm of careful philosophical analysis. First of all, the portrait of optimism provided by Reinhard consists primarily of commonplaces. Not even *once* does he quote directly from Leibniz's works (thus validating Emer de Vattel's reproach that Leibniz's critics did not consider it necessary to actually *read* his works), but seems merely to echo a kind of 'standard picture' common in the mid-eighteenth century and probably based directly on Crousaz's and Warburton's popular stereotypical anti-Leibnizian accounts of optimism as a fatalistic, deterministic doctrine. The principal commonplaces that constitute that popular picture are, as we saw before, the fashionable theme of the universal connection, or the "great chain" of the parts that compose the world as whole, and the subsequent motives of universal necessitarianism and moral fatalism. According to these, all the events that occur in the world are absolutely necessary (i.e. respond to general rational rules and principles of creation, as the Principle of Sufficient of Determinant Reason) and take place for the 'general good' (which in the end simply means: they take place on behalf of that universal rational order), including the emergence of physical and moral evils, as well as the actions of rational beings and of God' himself – who is naturally also subjected to the yoke of causality and the rule of the best order. All these motives can certainly be drawn from Leibniz's *Theodicy*; in this sense, Reinhard does not necessarily *lie* about some of the

---

27   *Cf.* Buschmann 1989b; Weinrich 1986: 78–9.

major tenets of "the system of the choice of the best". However, his depiction of those tenets remains incomplete and superficial, based mostly on the pseudo-philosophical clichés of his time.

Secondly, Reinhard's handling of the concepts and principles that he describes as Leibnizian – such as the dogma of the creation of the best, hypothetical necessity, the Principle of Determinant Reason, and moral intellectualism – is careless. He either just mentions those notions or even only hints at them, but never explains them. Accordingly, his criticisms are vague and, ultimately, rather unconvincing. Reinhard rejects the dogma of the best world by assembling his own theory of perfections and collisions, but does not explain what Leibniz actually means when he says this world is the best; he discards the complex doctrine of the hypothetical necessity of moral actions by pointing out that it contradicts our traditional ideas of freedom (i.e. by pointing out that well, it is complex) and by saying something that amounts to: 'it may be hypothetical, but it is still necessary'; he refutes the Principle of Determinant Reason on the grounds of an unpronounced 'what has been said by others'; and to intellectualism he opposes a sweeping moral voluntarism, which, as has become apparent, is itself problematic.

A third aggravating aspect of the *Examen* concerns its *originality*. As I pointed out and as is obvious from the preceding examination, Reinhard's admiration for the philosophical teachings of Christian August Crusius is a constant throughout his essay and evident both from the arguments used against optimism as well as from Reinhard's voluntarist solution to the problem of divine freedom and his obscure remarks concerning the Principle of Sufficient Reason. There is certainly nothing new under the sun (and this definitely applies to eighteen-century accounts and criticisms of Leibnizian metaphysics). Nonetheless, Reinhard could have at least mentioned Crusius in the *Examen*, given that virtually *all* the 'hard' arguments contained in it are, in fact, reruns of Crusius' own attacks against optimism.

At this point, one could ask whether Adolf Friedrich Reinhard's *Examen de l'optimisme* has *any* importance at all for an examination of early philosophical counter-optimism. I believe it does. Despite its many flaws, the *Examen* is theoretically relevant, or, more exactly, theoretically informative, in at least three ways. First, it reports on a kind of understanding of philosophical optimism – and, in broader sense, of Leibnizianism – that was popular in the eighteenth century (at least among the French and German intellectual circles connected to the Prussian Academy). It shows what theses were ascribed to optimism, as well as the dangers associated with them, such as the denial of the divine attribute of unlimited freedom, the introduction of a universal fatalism, etc. Secondly, the *Examen* illustrates the way in which critics argued against optimism, namely by trying to disprove the principle of the universal connection, or more importantly, by criticizing directly the dogma of the best of all possible worlds, the idea of a God coerced into action by something different from his own will, etc. And third, the *Examen* also shows the problems a counter-optimistic philosophy intending to explain the presence of evil in the world rationally (or even 'rationalistically') and in an orthodox manner, had to face, if it decided to advocate a radical moral voluntarism.

Further – and this is perhaps the most interesting aspect of Reinhard's work – the *Examen* is highly relevant for our understanding of the early history of the *popular* reception of philosophical optimism. As was the case with the reaction to the Academy's call for papers, the aftermath of the contest shows that optimism was neither a forgotten nor an obvious issue among French and German academic and intellectual circles in the middle of the eighteenth century. The work definitely did not go unnoticed after its publishing in 1755. Very much on the contrary, the *Examen* was translated *twice* into German in 1757[28] and provoked a number of critical reactions, some of them by representative figures of the Prussian intellectual establishment, like the above mentioned Jean Henri Samuel Formey[29] and the French mathematician and philosopher Pierre Le Guay Prémontval.[30] Both criticisms where published together with Reinhard's replies in a *Collection of Polemic Papers Concerning the Doctrine of the Best World* by the Hamburger theologian and historian Christian Ziegra.[31] And that is not all. In 1759 Moses Mendelssohn, who had already condemned

---

28 *Abhandlung von der Besten Welt. Welche den von der Königlichen-Preußischen Akademie der Wissenschaften zu Berlin für das 1755 Jahr ausgesetzten Preis erhalten* (trans. Johann Adolf Friedrich von Gentzkow), Greifswald, 1757; and *Vergleichung des Lehrgebäudes des Herrn Pope von der Vollkommenheit der Welt, mit dem System des Herrn von Leibnitz: Nebst einer Untersuchung der Lehre von der besten Welt. Eine Abhandlung, welche den, von der königl. Akademie der Wissenschaften und schönen Künste zu Berlin, aufgesetzten Preis vom Jahre 1755 davon getragen hat* (trans. Christian August Wichmann), Leipzig: Langenheim, 1757. This second translation contains an introduction and notes, in which translator replies to some of Formey's criticisms against the *Examen*.

29 Critical review of the *Examen de l'optimisme*, in *Nouvelle Bibliothèque Germanique* 18, I, Amsterdam: Schreuder & Mortier: 23–32.

30 Prémontval exposed his general criticism of Leibnizianism and Wolffianism in his *Vues philosophiques ou Protestations et déclarations sur les principaux objets des connaissances humaines*, Amsterdam: J.H. Schnieder, 1757. The second volume of this work opens with a letter addressed to Adolf Friedrich Reinhard, in which Prémontval criticizes the former's analysis of the notion of perfection in the *Examen*.

31 *Sammlung der Streitschriften über die Lehre von der besten Welt und verschiedene damit verknüpfte wichtige Wahrheiten, welche zwischen dem Verfasser der im Jahr 1755 von der Akademie zu Berlin gekrönten Schrift vom Optimismo und einigen berühmten Gelehrten gewechselt worden*, Rostock und Weimar: J.A. Berger & J. Boedner, 1759.

the contest of the Academy in 1755 together with Lessing, wrote another critical review of the *Examen*.[32] And in the same year, Immanuel Kant published a brief essay defending metaphysical optimism, specifically the dogma of the best of all possible worlds. Even though Kant's essay is not a direct answer to Reinhard's treatise, it attacks exactly those of Crusius' arguments against optimism on which the *Examen* is based.[33] Finally, Voltaire's famous reaction to the Lisbon Earthquake of 1755, the *Poème sur le désastre de Lisbonne* (1756), can in fact also be seen as a response to the question proposed by the Prussian Academy. As has been observed,[34] the occurrence of the Lisbon Earthquake is inseparable from Voltaire's counter-optimistic, pessimistic considerations. Yet, in the first place, these consist in the examination of optimism demanded by the Academy, as the subtitle of the *Poème* explicitly states: *Examen de cet axiome: "Tout est bien"*.

Therefore, Reinhard's *Examen* may not be particularly innovative regarding its theoretical value. From an 'institutional' point of view, however, it is perhaps one of the most important reactions to optimism before the Lisbon Earthquake, as it shows that the system of the best was in fact not only a matter of both academic and popular-intellectual interest, but also, and more interestingly, a matter of heated philosophical and theological debates even before Voltaire decided that the world might be less coherent than Leibniz claimed.

32   "Über Reinhard's *Examen de l'optimisme*" (*Briefe, die neueste Literatur betreffend*, letter 10, March 8, 1759), in: *Gesammelte Schriften* (ed. Georg Benjamin Mendelssohn), Leipzig: Brockhaus, 1844, vol. 4/1: 508–10.

33   "Versuch, einiger Betrachtungen über den Optimismus", in: *Kants gesammelte Schriften* (ed. Prussian Academy of Sciences), Berlin: Georg Reimer, 1912, vol. 2: 29–35. Kant wrote the essay as response to a dissertation on "*de mundo optimo*" written in 1759 by a certain Daniel Weymann, a fervent admirer of Crusius. The main purpose of Kant's essay was to "prove that there is indeed a possible world beyond which no better world can be thought" (Kuehn 2001: 122). Concerning the prehistory of Kant's essay see also Menzer 1912; Theis 2001. As Hübener writes: "Voltaire's *Candide* and Kants *Betrachtungen* – both written in 1759 – seem to constitute an endpoint" (Hübener 1978: 228).

34   Weinrich 1986: 76. See also Barber 1955: 210ff.

CHAPTER 6

Early Counter-optimism: Main Arguments and the Nature of the Conflict

1   Counter-optimism: An Inventory of Arguments

The critics examined in the preceding chapters address a number of aspects of optimism that they consider problematic or noxious. Some particular points are criticized more or less superficially, for example the Leibnizian notion of 'metaphysical evil' (for Budde and Knoerr – Chapter 2 – this notion implies that creatures are essentially evil, or better, that they are condemned to do and suffer evil by reason of being creatures and not God) or the dogma of 'universal connection' (which according to Adolf Friedrich Reinhard – Chapter 5 – leads to necessitarianism). There is, however, a set of central issues which these critics reject categorically and to which they return time and again in their criticisms. The most significant among these are the Leibnizian concept of 'the best of all possible worlds', the problem of the theoretical foundations of optimism, Leibniz's theory of uncreated eternal truths together with his understanding of the nature and scope of the Principle of Sufficient Reason, and the doctrine of hypothetical necessity, which is organically bound to the problem of divine freedom. These issues constitute a kind of *corpus* of 'counter-optimism' (which is how I have been calling early critical reaction to philosophical optimism). In this section, I will take a recapitulatory look at the critics' opinions regarding these issues. This will permit us to gain clarity about the common concerns, arguments and views of the examined critics, thus allowing us to approach the question what exactly the philosophical character of 'counter-optimism' might be.

1.1   *The Best of All Possible Worlds*

As I explained in Chapter 1, the notion of the best of all possible worlds and particularly the doctrine that *our* world is the best of all possible worlds is one of the main theoretical columns of philosophical optimism. Each one of the four critics examined previously rejects this doctrine in some way or another. Yet, their critiques are not identical, but come from at least two different fronts. Johann Franz Budde and Georg Christian Knoerr's, as well as Louis-Bertrand Castel's criticisms rest upon the belief that the notion of a best world contradicts not only empirical reality but, even more critically, the Christian dogma.

On the other hand, Christian August Crusius and Adolf Friedrich Reinhard reject the idea of the best of all possible worlds on the basis of its supposed conceptual invalidity.

Budde and Knoerr (Chapter 2) direct two main arguments against the doctrine of the best world. One of them maintains that the amount of evil in the world – or rather, the mere *presence* of evil in the world, contradicts the idea that the world could be the best possible. First, there *is* evil in creation, and second, the amount of evil in the world is greater than the amount of goodness. For these reasons, after the arrival of evil and suffering in the world through sin, this world, or at least the actual, *post-lapsum*-condition of the world, cannot be described as the best one among all possibles. Budde and Knoerr could, thus, be called 'empirical pessimists', since for them the idea of the best world is not necessarily logically inconsistent (in fact, Budde and Knoerr apparently accept that our world *was* the best of all possible world before sin), but simply unacceptable given the presence of evil. As I commented previously, for Leibniz it is relatively easy to refute such a 'pessimist' or 'empirical-pessimist' argument by maintaining that there is more good than evil in the world – a fact that we could verify easily if we could only assume a 'transcendent' perspective towards the universe, i.e. *God's* perspective.[1] If we could assume this viewpoint, it would be clear to us that the amount of goodness is superior to the amount of evil in the world, and that present evils are necessary for the rational harmony of the world. Further, as we already know well, goodness should not be understood in hedonistic but in rationalist terms, that is not as the physical pleasure of rational beings or the lacking of pain, etc., but as the particular pleasure produced by the contemplation of the harmony of the world.[2] If one accepts this kind of rationalist approach, empirical evils seem to be no crucial challenge for Leibnizian optimism.

But this is not Budde and Knoerr's strongest argument. Their most solid argument – solid at least at the beginning of the eighteenth century – is to maintain that the doctrine of the best world contradicts the Christian dogma of the Fall of Man. According to this doctrine, Adam's and Eve's first sin introduced evil into the world and changed its character in a fundamental way. Christ's advent is the result of the Fall, his death on the cross the divine sacrifice for our sins. Optimism, according to Budde and Knoerr, contradicts the

---

1   In this sense, as we saw in Chapter 1, Catherine Wilson writes: "Leibnizian optimism in necessarily directed toward an aspect of the world which is not directly available to perception and the sum of subjective pleasure is not in the end a good measure of its excellence" (Wilson 1983: 767). On the 'transcendent perspective' assumed by optimism see also Hübener 1978: 245.
2   *Cf.* Chapter 1, 1, 1.1; Chapter 3, 3, 3.2.

dogma of the Fall and makes Jesus' coming, as well as the necessity of salvation, pointless. Thus, Budde and Knoerr put forward against the Leibnizian concept of the best world neither a theoretical, nor an 'empirical' argument, but first and foremost a 'theological-dogmatic' one.

Louis-Bertrand Castel, the author of the critical review of the *Theodicy* published in the Jesuits' *Journal de Trévoux* in 1737 (Chapter 3), offers a similar empiric-dogmatic approach against Leibniz's theory of the best world. According to Castel, the doctrine of the best world overlooks the overwhelming presence of sin in the world. He writes:

> [H]ow could a man of spirit [...] have thought that a world in which there is evil and sin could be the best world that God could create? Sin alone is a great evil that all the perfection of a world infinitely superior to this one could not balance, and which has required nothing less than the coming and death of the Son himself in order to make this world, by a sort of [new] creation of a supernatural order, worthy of its creator [...]"
>
> CASTEL, 214

Exactly like Budde and Knoerr, Castel also criticizes the theory of the best based on two 'facts': on the one hand the empirical presence of evil, on the other the dogma of the redemption through Christ.

Regarding the second critical approach to the doctrine of the best world – the concept itself of a best or most perfect of all possible worlds is inconsistent – Crusius (Chapter 4) claims that a best world is either 'impossible' or 'unprovable'. In contrast to Budde and Knoerr's, as well as Castel's approach, Crusius does not consider the idea of a best world unviable due to the presence of evil in the world and the theological difficulties that the doctrine might give rise to. His problem is of a conceptual nature. The notion of 'the best possible world', according to Crusius, can mean two different things: either that the world contains all possible perfection or that this is the only world that permits God the attainment of some particular purpose. Now, on the one hand, Crusius argues, no world – or in general, no *created* thing – can contain all possible perfections, as all creatures are limited. Further, God, who limits the attributes of the world he decides to create, could have decided (in virtue of his wholly unlimited freedom) to give the world other attributes, thereby creating a completely different universe. On the other hand, if one assumes – as Crusius does – that God's freedom and power are absolutely unrestricted, it is absurd to say that a creature in some way *permits* God to achieve some purpose. Even if we assume that God has to accomplish some purpose, he could have done this by creating a different world (or by not creating any world at all).

Appealing to Rescher's and Rutherford's interpretations of the meaning of the concept of the best world, I tried to show in Chapter 4 that despite Crusius's theoretical attack, it is possible to understand the notion of the best world in ways that make Crusius's criticisms relatively harmless (since perfection, especially in the case of Rutherford's interpretation, is to be understood not as a static, quantitative notion but, so to speak, as a dynamic conception). Nevertheless, as I also commented in that chapter, for Crusius himself such a refutation might be irrelevant. Crusius's real problem does not seem to be Leibniz's concept of the best world, but, at the end of the day, his idea that this concept could be menacing for the belief in an absolutely free God, that means, for Crusius and others, a God whose decisions are wholly indifferent and arbitrary. This belief seems to be the major incentive behind his claim that the notion of the most perfect world is conceptually problematic. This fundamental problem has been mentioned several times during this work. And we shall return to it in the next pages.

Adolf Friedrich Reinhard's criticism of the notion of the best world goes in the same direction as Crusius's. As we saw in Chapter 5, for Reinhard the most perfect world is the one containing the most reality, or the one whose creation permits God to accomplish a particular end or a set of ends. Like Crusius, Reinhard argues, first, that there can be no creature which contains the biggest amount of reality, and second, that God, as an absolutely free being – an indifferent, arbitrary being – can always create a world more perfect or simply different – and equally perfect – to the world he created. Further, Reinhard's indifferent God is in no need of creating a particular world in order to achieve a particular purpose. Again, it seems evident that Reinhard's main argument *and* motivation against the concept of the best world is the appeal to God's supposed absolute freedom of choice.

1.2   *The Foundations of Optimism*

At least two of the examined critics argue that optimism is theoretically not well-founded: the Jesuit Castel and Crusius. For different reasons, both of them cast doubts on the consistency or solidity of the system of the best.

Louis-Bertrand Castel repeatedly addresses the idea that optimism rests on a kind of twofold intellectual illness on the part of Leibniz (as well as other eighteenth-century figures like Alexander Pope and [pre-Lisbon] Voltaire): on the one hand, exaggerated rationalism – according to which everything must occur for a reason – on the other, an equally exaggerated positive view of the world. As I commented in Chapter 3, although it could in fact be possible, at first glance, to consider optimism as essentially dogmatic in nature, a more careful approach shows not only that optimism rests on very specific and markedly rationalist assumptions, but also that it follows rather naturally from them. Optimism does not only seem to be consistent, but also a fundamental element within Leibnizian metaphysics. Leibniz's rationalism is, therefore, not just some sort of intellectual fever, but the outcome of the conviction, for example, of the universal validity of the Principle of Sufficient Reason. On the other hand, as I commented earlier, Leibniz's optimism does not ignore the presence of evil in the world, but seems to advocate a particularly rationalist, non-hedonistic understanding of what goodness and happiness mean.

For his part, Crusius maintains that the conclusion that this world is the best possible presupposes the belief in the existence of *one* best world among all possible worlds. Since he thinks that the concept of a best or most perfect world is impossible, optimism must also be flawed. To this one can reply, as I proposed in Chapters 1 and 4 with reference to Nicholas Rescher's and Donald Rutherford's interpretations of the concept of perfection, that the concept of the best world can be made viable. Again it can be shown that optimism is consistent (at least with its own presuppositions).

As was claimed a number of times in the last chapters, the problem of the theoretical consistency of optimism seems to boil down to the following: there is a set of theoretical, metaphysical and theological assumptions behind optimism that make it consistent. To present optimism as an ill-founded doctrine is misguided (or simply does not do it justice), since, if one accepts Leibniz's assumptions, optimism appears to have a rather consequent and solid theoretical skeleton. *If one accepts Leibniz's assumptions* ... And that is, of course, precisely what Leibniz's critics do not do. In particular, as we well know, the examined critics of Leibniz advocate a concept of God, and particularly, an understanding of what it means to say that God is omnipotent and *free*, that differ radically from Leibniz's. In the case of Castel and Crusius, the claim of the theoretical inconsistency of optimism seems to have much to do with their rejection of Leibniz's God and his notion of divine freedom. Castel maintains that Leibniz's rationalist stance is hyperbolic. Clearly, the concern behind this claim is the idea that Leibniz's idea of God as an essentially rational being seems to deny divine freedom. For this reason, Castel considers Leibniz's rationalism exaggerated. Something similar occurs with Crusius' rejection of a best world. For him, the belief in the existence of *one* best world among all possible worlds implies that God is limited in his actions, because he cannot just do *anything* he wants, without any (rational) reason at all.

1.3 *Leibniz's Theory of Uncreated Eternal Truths*

Budde and Knoerr's opinion concerning Leibniz's theory of uncreated eternal truths was examined in Chapter 2. For Budde and Knoerr, if the eternal truths are uncreated and independent of God's decrees, then God is not free, because, first, there is something in the world that is not subjected to divine rule, and second and more important, because God himself is subjected to that 'something'. For Budde and Knoerr, the existence of eternal principles that were *not* established by God but rather determine *his* behavior by setting parameters to his willing, means that God is determined by something *external* to himself and, thus, not completely free.

As I commented in that chapter, the rationalist-Leibnizian account of the nature of the eternal truths is certainly not unproblematic. It is possible to ask questions like, for example: If the eternal truths do not depend on God, what makes them true? Are the Leibnizian eternal truths some kind of Platonic Forms that God contemplates and which limit his actions? Leibniz, as I explained, would answer by demanding conceptual clarity. Eternal truths are not something external, Platonic Forms or something similar that forces God to act in one specific way. They are – on the contrary – the 'object of God's understanding', which means: when God follows them he is simply following *his own understanding*, i.e. *himself*.

Now of course, Budde and Knoerr's account of the nature of the eternal truths is not simply absurd, having a rather notable historical precedent, namely the Cartesian account of eternal truths as dependent on God's decrees. The Cartesian account is a parallel model to Leibniz's rationalist account of God and creation. Here, once again, the existence of two conflicting models of the functioning of the divine nature turns out to be a central motive behind the conflict between optimism and its early critics.

1.4 *The Principle of Sufficient Reason*

All critics examined previously seem to disapprove in one way or another of Leibniz's idea that everything that is or occurs has a reason. Their major concern is particularly the belief that even *God's* actions respond to reasons, i.e. that they are subjected to the Principle of Sufficient Reason. Thus, for example, the Jesuit critic Castel maintained that it is because of their ignorance of the workings of the divinity that philosophers like Leibniz maintain that "nothing can exist on the part of God himself and on the part of his will [...] without a sufficient reason" (Castel, 215), and Adolf Friedrich Reinhard, the winner of the polemical prize-contest of the Prussian Academy of Sciences, claims – albeit without arguments – that Leibniz's followers apply the Principle "in spite of the counter-evidence given against the way in which Leibnizians understand it" (*Examen*, 38).

The only really articulated criticism of the Leibnizian Principle of Sufficient Reason is offered by Christian August Crusius. As we saw in Chapter 4, Crusius, recognizing the Principle as a menace to the idea of freedom of choice, proposes a new definition for a *limitation* of the Principle's scope. He insists first of all that the Principle be called of *Determinant* Reason, "since to determine means to admit of only one possibility why a thing, given these circumstances, should be as it is" (*De usu*, §3/9), which is precisely what Leibniz's Principle states. Further, against Leibniz, Crusius claims that the Principle of Determinant Reason applies only to natural, empirical occurrences and to the sphere of logics, not to moral actions of rational beings. These actions only respond to *sufficient* causes ("a cause in which nothing is missing, which should be necessary for the production of an effect" [*De usu*, §44/120–1]), which do admit, in contrast to the determinant causes of physics and mathematics, alternative courses of action. In short, Crusius puts forward a theory according to which logical and natural events are subjected to a 'strong' or 'hard' (Leibnizian) version of the Principle of Sufficient/Determinant Reason, but moral events only to a 'soft' version of the Principle, which certainly explains why something occurs as it does, but does not determine that it occur otherwise.

If one accepts that Leibniz's belief in the universal validity of the Principle contradicts divine freedom, but still wants to guarantee a basic rationality for actions (i.e. their occurring for *some* reason), then Crusius's approach is at least *justifiable*. The problem is that Crusius's theory seems to be wholly arbitrary. For him, morality *cannot* be subjected to the Principle of Sufficient/Determinant Reason (understood in the Leibnizian sense), because that means automatically the disappearance of freedom of choice (understood in voluntarist fashion, as absolute indifference and indeterminacy). Therefore morality *is not* subjected to the Principle. Of course, Crusius cannot prove that this is the case. His only possible proof is to say: if the Principle is universally valid, then God is not free – thus opening the fallacious circle right from the start. Leibniz's approach, problematic as it might be, seems to be, in theoretical terms, more interesting than Crusius's theory: through answers like the theory of hypothetical necessity Leibniz wants to face up to the challenge of matching the Principle of Sufficient Reason and freedom of choice, without having to limit capriciously the Principle of Sufficient Reason.

1.5   *Hypothetical Necessity and Freedom*

The aversion of most of early critics (including critics like Samuel Clarke, who, given the tenor of this work, have not been examined here) towards Leibniz's theory of agency and the doctrine of hypothetical or moral necessity is well resumed by Louis-Bertrand Castel's rather simplistic rebuff of the Leibnizian doctrine of moral necessity (as opposed to metaphysical necessity). Castel writes:

> The necessity that our author draws from the divine wisdom is for him no more than a *moral* necessity. But isn't this necessity just as metaphysical as that of Spinoza? It is at least just as absolute as that one. Indeed, God is absolutely wise at all times, in every aspect, in all his actions. *It is a happy necessity* – Leibniz says – *which obliges the wise to do good*. The necessity which obliges God to do good and prevents him of doing evil is a very absolute and very natural necessity, and Leibniz calls it improperly *moral necessity*, only because it concerns the morality of actions. This is an abuse of the terms: God is only free to choose the best.
>
> CASTEL, 964–5

As it was noted in Chapter 3, for Castel necessity is simply necessity – no matter what appeasing adjective Leibniz could try to append to that treacherous word in order to 'save' freedom of choice. According to this problematic critical approach, the mere fact that willing is guided, directed, determined in some way; that God's decisions are bound to principles of reason (even if these are principles of *his own* rationality); that, because of this submission, God only can want to choose the best, etc. – all this amounts automatically to a denial of freedom. To talk about a kind of necessity that is not (an absolute) necessity makes, for radical critics like Castel, no sense at all.

Although all examined critics seem to reject Leibniz's attempts of guaranteeing freedom of choice by appealing to a theory of causation that does *not* exclude the possibility of alternative courses of action – i.e. a theory of *teleological causation* or of *final causes*, as it was described in Chapter 1 – all their critiques are, unfortunately, quite superficial (indeed they all seem to amount to repeating Castel's 'argument' that '*necessity is necessity*'). Perhaps Crusius's critique of hypothetical or moral necessity is – although not implicitly conclusive – at least a *clear* critique of the concept of hypothetical necessity.

As I commented in Chapter 4, for Crusius an act or an event is absolutely necessary if it follows directly from necessary conditions and if its opposite cannot be thought of. In turn, an act or an event is hypothetically necessary if it follows from a condition that is itself not necessary and if its opposite can be thought of (Crusius, *De usu*, §5/17–8). Now, for Crusius, such a distinction is nonsense ("merely verbal"). If, as Leibniz admits (or better: *establishes*), the Principle of Sufficient Reason (Principle of Determinant Reason) is universally valid, then everything occurs for a (necessary reason), i.e. there are no 'non-necessary reasons', everything is determined by so-called 'efficient' or 'moving' causes.

Now Crusius does not quite seem to do justice to the Leibnizian understanding of moral or hypothetical necessity as referring to a teleological causation, based not on efficient but on *final* causes. At least he does not mention anything about final causes or a kind of determination of actions based on purposes. And yet, although neither Crusius nor any of the other critics of optimism examined here seem to offer an adequate – that is, a fair – critique of hypothetical necessity, the origin of their claims is still understandable: if the Principle of Sufficient/ Determinant Reason has universal validity, then no matter how one tries to explain the fact that rational actions are only subjected to some kind of non-absolute, hypothetical, *lenient* necessity, the question of the real extent and efficacy of this explanation remains problematic. The main criminal in this story is obviously the Principle of Sufficient Reason and its consequences regarding the desired (by Leibniz's critics) indeterminacy of divine action. In this way, Crusius' decision to criticize the Principle is at least comprehensible.

1.6 *Counter-optimism and Voluntarism*

The claim that Leibniz's theory of rational agency denies freedom of choice and the subsequent rejection of that theory seem to be common denominators between the four examined critics.

In the case of Budde and Knoerr, the critique takes place in the form of a rejection of the Leibnizian doctrine of eternal ideas as uncreated principles reviewed some lines ago. For Budde and Knoerr, to maintain that eternal truths are independent of God's willing and moreover, that God himself is guided, regulated, by those truths or principles of reason, amounts to denying God's freedom, as they insist in regarding the Leibnizian eternal truths as 'external' entities that curtail the divine will.

According to Castel, by maintaining that God acts following principles of action like, for example, the "Rule of the Best", optimism transforms God into an "automaton", depriving him "of freedom of choice and of every other kind of freedom" (Castel, 209–10). The idea behind this reasoning is well known to us: if God has to obey any kind of parameters when acting, if he has to take account of them when deciding how to act, then he is not free, because he cannot do anything he wants, or better, because he cannot just will *anything* (since he can only want the best).

Crusius is more than explicit when judging the connection between philosophical optimism and freedom. According to him, the doctrine of the best world "eliminates divine and human freedom" (*Entwurf,* §388/750). As I have explained in several places of this work, given the theoretical and theological assumptions of optimism, God, having identified one world as the best possible, was compelled to create that particular world. Whereas for Leibniz the fact that God could only create one world, i.e. the best one, does justice to both

God's wisdom and his freedom (since, for Leibniz, freedom consists precisely in following the own wisdom of wanting the best[3]), for Crusius it amounts to denying divine freedom. For him, if divine freedom means anything at all, it must mean absolutely unrestricted and undetermined freedom of choice.

With Reinhard we seem to have a similar story. For him Leibniz's doctrine of God's determination to action by the representation of the good, and specifically the idea of the universal validity of the Principle of Sufficient Reason, threaten divine freedom by postulating reasons and bounds to God's willing. Reinhard considers radically that only if the existence of the world is regarded as an "arbitrary product of God's absolute freedom of the will", can divine freedom related to the creation of the world be preserved (*Examen*, 37). Although – as I remarked in Chapter 5 – Reinhard's criticism of Leibniz is often superficial, his motivation is clear: the primordial concern regarding the supposed disappearance of divine freedom under optimism.

As we have seen in the past chapters, not only the conviction that optimism is fatal for divine freedom is common to all the examined commentators. Also the theory of the complete indeterminacy and indifference of God's acts of will as an alternative to the Leibnizian theory of divine agency seems to be a fundamental shared view. I have called that alternative a *voluntarist* account of divine agency. As I have explained repeatedly following Steven Nadler's clarifications, voluntarism may be understood as the one major antagonist of a theory of divine agency that I have been calling an *intellectualist* theory, of which Leibniz's thought (as well as Malebranche's) is representative. There are certainly differences among the accounts of Leibniz's critics, especially between the degrees of philosophical clarity that those accounts offer. Yet it is quite manifest, on the one hand, that all four critics are moved by the same belief – optimism denies divine freedom – to criticize Leibniz and that this belief can be found rather easily at the root of most of their particular criticisms. On the other hand, it is clear that they all advocate, albeit with very different degrees of intelligibility, a similar view of the nature of God's way of operating – a view that can be described in each case as some kind of voluntarism.

Thus, Budde and Knoerr argue for a God who does not seem to be guided in his actions by principles independent of his will, whose decisions are not determined by the perception of an 'objective' good. "The nature of things is grounded in God's will" (*Doctrinae*, III, §5 [73]), they write. In their case – as in Descartes's – this means that God's actions of the will are wholly undetermined, and particularly that the eternal truths are not uncreated, immutable, necessary, etc., but depend wholly on God's willing and can, therefore, be

---

3 See for example in LC, L.V.7/GP VII, 390.

modified by him. In the special case of the creation of the world, God was not moved to create by the existence and identification of a best world among all possibles (i.e. he was not moved by principles of reason), but simply decided to create a world which, according to Budde and Knoerr, is not the best for itself, "but rather is the best [...] because God chose it" (*Doctrinae*, III, §5 [74]).

Although Castel is never explicit in his review of the *Theodicy* about his views concerning the nature of divine action, it seems reasonable to think that he advocates a theory according to which God's actions are arbitrary, not subjected to rational, objective parameters. Indeed, Castel criticizes the rationalist belief in the applicability of the Principle of Sufficient Reason to God's ways (Castel, 215–6), calls optimism "a spiritual Spinozism" that denies freedom (208–9), and mocks Leibniz's notion of 'choice', commenting that a necessary choice (in God's case, the choice of the best) is no free choice at all (448). As I noted in Chapter 3, whether this suffices to conclude that Castel explicitly propounds a form of voluntarism is unclear, but at least it seems quite probable he does.

According to Crusius, freedom cannot be defined – as Leibniz does – as the ability to choose the best; indeed, "what kind of choice is that where only one action is possible?" (*Entwurf*, §388/752–3). Crusius, just as the other examined critics seem to do, interprets Leibniz's theory of the determination of the divine will by reasons, i.e. by the intellectual representation of the good, as meaning that God is determined by something 'external' to him. Against Leibniz (or more precisely: against *this interpretation* of Leibniz), Crusius accepts that the will moves *on the basis* of representations, but claims that it always moves *itself* to action and, more importantly still, that it responds to no other reason than itself, being thus "neither externally nor internally compelled" (*Anweisung*, §38/44). In a passage of his major metaphysical work, the *Entwurf der nothwendigen Vernunftwahrheiten* quoted in Chapter 4, Crusius is quite clear about his voluntarist view of the will: "The will is in every soul the dominant power, by virtue of which all the rest of the faculties exist as means, and to which they are all [...] subordinated". Further, "the direction and the use of the powers of the understanding are subordinated to the will, as the experience confirms it. Certainly all volition presupposes thought. But the use of the understanding depends on the will in the following manner: when by some cause there already exist ideas on the basis of which the will can act, then the understanding can be moved to cogitate over those ideas and [...] make them more clear, complete and copious. [...] The longer this work is pursued [...], the greater will knowledge be extended. [...] In this way, the state of the understanding will be improved or deteriorated by the will" (*Entwurf*, §454/885–90).

As was the case with Budde and Knoerr, Reinhard also maintains that the world is "perfect because it is what it has to be according to God's intention" (*Examen*, 37), which in this context implies that God is not subjected to objective parameters of action, but created the world simply because he *wanted* to. As I showed in Chapter 5, Reinhard explicitly advocates what he called the doctrine of 'liberty of indifference', which corresponds to "what human beings have always considered just and good regarding ethics" (*Examen*, 37–8). By this Reinhard understands a theory according to which God is never determined by a particular reason, but is completely undetermined when willing: precisely the kind of indeterminacy or 'equipoise' of actions that Leibniz so roughly rejects, as according to him a rational being who did not have a compelling reason to act, who would be equally inclined towards different courses of actions, could not act at all.[4]

2   Classifying Counter-optimism: The Intellectualism-Voluntarism Schema

What kind of conflict is the conflict between optimism and its critics in the first half of the eighteenth century, before the famous Lisbon Earthquake of 1755? How should that conflict be classified, according to what philosophical categories? These are some of the questions that motivated the present work.

It seems to be difficult to adapt the conflict between philosophical optimism and its early critics (at least the ones examined in the past chapters) to schemata used traditionally to bestow a theoretically interesting structure on the history of early modern philosophy. This conflict, as I have tried to show in the previous pages, seems to be of quite a peculiar nature – a nature which I have approached by referring to the contrasting terms 'intellectualism' and 'voluntarism'.

The most customary and widespread classification of early-modern philosophical debates in which Leibniz played an important role is perhaps the schema *rationalism-empiricism*, referred to very briefly in Chapter 1. This schema tends to explain the history of modern philosophy primarily as the succession of epistemological conflicts. Put rather sketchily, according to this view the central motor of a considerable portion of post-Cartesian polemics is the concern for the nature and the possibility of knowledge, or more particularly, the question regarding the possibility of a solid foundation of our

---

4 See for example T, §§35, 46ff., 303/GP VI 122–3, 128ff., 296–7.

knowledge, as well as the question about the relationship between the content of our knowledge with the real configuration of the so-called 'external' world, etc.[5] Some of the favored concepts of the historians of philosophy that ascribe a central role to the rationalism-empiricism-model are 'reality', 'idea', 'mind', 'subject', 'object', 'perception', 'empirical knowledge', and the like. A similar esteem is shown towards labels like 'rationalist', 'empiricist', and in some cases 'skeptic' as a common antagonist of the first two (although this is not necessarily the case, since combinations between these labels are possible – one just has to think about the use that the 'rationalist' Descartes makes of the skeptic method of doubt or about the 'empiricist' Hume's purported skepticism towards the reality of the external world, personal identity, etc.). Apart from Leibniz, the most famous names behind this model are Descartes, Spinoza or Malebranche on the one side, and on the other Locke, Berkeley, and Hume, among many others.[6]

With regard to the specific idea that this is the best of all possible worlds a very different but equally traditional schema is also prominent: the *optimism-pessimism* schema. While the distinction between rationalism and empiricism involves generally a reference to the sources and the quality of our knowledge, the optimism-pessimism distinction refers predominantly to the moral character of the world in the face of undeniable evils. Some representative problems of this definition are: Is there more good than evil in the world? Is suffering a rule or an exception?, etc. Against the rationalist/optimist defense of the perfection of the world examined in the present work, thinkers traditionally labeled as 'pessimists' usually point to the empirical world, to its evils and deficiencies. The protagonists of the optimism-pessimism schema are not less notable than the protagonists of the conflict between rationalists and empiricists. The most famous among them are, representing optimism, Leibniz and others like Pope, Lessing and Mendelssohn, the early Kant, etc. Representing some kind of negative attitude towards the character of the empirical world or the quality of human life are thinkers like Bayle for the pre-Leibnizian period, Voltaire or the Hume of the *Dialogues Concerning Natural Religion* (1779) in the second half of the eighteenth century, and most famously: Arthur Schopenhauer in the nineteenth century.[7]

---

5 *Cf.* Markie 2017; Perler 2003; Chapter 1, 2, 2.2.
6 For some interesting definitions and critical assessments of the rationalism-empiricism-model, see Cottingham 1988: 1–4; Doney 1983; Engfer 1996; Perler 2003.
7 A particularly interesting work of intellectual history in which the schema optimism-pessimism is given a central role is the book *Evil in Modern Thought. An Alternative History of Philosophy* (Neiman 2002). There, Susan Neiman, intending explicitly to offer an alternative to the traditional rationalism-empiricism-model, reconstructs the history of modern

The conflict between Leibnizian optimism and its early critics involves aspects that seem to be explainable within both mentioned classifications. At the same time, the particular character of that conflict does not seem to fit completely into those traditional categories. For example, Christian August Crusius rejects the Leibnizian and Wolffian belief in the absolute validity of what seems to be a characteristic and fundamental principle of rationalism,[8] the Principle of Sufficient Reason. (This also seems to be the case with Louis-Bertrand Castel and Adolf Friedrich Reinhard, although their aversion towards the Principle is expressed with less clarity.) This critique, however, says nothing about his opinion about the source or the solidity of our knowledge, or anything that could enable us to characterize him as an empiricist. It neither justifies us in describing him as some kind of skeptic who doubts the validity of the Principle, or better, our capacity of gaining objective knowledge of that validity. Crusius does not doubt the objective validity or the possibility of our objective knowledge of the Principle of Sufficient Reason. Concerned fundamentally with God's freedom of choice he 'only' denies the *universality* of the Principle, rejecting the theory of the applicability of the Principle to the field of moral action. Similarly, Budde and Knoerr, in a manner that reminded us of Descartes, deny the theory of the independency and essential immutability of the eternal truths,[9] and claim that such principles depend on God's decrees. However, this denial does not seem to imply automatically a rejection of rationalism. (This is especially evident in Descartes's case.) What has been said about Crusius is also true regarding Budde and Knoerr's dissatisfaction with optimism: their problem is not an epistemological discussion on the nature or consistency of knowledge. Neither do they seem to be interested in the cosmological question whether the universe is essentially rational or not. Their main interest is God, their mission: to guarantee unequivocally divine freedom (understood in the radical terms explained in different places throughout the previous chapters).

Something similar seems to happen with regard to the schema optimism-pessimism. Although in the cases of Budde and Knoerr and Castel it is easy to find enough evidence that enables us to describe them as 'pessimist' critics – as we saw in the respective chapters, they maintain unambiguous that after the

---

thought from the perspective of the problem of evil in the world and the diverse answers that famous thinkers have given to it. Joshua Dienstag's *Pessimism: Philosophy, Ethics, Spirit* (Dienstag 2006) intends to make out the existence of a general worldview shared by thinkers usually considered as 'pessimists'. On the dialectics of optimism and pessimism see also Günther 1984; Mason 2006; Mauthner 1923; Vereker 1967; Vyberberg 1958.

8 See for example Carraud 2002; Lin & Melamed 2020.
9 See Chapter 2, 1, 1.1. *Cf.* Nadler 2008b: 191ff.; Perler 2006: 203ff.

Fall of Man there is more evil than good in this world – their pessimism does not seem to be their primordial argument against optimism. Their fundamental argument is their criticism of particular, characteristic tenets of Leibnizian thought. In the case of Budde and Knoerr, the critique of the Leibnizian theory of eternal ideas; in Castel's case his attack against what he considers an exaggerated rationalism on Leibniz's side. For the rest, neither Crusius nor Reinhard share this pessimistic view of the character of the world. Thus, for example, Crusius begins his critique of optimism by denying the validity of the concept of the best of all possible worlds. Yet he clearly states that the world is "very good" (*Entwurf*, §389/753). Again, the fundamental problem here is not whether the world is good, evil, the best or the worst. (Besides, the examined thinkers – representative of a more or less traditional theology and its acceptance of sin as an element of the world after the Fall – do not even seem to have any problem accepting that the world is not paradise and accepting the existence of evil in it). Their main bitterness towards Leibnizian optimism is the supposed annulment of divine freedom that it entails. In a few words, while 'pessimist' thinkers like Voltaire, Hume or Schopenhauer criticize the optimist doctrine of the best world by pointing to the (empirical) world, the life of human beings and their evils, the early 'counter-optimists' examined in the past chapters disapprove of optimism – but pointing towards God.

Thus, it seems clear that the examined authors, despite the differences of profoundness, approach, and form of their criticisms of optimism, share the disapproval of Leibniz's God as a fundamental motor of their critiques. They all reject the fact that Leibnizian metaphysics in general, and philosophical optimism in particular, promote theoretical claims that, in their opinion, lead to the limitation of divine freedom. Against Leibniz's theory of rational action – moreover, against his particular form of rationalist *theology* – these early critics either repudiate the basic rationalist 'attitude' of Leibnizian metaphysics (as is clear in Castel's case, whose critique implies the rejection of what I have identified as an intellectualist approach to moral agency), or they propose a 'positive' alternative to the intellectualist understanding of God's functioning (an alternative that was described in each case as a form of voluntarism, or the view that God is not subjected to rational 'external' principles and reasons in his willing).

It therefore seems adequate to explain – again quite sketchily – the peculiarity of the early philosophical reaction to Leibnizian optimism by emphasizing the fact that, while the main philosophical concern within the rationalism-empiricism schema is the nature of our knowledge and within the optimism-pessimism model the moral character of the empirical world, the early conflict between Leibniz's optimism and so-called 'counter-optimism' may be explained through the lens of the distinction between intellectualism and voluntarism; its main philosophical concern being not the nature of knowledge or the character the world, but the nature of divine agency and, particularly, the problem of divine freedom. For the specific task of classifying the group of critics that I have been calling 'counter-optimists', the traditional schemata do not seem to be comprehensive or thorough enough. The distinction intellectualism-voluntarism appears to be stronger when wanting to explain the nature of the conflict between philosophical optimism and its critics in the first half of the eighteenth century.

Now, nothing of this is new: Throughout this work I have been describing this distinction and applying it to particular clashes between philosophical optimism and its critics. At this point, however, that distinction seems to be not only relevant in order to understand *specific* aspects of early counter-optimism. More importantly, it now also seems to be helpful for understanding early counter-optimism *as such*. Until now, I have been referring to 'counter-optimism' as a rather hollow notion, the mere negation of the Leibnizian position. By tracing out the field in which the early critical reaction to optimism takes place; by identifying the conflict between intellectualism and voluntarism as an essential marker of that reaction – by doing all this, the concept of 'counter-optimism' receives, so to speak, a concrete *content*.

3 Some Comments on the Feasibility of Intellectualism and Voluntarism

In the previous chapters I pointed out some traditional problems – regarding particularly the question about the nature, the scope, and the possible or necessary limitations of God's freedom – of both the Leibnizian intellectualist position and the examined criticisms of optimism, which were shown to have clear voluntarist traits. If we were to summarize those problems, then we have, on the one hand, that Leibniz's main problem is (at least in the eyes of his critics) that his understanding of God and freedom as being essentially rational seems to deny what many people (or at least critics like the ones examined here) believe divine freedom to be: the ability to want and do anything at all. On the other hand, the 'counter-optimist' critics promote a voluntarist notion of divine freedom that would seem to rule out the possibility of considering that God and his actions are rational, or even *intelligible* in some manner. They promote a notion of freedom that seems to make God incomprehensible.

As we know well, according to Leibniz God is guided, determined, inclined in his actions by his wisdom (i.e. by the representations of his understanding):

"The will of God is not independent of the rules of wisdom" (T, §193/GP VI 231). As an essentially rational being God follows principles of reason (eternal truths that are, according to Leibniz, the object of the divine understanding). By virtue of these principles, God always does the best. Or in other terms: the final cause of his actions is always what he identifies as the best. For the case of the creation of the world, God was compelled to create this and no other world because he recognized it as the best among infinite worlds. Certainly, God had no other choice; certainly, God's actions *are* subjected to a kind of necessity (moral or hypothetical necessity): given his rationality, God had to create this and no other world. But for Leibniz this is no limitation of freedom. As we have read several times during the past chapters: "To be morally compelled by wisdom, to be bound by the consideration of good, is to be free" (T, §236/GP VI 258–9). Further, according to Leibniz, moral necessity does not exclude *per se* alternative possibilities;[10] it 'only' implies that when presented with different alternatives of choice, God will always choose the best. Leibniz's notion of the divine agency is intimately connected to his belief in the fundamental rationality and subsequent comprehensibility (at least in principle) of God and his creation. Since Leibniz believes that God is rational, that his acts are also subjected to the Principle of Sufficient Reason, he has to accept that divine actions are subject to a particular kind of necessity. As I remarked in Chapter 1, if God's decision of creating the world did not follow from rational principles and reason, "his decision would be wholly arbitrary and the existence of the world unintelligible" (Seeskin 1994: 324).

For many contemporary critics, Leibniz's notions of freedom, moral necessity, etc., are problematic. For the critics examined in the past Chapter, they are nonsense. They appear to believe that an agent is free only if the acts of his will are completely independent of the limitations or even the guidance imposed to them by the understanding, i.e. by its representations, by eternal truths or any other kind of principles of reason. As we have seen in the previous chapters, critics usually consider that those elements (even the understanding) are 'external' constraints to the will. Thus Budde and Knoerr write: "The nature of things is grounded on God's will" (*Doctrinae*, III, §5 [73]) and "God did not choose the world because the world is the best, but rather this is the best world because God chose it" (§5 [74]); and Castel claims: "By subjecting him [God] to the Rule of the Best, [Leibniz] deprives God of freedom of choice and of every kind of freedom" (Castel, 209–10). Further, critics consider that Leibniz's idea that God is free precisely because he follows the dictates of his own wisdom and, therefore, only wants and does the good, is unacceptable.

---

10   *Cf.* Chapter 1, 3, 3.2.

In this kind of freedom, they argue, there is not real choice at all. As Crusius maintains: "[W]hat kind of choice is that where only one action is possible? God is not free because he recognizes and knows the good, which he wants necessarily [...], but because in one particular situation he can act or not, in this or that manner" (*Entwurf*, §388/752–3); and Crusius's follower, Reinhard: "If God's perfections contain the determinant reason of divine volitions, then there is no freedom; each one of his actions is just as necessary as the mathematical truths" (*Examen*, 38).

Consequently, the critics maintain that *real* freedom means that God is arbitrary in his actions (that is, God is bound by no rational principles or reasons to action) and, therefore, his decisions are indifferent (that is, when presented with different alternatives of action in a particular situation, God can, strictly speaking, choose *any* course of action). For the case of the creation of the world, this means that God could have created *any* world he wanted, i.e. he could have given the world very different attributes (and he could also have wanted no world at all). As Reinhard writes: "God has established freely the amount of perfection of the created world" (*Examen*, 48).

According to the voluntarist view God did not create the world because of its inherent, objective goodness. For Leibniz, as we saw in Chapter 1, this is the best possible world because of objective reasons, for which God chose it among infinite alternatives. For his critics, the truth is exactly the other way around: God did not choose this world because he considered it to be good. He simply created a world that is (or was, as Budde and Knoerr and Castel think) the best world (or a "very good world", as Crusius believes), simply because God created it. As Budde and Knoerr maintain, "everything that God chooses is the best in a moral way", but "it is not morally the best for itself, but on account of God's choice" (*Doctrinae*, III, §5 [72]).

If one considers that God's will is free only if it is completely independent from all rational guidance, from all intellectual 'regulation', or, what is the same, that any rational guidance of the will automatically denies its freedom; if one consider this, then the disapproval of Leibniz and the voluntarist position, like the one the examined critics defend, are at least reasonable. Now – as I commented at the end of Chapter 5 – that position seems to lead to some rather thorny questions. And depending on the way in which one answers these questions, they in turn seem to lead to a paradox regarding the consistency of voluntarism.

The questions concern, on the one hand, the problem of the functioning of God's willing: If God is not bound by principles of reason, by the representation of the good, how does he even come to act? How does the will focus on the object that it wills? If confronted with different possible courses of action, which are the criteria by which God decides to choose one particular option, to pass from inactivity to choice? On the other hand, they concern the limits of God's willing: If God is not bound by principles of reason, not even by the representation of the good, is he then, at least in principle, capable of doing evil? Does God act in a good way only accidentally, or more exactly: only in a contingent manner?

Interestingly enough, the examined critics do not have a clear answer for the first group of questions – at least not within their criticism of optimism. At least there, the question concerning the functioning of God seems to remain a mystery. Oddly, this is almost understandable, since what those critics seem to believe is precisely that God is *not* rational, or that his rationality is completely different to ours, or that he is not comparable in any way to the way in which human beings work, etc. It would thus seem that the examined voluntarist critics, in order to defend a very broad concept of freedom, end up by giving away the possibility of explaining God as a rational being.

And yet – as regards the second group of questions – our critics do deny that God is able to do evil. Further, they do admit that God always does the good. And even further: they do acknowledge a kind of necessity for God's choices, a necessity that binds God to always want and do the good! Budde and Knoerr maintain that God can only know and subsequently do the best – and this with necessity. They write:

> The manner in which the divine wisdom causes that only the best world is created, implies also that only the best is known, an this namely with necessity. Indeed, such as God, in virtue of the fact that he is the wisest being, desires only the best world, he also knows the best, since the rest is nothing, and God cannot know nothing [...] Furthermore, God's wisdom renders the moral wisdom in God geometric, since God possesses geometric necessity in a manner that is morally necessary. Every creature, however created, has moral necessity in geometric manner, i.e. such that, if the creature would not be good or, which means to be morally good, would not do good, it would not be this creature. On the contrary, God is good because he is God and he does what is good. Therefore, since it is morally and, according to God's nature, geometric necessary to create only the best world, there is also the moral and, consequentially, the geometric necessity in God to know only the best [world] [...].
>
> [*Porro sapientia divina, dum, ut optimus tantum mundus crearetur, facit, ita ut etiam non, nisi optimus cognoscatur, facit, idque necessario. Nam*

dum Deus, quia sapientissimus est, optimum mundum tantum vult; optimum etiam cognoscit; quia cetera omnia nihil sunt, Deus autem nihil non cognoscit. [...] Porro sapientia Dei in Deo, moralem necessitatem facit geometricam; quia Deus necessitate geometrica, moralem necessitatem habet. Nulla enim creatura, qualis qualis sit, moralem necessitatem habet geometrice, id est, ita, ut si bona non esset, aut quod moraliter bonum est, non ageret, plane non esset ea creatura, quae est, sed Deus, quia Deus est, bonus est & quod bonum est, agit. Hinc etiam quia necessitas moralis & ratione Dei geometrica est, mundum optimum tantum creare; etiam in Deo necessitas moralis & consequenter geometrica est, optimum tantum in ideis habere, quia qui aliquid, quod plane possibile non est, in ideis habet & considerat, sapiens dici nequit.]
  Doctrinae, III, §4 [66]

Also Crusius, as Stefan Lorenz explains, introduces in a *Dissertatio de decoro divino* (1739) which is unfortunately not included in his complete works, a kind of 'control' to God's actions in order to avoid an absolute arbitrariness on the part of God. That control is called by Crusius '*decorum divinum*': a divine 'adequateness' or 'reasonableness'. According to this norm, God is obliged to act in accordance to his own perfection, which prevents him from wanting and doing evil.[11] Reinhard, as we saw previously, also establishes a control to God's actions. Following clearly Crusius's approach, Reinhard writes:

> From this it can be observed that God's freedom does not extend to all things. He is not free to act against his own perfection or against the fundamental perfection of things. His freedom extends only to what is indifferent; freedom can be exercised only in such cases in which different possible ways of acting are present. Thus freedom extends only to the arbitrary fixing of the ends; to the choice between the different, equally appropriate ways of attaining those ends; the choice between possible systems that are suitable to divine wisdom; the arbitrary determination of contingent perfections and indifferent circumstances; the arbitrary distribution of the degree of perfection that each individual must have, etc. The object of divine freedom is nothing but general good; its

---

11   *Cf.* Lorenz 1997: 174. Lorenz refers the criticism of Wilhelm Gass (Gass 1867: 165f.), who maintans that the *decorum divinum*, at least in the voluntarist manner in which Crusius introduces it, remains a subjective principle with no objective validity. Once again, this subjective character seems to be understandable, since the critics here examined consider any objective parameter to be a limitation of God's freedom.

exercising consists of the determination of that which can occur in more than only one way. This is the genuine notion of freedom [...]

[*Cela fait voir que la liberté de Dieu ne s'étend pas sur toutes choses. Il n'a point de liberté pour agir contre sa propre perfection, essentielle des choses. La liberté ne s'étend que sur ce qui est indifférent; elle ne peut être exercée que là où il y a plusieurs manières d'agir également possibles. Ainsi la liberté ne regarde que la condition arbitraire des fins, le choix entre plusieurs moyens également propres à ces fins, le choix entre plusieurs systèmes possibles & dignes de la sagesse divine, la détermination arbitraire des perfections accidentelles, des circonstances indifférentes, la répartition arbitraire du dégrée de perfection que doit avoir chaque individu, etc. L'objet de la liberté divine n'est que le bien en général; son exercice ne consiste que dans la détermination de ce qui peut être de plusieurs manières. Voici la notion génuine de la liberté* [...]]]

Examen, 39–40

The paradox is evident. The examined voluntarist critics reject Leibniz's understanding of the divine nature and his notion of moral necessity by maintaining that any rational determination of God's willing denies divine freedom of choice. This opens the door to the possibility of complete arbitrariness and evil choices on God's part. In order to avoid these risks, the voluntarists introduce new forms of necessity, which are not even different in terminology to the Leibnizian account (Budde and Crusius: "[...] since God possesses geometric necessity in a manner that is morally necessary [...]"; Reinhard: "The object of divine freedom is nothing but general good; its exercising consists of the determination of that which can occur in more than only one way"). They say that God is limited by his own perfection, that he can only want what is in accordance with his own nature, that he wants only the best, etc. It is this not the same thing that Leibniz maintains, that "to be morally compelled by wisdom, to be bound by the consideration of good, is to be free", that eternal ideas are the object of God's understanding, that God is directed in his willing by his own wisdom, etc.? The paradox is thus: in order to avoid the risks caused by the rejection of Leibniz's parameters, our voluntarist critics are obliged to establish limitations to God's willing that seem to bring them back to Leibniz's account.

It is not my intention here to decide which of the two models of divine agency – Leibnizian intellectualism on the one hand, the kind(s) of voluntarism defended by Leibniz's counter-optimist critics on the other – is better or explains God's nature and the meaning of divine freedom more adequately. As

I explained in Chapter 1, and as Wolfgang Hübener has shown,[12] the Leibnizian understanding of God seems to have a lot in common with the traditional Christian understanding of God. Further, from a theoretical point of view, the Leibnizian model *explains* more. And if the task of philosophy is to explain the world rationally, then Leibniz seems to prevail. And yet, one could say that idea – the task of philosophy is to explain rationally the world – already presupposes too much, namely that the world is rationally explainable. At least for the particular case of God, the voluntarist critics do not seem to consider it dramatic that God may *not* be explained rationally. Not to speak of the problems and dissatisfactions, commented on in the past chapters, that Leibniz's definition of freedom and his theory of moral necessity might contain.

---

12   Hübener 1978: 239ff.

Conclusions

The objective of this work was to examine the early critical reception of philosophical optimism – Leibniz's theory of 'the best of all possible worlds' – between 1710 and 1755. These years mark the publication of the first edition of the *Theodicy*, Leibniz's main work on optimism, and the Lisbon Earthquake on November 1, 1755. As was mentioned in the Introduction, it has been customary among an important number of historians of ideas to say that the earthquake represents the major turning point in the history of optimism in the eighteenth century. According to this 'standard picture', the accounts of the horrors of caused by the earthquake persuaded Voltaire to write two famous literary condemnations of optimism: the *Poème sur le désastre de Lisbonne* (1756) and, later, *Candide ou l'optimisme* (1759), which led to what has been described by different commentators as the major crisis and even the death of philosophical optimism.

The primordial questions around which the present investigation has taken shape were, on one side, in terms of the history of ideas, the problem of the veracity of that traditional picture of the development of optimism in the eighteenth century: Where there philosophically relevant criticisms of Leibniz's doctrine of the best of all possible worlds *before* Voltaire's famous reactions to the Earthquake? On the other, regarding the theoretical nature of those criticisms, the question of the motives, nature, and consistency of the arguments directed by early commentators against optimism: Which are the central tenets, main arguments, and possible theoretical problems of those early criticisms? Further, this work also pretended to identify the points that early critiques might have in common, and to find out to what extent the general concept used here to refer to those critiques, 'counter-optimism', could be given a philosophically stimulating content that might permit to identify and understand the particular nature of the conflict between optimism and its critics before 1755. As was explained in the Introduction, the first question has been examined in the past years by a number of commentators who have shown that there was indeed a rich reaction to optimism in the first decades after the publication of the *Theodicy*. Yet these studies are, despite their undeniable interest and importance not only for the present work, either quite brief and general reviews of the state of affairs,[1] or more extensive and detailed reports[2] that, nevertheless, fail to give account of the theoretical

---
1 *Cf.* Fonnesu 1994 and 2006; Hübener 1978.
2 *Cf.* Lorenz 1997.

motivation and common philosophical and theological concerns that early critics clearly share.

•••

The present work has shown that there definitely was a philosophically interesting, critical reaction to Leibnizian optimism before the Lisbon Earthquake. The reaction was illustrated here through the examination of four representative criticisms by the German Lutheran theologians Johann Frank Budde and Georg Christian Knoerr, the French Jesuit Louis-Bertrand Castel, the philosopher and theologian Christian August Crusius, and Adolf Friedrich Reinhard, winner of the contest on optimism of the Prussian Academy of Sciences in Berlin for the earthquake-year 1755. It was shown that critical reaction by these authors has a very particular theoretical nature that does not seem to fit easily into classifications used traditionally to explain the development of early modern philosophy, such as the well-known schemata of 'rationalism vs. empiricism' and 'optimism vs. pessimism'. This made it clear that the conflict between Leibniz's optimism and its early critics differs not only from the more popular epistemological conflicts of the seventeenth and early eighteenth centuries – for which names like Descartes, Spinoza, Malebranche, Leibniz, Locke, Berkeley or Hume are representative – but also from the post-Lisbon reaction to the optimist idea that the world is the best possible, a reaction which seems to make more emphasis on the problem of evil, the moral character of the world, and the quality of human life than on the problem of divine freedom, and which, apart from Voltaire, is related to famous thinkers like Hume and Schopenhauer.

The 'very particular theoretical nature' of the early reaction to optimism was thus reviewed critically by appealing to the opposing concepts of 'intellectualism' and 'voluntarism', which were borrowed, with slight terminological modifications, from Steven Nadler's studies of the notions of God that dominated early modern thought. As it was explained a number of times in the past chapters, an intellectualist theory maintains, in a few words, that God *acts following reasons*. For intellectualism moral, i.e. *rational* beings act following the perceptions or representations provided to them by their own understanding. In God's case the reason which inclines him to act is always goodness, the representation of what is *objectively* good (or more exactly: the best), which he identifies by virtue of his understanding. The intellect or understanding is thus, so to speak, the guide of God's willing. By contrast, voluntarist accounts consider that God is essentially different from other rational beings. In fact, they consider, as Nadler writes, that "God transcends practical rationality altogether". Whereas for intellectualists God acts at all times for good reasons, voluntarists – in order to guarantee a rather radical conception of freedom of choice – maintain that "God's will is absolute and completely unmotivated by (logically) independent reasons" (Nadler 2011a: 525–6). The origin of this clash is clearly the concern of making sense of God's rationality *and* his freedom of choice. While intellectualists claim that rationality does not contradict or rule out freedom – moreover: that acting rationally is *exactly* what it means to act freely – voluntarists believe that maintaining that God acts for reasons amounts to setting limits for him and his actions, thus denying absolute freedom. Of course, a further problem is that voluntarists understand freedom in quite a different way to intellectualists: not as the capacity of acting according to good reason (or choosing the best alternative of action), but as complete indeterminacy and arbitrariness of choice.

A fundamental conclusion of this work is, therefore, that the contraposition intellectualism-voluntarism seems to provide us with an adequate theoretical instrument to explain the conflict between Leibniz's philosophical optimism and the examined critics. Against Leibniz's theory of divine agency – which in Chapter 1, for reasons there explained, was identified as an intellectualist approach to rational moral agency – our four critics maintain usually one or both of two complementary attitudes:

i) They *reject* Leibniz's God either directly or through the rejection of tenets of Leibnizian metaphysics related organically to Leibniz's intellectualist concept of God. Some of these are Leibniz's theory of eternal truths, his understanding of the nature and scope of the Principle of Sufficient Reason, or his theory of hypothetical or moral necessity.

ii) They explicitly *advocate* an alternative concept of God, or more exactly, of divine freedom. This concept was shown for each one of the studied critics to correspond to a voluntarist approach to the divine nature.

Further, it was also clear from the previous examination that the concern about the supposed denial of divine freedom by optimism is the main motivation behind the particular criticisms of other aspects of Leibnizian metaphysics by the 'counter-optimists'.

•••

The conclusions of this work regarding the characteristics of an early critical reaction to philosophical optimism are relevant in at least two distinct ways. These somewhat correspond to what Bernard Williams has described as the principal difference between 'the history of ideas' and the 'history of philosophy'. According to Williams, the first examines the meaning of a work, a doctrine, a philosophical argument or such in the moment it was exposed. As Williams puts it: "For the history of ideas, the question about a work *what does it mean?* is centrally the question *what did it mean?*" (Williams 2005: xiii). On the other hand, for the history of philosophy the central question about the meaning of a philosophical work or system is the question what *does* it mean (or *could* mean): "the history of philosophy is more concerned to relate a philosopher's conception to present problems" (Williams 2006: 256). Thus, regarding the history of the ideas that gave form to the early modern European intellectual debate, in this work it was shown that optimism was no unchallenged paradigm in the first half of the eighteenth century. The history of philosophical optimism appears to be intellectually richer as has been considered traditionally and to concern quite more than only the question whether the world is good or a complete disaster.

As I pointed out at the beginning of this section, it is possible to talk about a kind of customary, 'standard picture' of optimism among historians of ideas. According to it, Leibnizian optimism was a more or less unopposed philosophical paradigm regarding the explanation of evil in the world at the beginning of the eighteenth century in France and Germany. This paradigm supposedly experienced its first and most fatal blow immediately after the Lisbon Earthquake in 1755 and Voltaire's anti-optimist reaction above mentioned.[3]

Interesting and informative as the 'standard picture' may be, there are other possible readings of the history of philosophical optimism. One of them has been made somewhat eminent in the last decades by the German philosopher Odo Marquard.[4] Marquard maintains that the Lisbon Earthquake certainly provoked a crisis of the Leibnizian idea that this is the best of all possible worlds (as well as of Alexander Pope's literary motto "everything what is, is right", referred to in Chapters 3 and 5). Yet, the aftermath of the earthquake did not wholly destroy the optimistic paradigm or better, the particular *rationalist approach* to reality that underlies philosophical optimism. The idea of an essentially rational, comprehensible, and positive reality outlived the Lisbon disaster and Voltaire's criticisms, perhaps not in the traditional metaphysical form given to it by Leibniz, but in a more dynamic, history-aware form that survived at least until the end of the nineteenth century. As Marquard explains, the crisis of optimism led to "a kind of post-theistic theodicy with futurising über-optimism" (Marquard 2007: 97). This "futurising über-optimism" is best represented by

---

[3] Interesting recent reactions against this 'standard picture' are Nichols 2014 and Strickland 2019.
[4] See Marquard 1981, 1986, and specially 2007.

the *Geschichtsphilosophie* (or Philosophy of History – particularly prominent at the end of the eighteenth and during the nineteenth century, and for which famous names such as Bossuet, Turgot, Voltaire, Condorcet, Kant, Fichte, Hegel or Marx are representative) and by two theses intimately related to it: i) the world is understood not anymore as a creation of God but as creation of man (namely as a *historical* development), and ii) history is a process "with a problematical present but a good future". According to Marquard, the system of optimism survived the crisis caused by the earthquake in the form of "theodicy motives" typical for modern thought. These are called by Marquard the motives of "autonomisation" (*"Autonomisierung"*), the "good-making" of evil (*"Malitätsbonisierung"*), the motive of "compensation" (*"Kompensation"*),[5] as well as the central notion of 'progress'.

This stimulating account cannot be examined in detail here. However, one thing must be clear: versions of the history of optimism which diverge from the 'standard picture' are possible. Thus, for the mentioned case, while the 'standard picture' preaches the decease of philosophical optimism after the catastrophe in Lisbon, Odo Marquard identifies the persistence of several motives of optimism – or more particularly, motives of a special form of theistic rationalism that underlies the system of the best – after 1755, defending the thesis of a kind of 'never-ending optimism' that survives the intellectual earthquake produced by Voltaire in a history-oriented form. Clearly, the standard theory of the end of optimism resulting from the Lisbon Earthquake and Marquard's proposal of a "futurising über-optimism", far from being contradictory, are in fact complementary theses, or more exactly, Marquard's thesis is a correction, an enriching clarification, of the 'standard picture'. The Lisbon Earthquake certainly provoked a profound and decisive crisis of optimism. However, the intellectual basis, the philosophical intention of the system of the best survived rather vigorously all through the following centuries.[6]

The thesis defended in the present study can be judged as a further enriching reading of the history of optimism. In its perhaps most condensed form, this thesis reads: Leibnizian optimism was no unhampered paradigm in the first half of the eighteenth century in France and Germany. On the contrary, some of its central theories and principles – like the notion of a best possible world, the belief in the universal validity of rational principles like the Principle of Sufficient Reason, the idea of the necessarily positive moral character of creation, and first among all, the particular rationalist (and specifically:

---

5 *Cf.* Marquard 1986.
6 On the, acceptance and influence of Odo Marquard's theses on the crisis of optimism and the origins of the Philosophy of History, see for example: Caro 2012; Dörpinghaus 1997: 108ff.

intellectualist) concept of God that underlies optimism – were challenged with arguments that are definitely worthy of attention and philosophical interest. Thus, while Marquard's idea of a survival of several motives of optimism straightens out the 'standard picture' regarding the period following the Lisbon Earthquake, the previous chapters show that the standard view of the history of optimism must also be enjoyed with some prudence concerning the period *before* the earthquake. Optimism was criticized before 1755. This critique was directed against central tenets of the doctrine that this is the best of all possible worlds. Even more interestingly, it was directed against the core of optimism's theoretical foundation: the idea of God as a rational being that acts according to reasons, of Leibniz's understanding of the way in which God works and what divine freedom means. As was explained in the previous chapter, the nature of the criticisms directed against optimism in the period between the publication of the *Theodicy* in 1710 and the Lisbon Earthquake of 1755 was very different to that of the critiques after the earthquake, which concerned mainly the moral character of the world supposedly created by an omnipotent and good God and the sufferings of mankind. Early criticisms are therefore interesting for themselves and constitute a further version of the development of the idea of the best world which complements both the 'standard picture' of the history of optimism *and* Marquard's theories.

With regard to the more specific history of the reception of Leibnizian thought, the thesis of a rather active 'counter-optimist' reaction at the beginning of the eighteenth century also shows that the response of and the very intense debates around Leibniz's thought, both in France and Germany, were still richer than normally supposed. As has been pointed out here, the conflict between Leibnizian optimism and its first critics has a value for itself. This conflict was not only, and specially, *not mainly*, the struggle between those who think, in the light of the problem of evil, that the world is good and those who consider it a valley of tears. Nor was it a clash between the two epistemological attitudes that determine a considerable part of early modern philosophical polemics, rationalism and empiricism. Also, 'counter-optimism' does not seem to have been some skeptical attack on the belief in reason, in some way heir of the skeptical crisis, famously described by Richard Popkin, that is, allegedly, also representative for the early modern period.[7] The battle between philosophical optimism and 'counter-optimism' was fundamentally a clash between two different approaches to the nature of God and, more particularly, to the problem of what it means to say that God is free. This quarrel has been described in this work with the aid of the less famous and nevertheless fundamental theoretical

---

7   *Cf.* Popkin 2003.

schema of 'intellectualism vs. voluntarism'. Of course, the fact that the conflict around optimism has such a clearly theological ingredient does not make the conflict less interesting for the history of modern philosophy. On the contrary, it shows that, if one looks a little deeper, that history can still contain surprises.

Concerning the theoretical interest of this work and the question that according to Bernard William's above mentioned distinction is the central question of the 'history of philosophy' (what *does* it mean – what does a philosophical work or a doctrine of the past mean nowadays?), the past chapters have sought to explain what kind of arguments were put forward against central tenets of Leibnizian metaphysics and particularly against Leibniz's understanding of rational, moral agency (in the present case: *divine* agency). Early criticisms of Leibnizian thought offer clear examples of the kind of problems that Leibniz's contemporaries had with basic notions and doctrines of the philosopher's rationalist worldview – and also of the kind of problems that such rationalist notions and doctrine might *actually* have or imply. These problematic or, at least, not self-evident aspects are, among others, the intellectualist notion of God, the doctrine of the universal validity of the Principle of Sufficient Reason, the theory of uncreated, unmodifiable eternal truths of principles of reason, the concept of hypothetical or moral necessity, the understanding of freedom as being "morally compelled by wisdom, [...] bound by the consideration of good" (T, §236/GP VI 258–9), etc. All these were shown by the examined critics to be knotty issues of Leibnizian philosophy. But what is more: they were also shown to be, for themselves, knotty aspects of a rationalist/intellectualist approach to reality. Thus, whether one assumes or rejects a theistic model, whether one accepts or not the reasons of the examined critics, their doubts point out important problems with which a rationalist philosophy – not only Leibniz's – must necessarily deal.

Further, it was also shown that the voluntarist alternative that early critics offer in order to 'save' divine freedom is in itself not less, and perhaps even more, problematic than the Leibnizian intellectualist approach. The theoretical relevance of an examination of so-called early 'counter-optimism' is therefore evident: the problems stressed by early critics of optimism seem to be of importance not only concerning the conflict between Leibniz and his detractors. Within a philosophical framework that pursues the examination of the pretensions and possibilities of rationalism, and includes the reference to approaches like the ones we have described here by using the categories of 'intellectualism' and 'voluntarism', the study of early counter-optimism is also relevant with regard to the quest of making sense of the idea of freedom. And it might be added: this is an enduring quest that goes beyond the temporal and theoretical limits of early modern philosophy.

Bibliography

Primary Literature

Leibniz's Works
[A] *Sämtliche Schriften und Briefe* (ed. Prussian Academy of Sciences u.a.), Darmstadt-Leipzig-Berlin): Akademie Verlag, 1923 ff. (Edition still in progress.)
[GP] *Die philosophischen Schriften von Leibniz* (ed. Carl I. Gerhardt), 7 vols, Berlin: Weidmannsche Buchhandlung, 1875–1890. Reprint: Hildesheim: Georg Olms, 1978.
[GR] *G. W. Leibniz: Textes inédits d'après les manuscrits de la Bibliothèque provinciale d'Hanovre* (ed. Gaston Grua), Paris: Presses Universitaires de France, 1948. Reprint: New York: Garland, 1985.
[GW] *Briefwechsel zwischen Leibniz und Christian Wolff* (ed. Carl I. Gerhardt), Halle: H. W. Schmidt, 1860. Reprint: Hildesheim: Georg Olms, 1963.

English Translations of Leibniz's Works
[Confessio] *Confessio philosophi. Papers Concerning the Problem of Evil, 1671–1678* (original Latin text with an English translation by Robert C. Sleigh), New Haven-London: Yale U.P., 2005.
[DM] *Discourse on Metaphysics and Other Essays* (trans. Daniel Garber & Roger Ariew), Indianapolis: Hackett, 1991.
[LA] *The Leibniz-Arnauld Correspondence: With Selections from the Correspondence with Ernst, Landgrave of Hessen-Rheinfels* (*The Yale Leibniz Series*) (ed. and trans Stephen Voss), New Haven-London: Yale U.P., 2016.
[LC] *The Leibniz-Clarke Correspondence* (ed. Henry Gavin Alexander), Manchester: Manchester U.P., 1956.
[LDB] *The Leibniz-Des Bosses Correspondence* (ed. and trans. Brandon C. Look & Donald Rutherford), New Haven-London: Yale U.P., 2007.
[LTS] *Leibniz and the Two Sophies: The Philosophical Correspondence* (ed. and trans. Lloyd Strickland), Toronto: ITER, 2011.
[Loemker] *Philosophical Papers and Letters* (ed. and trans. Leroy Loemker), Dordrecht: Kluwer, 1989.
[M] *Monadology*, in: *Discourse on Metaphysics and Other Essays* (trans. Daniel Garber & Roger Ariew), Indianapolis: Hackett, 1991.
[NE] *New Essays on Human Understanding* (ed. and trans. Peter Remnant & Jonathan Bennett), Cambridge: Cambridge U.P., 1981.
[NS] *Leibniz's 'New System' and Associated Contemporary Texts* (ed. and trans. Roger S. Woolhouse & Richard Franks), New York: Oxford U.P., 2006.
[PNG] *Principles of Nature and Grace Based on Reason*, in: *Philosophical Papers and Letters* (ed. and trans. Leroy Loemker), Dordrecht: Kluwer, 1989.

[T] *Theodicy: Essays on the Goodness of God, the Freedom of Man and the Origin of Evil* (ed. Austin Farrer, trans. E. M. Huggard), La Salle: Open Court, 1985.

[UOT] *The Ultimate Origin of Things*, in: *Philosophical Papers and Letters* (ed. and trans. Leroy Loemker), Dordrecht: Kluwer, 1989.

Works by the Authors Examined in Chapters 2–6

Baumeister, Friedrich Christian [*Historiae*], *Historia doctrinae recentius controversae de mundo optimo*, Leipzig und Görlitz: Richter, 1741.

Budde, Johannes Franz [*Bedencken*], *Bedencken über die Wolffianische Philosophie mit Anmerckungen von Christian Wolffen* (1724), in: Christian Wolff, *Gesammelte Werke* (ed. Jean École), Hildesheim-New York: Georg Olms, 1980, vol. 17.

Budde, Johannes Franz & Knoerr, Georg Christian [*Doctrinae*], *Doctrinae orthodoxae de origine mali contra recentorium quorundam hypotheses modesta assertio, auctore et respondente Georgio Christiano Knoerreo*, Jena: Müller, 1712.

Castel, Louis Bertrand [Castel], [Review of the second edition of the *Theodicy* (1734)], in: *Mémoires pour l'histoire des Sciences et des beaux arts = Mémoires de Trévoux* 37 (1737): 6–36, 198–241, 444–71 and 954–91. Reprint: Geneva: Slatkine Reprints, 1968.

Crusius, Christian August [*De usu*], *Dissertatio philosophica de usu et limitibus principii rationis determinantis, vulgo sufficientis* (1745), in: *Die philosophischen Hauptwerke* (ed. Sonia Carboncini and Reinhard Finster), Hildesheim-New York: Georg Olms, 1987, vol. 4.1: 182–237.

Ausführliche Abhandlung von dem rechten Gebrauche und der Einschränkung des sogenannten Satzes vom zureichenden, oder besser, determinierenden Grunde (trans. Christian Friedrich Krause), Leipzig: Langenheim, 1744.

*[*Anweisung*], *Anweisung, vernünftig zu leben. Darinnen nach Erklärung der Natur des menschlichen Willens die natürlichen Pflichten und allgemeinen Klugheitslehren im richtigen Zusammenhange vorgetragen werden* (1744), in: *Die philosophischen Hauptwerke* (ed. Giorgio Tonelli), Hildesheim-New York: Georg Olms, 1969, vol. 1.

*[*Entwurf*], *Entwurf der nothwendigen Vernunftwahrheiten, wiefern sie den zufälligen entgegen gesetzt werden* (1745), in: *Die philosophischen Hauptwerke* (ed. Giorgio Tonelli), Hildesheim-New York: Georg Olms, 1964, vol. 2.

Reinhard, Adolph Friedrich [*Examen*], "Le système de Mr Pope sur la perfection de monde, comparé à celui de Mr de Leibnitz, avec un examen de l'optimisme", in: *Dissertation qui a remporté le prix proposé par l'Académie Royale des sciences et belles lettres de Prusse, sur l'optimisme, avec les pièces qui ont concouru*, Berlin: Haude & Spener, 1755.

---

* German translations

*i) *Abhandlung von der Besten Welt. Welche den von der Königlichen-Preußischen Akademie der Wissenschaften zu Berlin für das 1755 Jahr ausgesetzten Preis erhalten* (trans. Johann Adolf Friedrich von Gentzkow), Greifswald, 1757.

*ii) *Vergleichung des Lehrgebäudes des Herrn Pope von der Vollkommenheit der Welt, mit dem System des Herrn von Leibnitz: Nebst einer Untersuchung der Lehre von der besten Welt. Eine Abhandlung, welche den, von der königl. Akademie der Wissenschaften und schönen Künste zu Berlin, aufgesetzten Preis vom Jahre 1755 davon getragen hat* (trans. Christian August Wichmann), Leipzig: Langenheim, 1757.

Tournemine, René-Joseph [Tournemine], [Review of the first edition of the *Theodicy* (1710)], in: *Mémoires pour l'histoire des Sciences et des beaux arts* = *Mémoires de Trévoux* 13 (1713): 1178–1199. Reprint: Geneva: Slatkine Reprints, 1968.

Other Authors

Augustine of Hippo [*Conf.*], *Confessions*, in: *Confessions and Enchiridion* (trans. Albert Cook Outler), London: S.C.M. Press, 1964.

Augustine of Hippo [*Ench*], *Enchiridion*, in: *Confessions and Enchiridion* (trans. Albert Cook Outler), London: S.C.M. Press, 1964.

Augustine of Hippo [*Lib. arb.*], *On Free Choice of the Will* (trans. Thomas Williams), Indianapolis: Hackett, 1993.

Augustine of Hippo [*Civ.*], *Concerning the City of God against the Pagans* (trans. Henry Bettenson), London: Penguin, 2003.

Aquinas, Thomas [*De malo*], *On Evil* (trans. R. Regan), Oxford: Oxford U.P., 2003.

Bayle, Pierre [OD], *Œuvres diverses* (5 vols., ed. Elisabeth Labrousse), Hildesheim: Georg Olms, 1964–1990.

Bayle, Pierre, [*Dictionnaire*] *Dictionnaire historique et critique* (16 vols., ed. A.J.Q. Beuchot), Paris: Desoer, 1820–1824. Reprint: Boston: Adamant Media Corporation, 2006. Electronic edition: http://www.lib.uchicago.edu/efts/ARTFL/projects/dicos/BAYLE/search.fulltext.form.html.

Bayle, Pierre, *Historical and Critical Dictionary. Selections* (ed. and trans. Richard H. Popkin), Indianapolis: Hackett, 1991.

Bayle, Pierre, *Pierre Bayle – Pour une histoire critique de la philosophie. Choix d'articles philosophiques du* Dictionnaire historique et critique (ed. J.-M. Gros), Paris: Honoré Champion, 2001.

Crousaz, Jean Pierre de (1737), *Examen de l'essai de M. Pope sur l'homme*, Lausanne: M. M. Bousquet.

Descartes, René [AT], *Ouvres de Descartes* (12 vols., ed. Charles Adam & Paul Tannery), Paris: J. Vrin, 1974–1983.

---

* German translations

Descartes, René [CSM], *The Philosophical Writings of Descartes* (3 vols., ed. and trans. John Cottingham, Robert Stoothoff & Douglas Murdoch), Cambridge: Cambridge U.P., 1985.

Formey, Jean Henri Samuel, [Review of Reinhard's *Examen de l'optimism*], in: *Nouvelle Bibliothèque Germanique* (ed. Jean Henri Samuel Formey), vol. 18, part I, Amsterdam: Schreuder & Mortier, 1755: 23–32.

Gottsched, Johann Christoph, *Beweis, dass diese Welt unter allen die beste sei* (1742), in: *Ausgewählte Werke* (ed. P.M. Mitchell), Berlin-New York: Walter de Gruyter, 1968–1987, vol V/2: 536–60.

Gottsched, Johann Christoph *De optimismi macula diserte nuper Alexandro Popio anglo, tacite autem G.G. Leibnitio, perperam licet, inusta*, Leipzig: Breitkopf, 1753.

Hume, David, *Dialogues Concerning Natural Religion* (1779), in: *Dialogues and Natural History of Religion* (ed. by J.A.C. Gaskin), Oxford-New York: Oxford U.P., 1993.

Kant, Immanuel, "Versuch, einiger Betrachtungen über den Optimismus" (1759), in: *Kants gesammelte Schriften* (ed. Prussian Academy of Sciences), Berlin: Georg Reimer, 1912, vol. 2: 29–35.

Lessing Gotthold Ephraim & Mendelssohn, Moses, *Pope ein Metaphysiker!* (1755), in: Gotthold Ephraim Lessing, *Sämtliche Schriften* (ed. Karl Lachmann), Stuttgart: Göschen, 1886–1924, vol. 6: 409–45.

Malebranche, Nicolas [OCM], *Oeuvres complètes de Malebranche* (20 vols., ed. André Robinet), Paris: J. Vrin, 1958–1978.

Mendelssohn, Moses, "Über Reinhard's *Examen de l'optimisme*" (*Briefe, die neueste Literatur betreffend*, letter 10, March 8, 1759), in: *Gesammelte Schriften* (ed. Georg Benjamin Mendelssohn), Leipzig: Brockhaus, 1844, vol. 4/1: 508–10.

Plotinus [*Enn.*], *The Enneads* (trans. Stephen MacKenna), London: Faber & Faber, 1962.

Pope, Alexander [*Essay*], *An Essay on Man*, in: *The Poems of Alexander Pope – The Twickenham Edition* (10 vols., ed. John Butt), London: Methuen, 1954–1967, vol. 3.1.

Pope, Alexander [*Letters*], *Selected Letters* (ed. Howard Erskine-Hill), New York: Oxford U.P., 2000.

Prémontval, Pierre Le Guay, *Vues philosophiques ou Protestations et déclarations sur les principaux objets des connaissances humaines*, Amsterdam: J.H. Schnieder, 1757.

Spinoza, Benedictus, *A Spinoza Reader: The Ethics and Other Works* (ed. and trans. Edwin Curley), Princeton: Princeton U.P., 1994.

Voltaire, *Oeuvres complètes* (general ed. Nicholas Cronk), Geneva-Oxford: Institut et Musée Voltaire & Voltaire Foundation, since 1968, still not concluded.

Warburton, William, *A Vindication of Mr. Pope's Essay on Man*, London: Knapton, 1739.

Weismann, Christian Eberhard, *Schediasmata academica sive dissertationes varii argumenti nostrorum maxime temporum controversii absque studio partium expendendis accomodatae*, Tübingen: Cotta, 1725.

Wolff, Christian [*Deutsche Metaphysik*], *Vernünftige Gedanken von Gott, der Welt und der Seele des Menschen, auch allen Dingen überhaupt* (1719), in: *Gesammelte Werke* (ed. Jean École et al.) Hildesheim: Georg Olms, 1962ff, vol. I/2.

Wolff, Christian [*Latin Ontology*], *Philosophia prima sive ontologia methodo scientifica pertractata qua omnis cognitionis humanae principia continentur* (1730), in: *Gesammelte Werke* (ed. Jean École et al.) Hildesheim: Georg Olms, 1962ff, vol. II/3.

Ziegra, Christian (ed.), *Sammlung der Streitschriften über die Lehre von der besten Welt und verschiedene damit verknüpfte wichtige Wahrheiten, welche zwischen dem Verfasser der im Jahr 1755 von der Akademie zu Berlin gekrönten Schrift vom Optimismo und einigen berühmten Gelehrten gewechselt worden*, Rostock-Weimar: J.A. Berger & J. Boedner, 1759.

Secondary Literature

Abashnik, Vladimir (2010), "Johann Franz Budde", in: Heiner F. Klemme & Manfred Kuehn (eds.), *The Dictionary of Eighteenth-Century German Philosophers*, London: Continuum, 2010, vol. 1: 164–9.

Abercrombie, Nigel (1936), *The Origins of Jansenism*, Oxford: Clarendon Press.

Adams, Marilyn McCord (1998), "Problem of Evil", in: Edward Craig (ed.), *Routledge Encyclopedia of Philisophy*, London-New York: Routledge, vol. 3: 466–73.

Adams, Marilyn McCord (1999), "Ockham on Will, Nature, and Morality", in: Paul Vincent Spade (ed.), *The Cambridge Companion to Ockham*, Cambridge: Cambridge U.P.: 245–72.

Adams, Marilyn McCord & Adams, Robert Merrihew (eds.) (1994), *The Problem of Evil*, Oxford: Oxford U.P.

Adams, Robert Merrihew (1994), *Leibniz: Determinist, Theist, Idealist*, New York: Oxford U.P.

Adams, Robert Merrihew (2005), "Moral Necessity", in: Donald Rutherford & J.A. Cover (eds.), *Leibniz: Nature and Freedom*, Oxford: Oxford U.P.: 181–93.

Ahnert, Thomas (2004), "Newtonianism in Early Enlightenment Germany, c. 1720 to 1750: Metaphysics and the Critique of Dogmatic Philosophy", in: *Studies in History and Philosophy of Science* 35, 3: 471–91.

Aiton, Eric J. (1985), *Leibniz. A Biography*, Bristol-Boston: Adam Hilger.

Alfaric, Prosper (1918), *L'évolution intellectuelle de saint Augustin*, vol. 1: *Du Manichéisme au Néoplatonisme*, Paris: Nourry.

Allard, Emmy (1985, 11914), *Die Angriffe gegen Descartes und Malebranche im Journal de Trévoux 1701–1715*, Hildesheim: Olms.

Alletz, Pons Augustin (1771), *L'Esprit des journalistes de Trévoux; ou, Morceaux précieux de littérature, répandus dans les Mémoires pour l'histoire des sciences & des Beaux*

Arts, depuis leur origine en 1701 jusqu'en 1762. Contenant ce qu'il y a de plus neuf & de plus curieux, soit pour les ouvrages dont ces littérateurs ont rendu compte, 4 vols, Paris: Hansy.

Altmann, Alexander (1969), *Moses Mendelssohns Frühschriften zur Metaphysik*, Tübingen: J.C.B. Mohr (Paul Siebeck).

Ammicht-Quinn, Regina (1992), *Von Lissabon nach Auschwitz. Zum Paradigmawechsel in der Theodizeefrage*, Freiburg: Universitätsverlag.

Anapolitanos, Dionysios A. (1999), *Leibniz: Representation, Continuity and the Spatio-temporal*, Dordrecht: Kluwer.

Antognazza, Maria Rosa (2009), *Leibniz; an Intellectual Biography*, New York: Cambridge U.P.

Antognazza, Maria Rosa (2014), "Metaphysical Evil Revisited", in: Larry M. Jorgensen & Samuel Newlands (eds.), *New Essays on Leibniz's Theodicy*, Oxford: Oxford U.P.: 112–34.

Babcock, William S. (1991), "Augustine on Sin and Moral Agency", in: William S. Babcock (ed.), *The Ethics of St. Augustine*, Atlanta: Scholars Press.

Barber, William Henry (1955), *Leibniz in France: From Arnauld to Voltaire. A Study in French Reactions to Leibnizianism, 1670–1760*, Oxford: Clarendon Press.

Barreira de Campos, Isabel (1998), *O grande terremoto (1755)*, Lisbon: Parceira.

Basker, James (2003), "Criticism and the Rise of Periodical Literature", in: Hugh Barr Nisbet & Claude Rawson (eds.), *The Cambridge History of Literary Criticism*, Cambridge: Cambridge U.P., vol. IV: 316–32.

Bennett, Jonathan (1994), "Descartes's Theory of Modality", in: *The Philosophical Review* 103, 4: 639–67.

Besterman, Theodore (1956), "Voltaire et le désastre de Lisbonne: ou, la mort d l'optimisme", in: *Studies on Voltaire and the Eighteenth Century* 2, 7–24.

Billicsich, Friedrich (1936–1959), *Das Problem des Übels in der Philosophie des Abendlandes*, 3 vols, Vienna: A. Sexl.

Blumenfeld, David (1975), "Is the Best Possible World Possible?", in: *Philosophical Review* 84: 163–77.

Blumenfeld, David (1994), "Freedom, Contingency, and Things Possible in Themselves", in: Roger S. Woolhouse (ed.), *Gottfried Wilhelm Leibniz – Critical Assessments*, vol. 4, London: Routledge: 303–22.

Blumenfeld, David (1995), "Perfection and Happiness in the Best Possible World", in: Nicholas Jolley (ed.), *Cambridge Companion to Leibniz*, Cambridge: Cambridge U.P.: 382–410.

Bobzien, Susanne (1998), *Determinism and Freedom in Stoic Philosophy*, Oxford: Oxford U.P., 1998.

Bost, Hubert (1994), *Pierre Bayle et la religion*, Paris: Presses Univ. de France.

Bost, Hubert (2006a), *Pierre Bayle*, Paris: Fayard.

Bost, Hubert (2006b), *Pierre Bayle historien, critique et moraliste*, Turhout: Brepols.
Bost, Hubert & De Robert, Philippe (ed.) (1996), *Pierre Bayle, citoyen du monde: de l'enfant du Carla à l'auteur du Dictionnaire* (Actes du colloque du Carla-Bayle, 13–15 septembre 1996), Paris: Champion.
Bots, Hans (ed.) (1998), *Critique, savoir et érudition à la veille des Lumières. Le Dictionnaire historique et critique de Pierre Bayle (1647–1706)*, Amsterdam-Maarssen: APA-Holland U.P.
Bots, Hans & Van Bunge, Wiep (2006), *Pierre Bayle (1647–1706), le philosophe de Rotterdam: Philosophy, Religion and Reception*, Leiden: Brill.
Bracht, Katharina (2005), "Securitas libertatis. Augustins Entdeckung der radikalen Entscheidungsfreiheit als Ursprung des Bösen" (Inaugural speech, Faculty of Theology of the Humboldt University in Berlin, February of 2004), Berlin: Humboldt-Universität zu Berlin.
Bracken, Harry (1964), "Bayle Not a Sceptic?", in: *Journal of the History of Ideas* 25: 169–80.
Braun, Theodore E.D. & Radner, John B. (eds.) (2005), *The Lisbon Earthquake of 1755: Representations and Reactions*, Oxford: Voltaire Foundation.
Breidert, Wolfgang (1993), "Einleitung", in: Alexander Pope, *Vom Menschen/Essay on Man* (English/German, ed. Wolfgang Breidert), Hamburg: Felix Meiner: vii–xxvii.
Breidert, Wolfgang (1994), *Die Erschütterung der vollkommenen Welt*, Darmstadt: Wissenschaftliche Buchgesellschaft Darmstadt.
Broad, C.D. (1975), *Leibniz: An Introduction*, Cambridge: Cambridge U.P.
Brooks, Richard A. (1964), *Voltaire and Leibniz*, Genf: Droz.
Brown, Peter (1967), *Augustine of Hippo*, London: Faber.
Burrel, Peter (1981), "Pierre Bayle's *Dictionnaire historique et critique*", in: A. Kafker (ed.), *Notable Encyclopedias of the Seventeenth and Eighteenth Centuries: Nine Predecessors of the "Encyclopédie"*, Oxford: The Voltaire Foundation: 83–103.
Bury, John B. (1920), *The Idea of Progress: An Inquiry into its Origin and Growth*, London: Macmillan.
Buschmann, Cornelia (1987), "Philosophischen Preisfragen und Preisschriften der Berliner Akademie. Ein Beitrag zur Leibniz-Rezeption im 18. Jahrhundert", in: *Deutsche Zeitschrift für Philosophie* 7: 779–87.
Buschmann, Cornelia (1989a), "Wolffianismus in Berlin", in: Wolfgang Förster (ed.), *Aufklärung in Berlin*, Berlin: Akademie-Verlag: 73–101.
Buschmann, Cornelia (1989b), "Die Philosophischen Preisfragen und Preisschriften der Berliner Akademie der Wissenschaften im 18. Jahrhundert", in: Wolfgang Förster (ed.), *Aufklärung in Berlin*, Berlin: Akademie-Verlag: 165–228.
Calinger, Ronald S. (1969), "The Newtonian-Wolffian Controversy: 1740–1759", in: *Journal of the History of Ideas* 30, 3: 319–30.
Campo, Mariano (1953), *La genesi del criticismo kantiano*, Varese: Magenta.

Carboncini, Sonia (1986), "Christian August Crusius und die Leibniz-Wolffsche Philosophie", in: Albert Heinekamp (ed.), *Beiträge zur Wirkungs- und Rezeptionsgeschichte von Gottfried Wilhelm Leibniz* (*Studia leibnitiana supplementa* 26), Stuttgart: Franz Steiner: 110–25.

Carboncini, Sonia (1987), "Einleitung", in: Crusius, Christian August, *Die philosophischen Hauptwerke* (ed. Giorgio Tonelli), Hildesheim-New York: Georg Olms, vol. 4.1: i–xxxvi.

Carboncini, Sonia (1989), "Die thomasianisch-pietistische Tradition und ihre Fortsetzung durch Christian August Crusius", in: Werner Schneiders (ed.), *Christian Thomasius 1655–1728. Interpretationen zu Werk und Wirkung. Mit einer Bibliographie der neueren Thomasius-Literatur*, Hamburg: Felix Meiner: 287–304.

Carboncini, Sonia (1991), *Transzendentale Wahrheit und Traum. Christian Wolffs Antwort auf die Herausforderung durch den Cartesianischen Zweifel*, Stuttgart-Bad Cannstatt: Frommann-Holzboog.

Carlson, Andrew (2001), *The Divine Ethic of Creation in Leibniz*, New York: Peter Lang.

Caro, Hernán D. (2010), "Was bleibt von Leibniz' Theodizee? – Ein Gespräch mit Wilhelm Schmidt-Biggemann", in: *Information Philosophie* 5/2010: 26–31.

Caro, Hernán D. (2011), "Evil, Philosophy, and God's Mysterious Ways – A Conversation with Steven Nadler on Early Modern Philosophy", unpublished. Available at: http://hu-berlin.academia.edu/HernanCaro/Papers/1091971/Conversation_with_Steven_Nadler_on_Evil_and_Early_Modern_Philosophy.

Caro, Hernán D. (2012), "Pierre Bayle y el problema del mal, o la demolición de la teodicea clásica", in: Ángela Uribe & Camila de Gamboa (eds.), *Fuentes del mal*, Bogotá: Universidad Nacional de Colombia.

Carraud, Vincent (2002), *Causa sive Ratio: la Raison de la Cause, de Suarez à Leibniz*, Paris: PUF.

Catechism of the Catholic Church (1994), London: Burns & Oates.

Chappell, Vere, Della Rocca, Michael & Sleigh, Robert C. (1998), "Determinism and Human Freedom", in: Daniel Garber & Michael Ayers (eds.), *The Cambridge History of Seventeenth-Century Philosophy*, vol. 2, Cambridge: Cambridge U.P.: 1195–278.

Ciafardone, Raffaele (1982), "Über den Primat der praktischen Vernunft vor der theoretischen bei Thomasius und Crusius mit Beziehung auf Kant", in: *Studia leibnitiana* 14: 127–35.

Copleston, Frederick (1999, 11958), *A History of Philosophy*, vol. 4: *Descartes to Leibniz*, Cornwall: Burns & Outes.

Cottingham, John (1988), *The Rationalists*, Oxford-New York: Oxford U.P.

Cress, Donald (1989), "Augustine's Privation Account of Evil: A Defense", in: *Augustine Studies* 20: 109–28.

Cross, F.L. & Livingstone, Elizabeth A. (eds.) (2005), *The Oxford Dictionary of the Christian Church*, New York: Oxford U.P.

Cunning, David (2018), "Descartes's Modal Metaphysics", in: Edward N. Zalta (ed.), *The Stanford Encyclopedia of Philosophy (Spring 2018 Edition)*. Available at: https://plato.stanford.edu/entries/descartes-modal/. Last view: May 2020.

Curley, Edwin M. (1984), "Descartes on the Creation of the Eternal Truths", in: *The Philosophical Review* 93, 4: 569–97.

Delpla, Isabelle & De Robert, Philippe (eds.) (2003), *La raison corrosive: études sur la pensée critique de Pierre Bayle*, Paris: Champion.

Desautels, Alfred (1956), *Les mémoires de Trévoux et le mouvement des idées au XVIIIe siècle, 1701–1734*, Rome: Instituti Historici Societatis Jesu.

Devillairs, Laurence (1998), *Descartes, Leibniz, les vérités éternelles*, Paris: Presses Universitaires de France.

Dibon, Paul (ed.) (1959), *Pierre Bayle. Le philosophe de Rotterdam. Etudes et documents*, Amsterdam-London-New York-Princeton: Elsevier-Vrin.

Dienstag, Joshua F. (2006), *Pessimism: Philosophy, Ethic, Spirit*, Princeton: Princeton U.P.

Doering, Heinrich (1832), *Die gelehrten Theologen Deutschlands im achtzehnten und neunzehnten Jahrhundert*, 2 vols, Neustadt: Johann Karl Gottfried Wagner.

Doney, Willis (1983), "Rationalism", in: *Southern Journal of Philosophy* 21, Supplement 1: 1–14.

Dörpinghaus, Andreas (1997), *Mundus pessimus: Untersuchungen zum philosophischen Pessimismus Arthur Schopenhauers*, Würzburg: Königshausen und Neumann.

Dumas, Gustave (1936), *Histoire du Journal de Trévoux, depuis 1701 jusqu'en 1762*, Paris: Boivin & Co.

Eifert, Christiane (2002), "Das Erdbeben von Lissabon 1755. Zur Historizität einer Naturkatastrophe", in: *Historische Zeitschrift* 274/3: 633–64.

Engfer, Hans-Jürgen (1996), *Empirismus versus Rationalismus? Kritik eines philosophischen Schemas*, Paderborn: Schöningh.

Erhard, Jean & Roger, Jacques (1965), "Deux périodiques français au XVIIIes siècle: le 'Journal des Savants' et les 'Mémoires de Trévoux'. Essai d'une étude quantitative", in: *Livre et société dans la France du XVIIIe siècle*, Paris-The Hague: Mouton & CO: 33–59.

Evans, Gillian Rosemary (1983), *Augustine on Evil*, Cambridge: Cambridge U.P.

Fabbianelli, Faustino (2003), "Leibniz, Budde et Wolff. Trois modèles de théodicée", in: *Revue philosophique de la France et de l'étranger* 128: 293–396.

Faye, Emmanuel (ed.) (2000), *Cartésiens et augustiniens au XVIIe siècle (Corpus 37)*, Paris: Centre d'Études d'Histoire de la Philosophie Moderne et Contemporaine-Université Paris X.

Flasch, Kurt (1994), *Augustin. Einführung in sein Denken*, Stuttgart: Reclam.

Flasch, Kurt (2008), *Kampfplätze der Philosophie. Große Kontroversen von Augustin bis Voltaire*, Frankfurt am Main: Vittorio Klostermann.

Flew, Antony (1973), "Compatibilism, Free Will and God", *Philosophy* 48: 231–44.

Fonnesu, Luca (1994), "Der Optimismus und seine Kritiker im Zeitalter der Aufklärung", in: *Studia leibnitiana* 26, 2: 131–62.

Fonnesu, Luca (2006), "The Problem of Theodicy", in: Knud Haakonssen (ed.), *The Cambridge History of Eighteenth-Century Philosophy*, Cambridge: Cambridge U.P., vol. II: 749–70.

Forget, Jacques (1913), "Jansenius and Jansenism", in: Charles G. Herbermann (ed.), *The Catholic Encyclopedia*, 15 vols, New York: Appleton.

Frank, Gustav (1876), "Buddeus, Johann Franz", in: *Allgemeine Deutsche Biographie* (ed. Bavarian Academy of Sciences), Leipzig: Duncker & Humblot, vol. 3: 500–1.

Franke, Ursula (1992), "Mundus optimus – eine hermeneutische Kategorie. Leibniz' Verteidigung der Sache Gottes gegen Pierre Bayle", in: Heinekamp, Albert & Robinet, André (eds.), *Leibniz: le meilleur des mondes. Table ronde organisée par le Centre National de la Recherche Scientifique, Paris et la Gottfried Wilhelm-Leibniz-Gesellschaft, Hannover. Domaine de Seillac (Loir-et-Cher), 7 au 9 Juin 1990* (*Studia leibnitiana* Sonderheft 21), Stuttgart: Franz Steiner: 153–62.

Frankfurt, Harry (1977), "Descartes on the Creation of the Eternal Truths", in: *The Philosophical Review* 86, 1: 36–57.

Gass, Wilhelm (1867), *Geschichte der protestantischen Dogmatik in ihrem Zusammenhange mit der Theologie überhaupt*, vol. 4, Berlin: Georg Reimer.

Gawlick, Gunther & Kreimendahl, Lothar (2002), "Einleitung", in: Pierre Bayle, *Historisches und kritisches Wörterbuch. Eine Auswahl der philosophischen Artikel* (ed. and trans. Gunther Gawlick & Lothar Kreimendahl), Hamburg: Felix Meiner.

Gawlick, Gunther (2007), "Spinozismus", in: Joachim Ritter, Karlfried Gründer & Gottfried Gabriel (eds.), *Historisches Wörterbuch der Philosophie*, Basel: Schwabe, vol. 9: 1398–1401.

Geerlings, Wilhelm (2002), *Augustinus. Leben und Werk. Eine bibliographische Einführung*, Paderborn: Schöningh.

Geyer, Carl-Friedrich (1982), "Das 'Jahrhundert der Theodizee'", in: *Kant-Studien* 73: 393–405.

Goubet, Jean-François (2009), "La première réception wolffienne de la *Théodicée* leibnizienne", in: Paul Rateau (ed.), *L'idée de théodicée de Leibniz à Kant: héritage, transformations, critiques*, Stuttgart: Steiner: 103–12.

Günther, Horst (1984), "Optimismus", in: Ritter, Joachim & Gründer, Karl (eds.), *Historisches Wörterbuch der Philosophie*, Basel-Stuttgart: Schwabe & Co., vol. 6: 1241–6.

Günther, Horst (2005), *Das Erdbeben von Lissabon und die Erschütterung des aufgeklärten Europa*, Frankfurt am Main: Fischer.

Habel, Thomas (2007), *Gelehrte Journale der Aufklärung. Zur Entstehung, Entwicklung und Erschließung deutschsprachiger Rezensionszeitschriften des 18. Jahrhunderts*, Bremen: Lumière.

Harnack, Adolf von (1886–1890), *Lehrbuch der Dogmengeschichte*, Tübingen: Mohr.

Harnack, Adolf von (1900), *Geschichte der Königlich Preußischen Akademie der Wissenschaften zu Berlin*, Berlin: Reichsdruckerei, vol. I/1. Reprint: Hildesheim-New York: Georg Olms, 1970.

Harrison, Simon (2006), *Augustine's Way Into the Will. The Theological and Philosophical Significance of* De Libero Arbitrio, New York: Oxford U.P.

Hart, Trevor (1997), "Redemption and Fall", in Gunton, Colin (ed.), *The Cambridge Companion to Christian Doctrine*, Cambridge: Cambridge U.P.: 189–206.

Hartkopf, Werner (1990), *Die Berliner Akademie der Wissenschaften – Ihre Mitglieder und Preisträger 1700–1990*, Berlin: Akademie-Verlag.

Hazard, Paul (1949), *Die Herrschaft der Vernunft: das europäische Denken im 18. Jahrhundert*, Hamburg: Hoffmann & Campe.

Hazard, Paul (1973), *The European Mind 1680–1715*, Harmondsworth: Penguin.

Heimsoeth, Heinz (1926), *Metaphysik und Kritik bei Chr. A. Crusius. Ein Beitrag zur ontologischen Vorgeschichte der Kritik der reinen Vernunft im 18. Jahrhundert*, Berlin: Deutsche Verlagsgesellschaft für Politik und Geschichte.

Heinekamp, Albert (ed.) (1968), *Beiträge zur Wirkungs- und Rezeptionsgeschichte von G.W. Leibniz* (*Studia leibnitiana* Sonderheft 26), Stuttgart: Franz Steiner.

Heinekamp, Albert (ed.) (1984), *Leibniz-Bibliographie. Die Literatur über Leibniz bis 1980*, Frankfurt am Main: Vittorio Klostermann.

Heinekamp, Albert & Robinet, André (eds.) (1992), *Leibniz: le meilleur des mondes. Table ronde organisée par le Centre National de la Recherche Scientifique, Paris et la Gottfried-Wilhelm-Leibniz-Gesellschaft, Hannover. Domaine de Seillac (Loir-et-Cher), 7 au 9 Juin 1990* (*Studia leibnitiana* Sonderheft 21), Stuttgart: Franz Steiner.

Heinrich, Dieter (1963), "Über Kants früheste Ethik. Versuch einer Rekonstruktion", in: *Kant-Studien*, 54, 4: 404–31.

Hellwig, Marion (2008), *Alles ist gut: Untersuchungen zur Geschichte einer Theodizee-Formel im 18. Jahrhundert in Deutschland, England und Frankreich*, Würzburg: Königshausen & Neumann.

Hermanni, Friedrich (1998), "Die Positivität des Malum. Die Privationstheorie und ihre Kritik in der neuzeitlichen Philosophie" in: Friedrich Hermanni & Peter Koslowski (eds.), *Die Wirklichkeit des Bösen*, München: Wilhelm Fink: 49–72.

Hettche, Matt & Corey, Dick (2019), "Christian Wolff", in: Edward N. Zalta (ed.), *The Stanford Encyclopedia of Philosophy* (*Winter 2019 Edition*). Available at: https://plato.stanford.edu/entries/wolff-christian/. Last view: May 2020.

Heyd, Michael (1977), "A Disguised Atheist or a Sincere Christian? The Enigma of Pierre Bayle", in: *Bibliothèque d'humanisme et Renaissance* 39: 125–37.

Hick, John (1966), *Evil and the God of Love*, London: Macmillan.

Hirsch, Eike Christian (2000), *Der berühmte Herr Leibniz. Eine Biographie*, Munich: C.H. Beck.

Howard-Snyder, Daniel (ed.) (1996), *The Evidential Argument from Evil*, Bloomington-Indianapolis: Indiana U.P.

Hübener, Wolfgang (1978), "Sinn und Grenzen des Leibniz'schen Optimismus", in *Studia leibnitiana* 10, 2: 222–46.

Israel, Jonathan (2002), *Radical Enlightenment: Philosophy and the Making of Modernity 1650–1750*, Oxford: Oxford U.P.

Israel, Jonathan (2006), *Enlightenment Contested: Philosophy, Modernity, and the Emancipation of Man 1670–1752*, Oxford: Oxford U.P.

Janowski, Zbigniew (2001), *Cartesian Theodicy: Descartes' Quest for Certitude*, Dordrecht: Kluwer.

Janssen, Hans-Gerd (1989), *Gott-Freiheit-Leid: das Theodizeeproblem in der Philosophie der Neuzeit*, Darmstadt: Wissenschaftliche Buchgesellschaft Darmstadt.

Johnson, Oliver A. (1954), "Human Freedom in the Best of All Possible Worlds", in: *The Philosophical Quarterly* 4, 15: 147–55.

Jolivet, Régis (1936), *Le problème du mal d'après saint Augustin*, Paris: Beauchesne.

Jolley, Nicholas (1998), "The Relation between Theology and Philosophy", in: Daniel Garber & Michael Ayers (eds.), *The Cambridge History of Seventeenth-Century Philosophy*, Cambridge: Cambridge U.P.: 363–92.

Jolley, Nicholas (2005), *Leibniz* (Routledge Philosophers), New York: Routledge.

Jorgensen, Larry M. & Newlands, Samuel (eds.) (2014), *New Essays on Leibniz's Theodicy*, Oxford: Oxford U.P.

Jossua, Jean-Pierre (1977), *Pierre Bayle ou l'obsession du mal*, Paris: Aubier Montaigne.

Journet, Charles (1961), *Le Mal*, Paris: Desclée de Brower.

Kahl-Furthmann, Gertrud (1976), "Der Satz vom zureichenden Grunde. Von Leibniz bis Kant", in: *Zeitschrift für philosophische Forschung* 30, 1: 107–22.

Kanzian, Christian (1993), "Kant and Crusius 1763", in: *Kant-Studien* 84, 4: 399–407.

Kaufman, Dan (2005), "God's Immutability and the Necessity of Descartes's Eternal Truths", in: *Journal of the History of Philosophy* 43, 1: 1–19.

Kemmerer, Arthur (1958), *Das Erdbeben von Lissabon in seiner Beziehung zum Problem des Übels in der Welt*, Frankfurt am Main: Phil. F. Diss.

Kearns, Edward John (1979), *Ideas in Seventeenth-Century Thought*, Manchester: Manchester U.P.

Kendrick, Thomas D. (1956), *The Lisbon Earthquake*, London: Methuen.

Kent, Bonnie (2007), "Evil in Later Medieval Thought", in: *Journal of the History of Philosophy* 45, 2: 177–205.

Kirwan, Christopher (1999), *Augustine. The Arguments of the Philosophers*, London-New York: Routledge.

Kondylis, Panajotis (1981), *Die Aufklärung im Rahmen des neuzeitlichen Rationalismus*, Stuttgart: Klett-Cotta.

Koyré, Alexandre (1922), *L'idée de Dieu et les preuves de son existence chez Descartes*, Paris: E. Leroux.

Krause, Karl Ernst Hermann (1889), "Reinhard, Friedrich", in: *Allgemeine Deutsche Biographie* (ed. Bavarian Academy of Sciences), Leipzig: Duncker & Humblot, vol. 28: 35–6.

Kreimendahl, Lothar (1993), "Das Theodizeeproblem und Bayles fideistischer Lösungsversuch", in: Richard H. Popkin & Arno Vanderjagt (ed.), *Scepticism and Irreligion in the Seventeenth and Eighteenth Centuries*, Leiden: Brill: 267–81.

Kreimendahl, Lothar (ed.) (1995), *Aufklärung und Skepsis. Studien zur Philosophie und Geistesgeschichte des 17. und 18. Jahrhunderts*, Stuttgart-Bad Cannstatt: Frommann-Holzboog.

Kreimendahl, Lothar (2009), "Bayles Destruktion der rationalen Theologie", in: *Aufklärung. Interdisziplinäres Jahrbuch zur Erforschung des 18. Jahrhunderts und seiner Wirkungsgeschichte* 21 ("Religion", ed. Robert Theis): 9–27.

Kremer, Elmar J. (2001), "Leibniz and the 'Disciples of Saint Augustine' on the Fate of Infants Who Die Unbaptized", in: Kremer, Elmar & Latzer, Michael John (eds.), *The Problem of Evil in Early Modern Philosophy*, Toronto: University of Toronto Press: 119–37.

Krieger, Martin (1993), *Geist, Welt und Gott bei Christian August Crusius. Erkenntnistheoretisch-psychologische, kosmologische und religionsphilosophische Perspektiven im Kontrast zum Wolffschen System*, Würzburg: Königshausen & Neumann.

Kuehn, Manfred (2001), *Kant. A Biography*, New York: Cambridge U.P.

Labrousse, Elisabeth (1983), *Bayle* (Past Masters), Oxford-New York: Oxford U.P.

Labrousse, Elisabeth (1985, 1963), *Bayle I: Du pays de Foix à la cité d'Erasme*, Dordrecht: Nijhoff.

Labrousse, Elisabeth (1993), "Pierre Bayle", in: J.-P. Schobinger (ed.), *Die Philosophie des 17. Jahrhunderts*, vol. 2 (*Grundriss der Geschichte der Philosophie* [*begr. von F. Überweg*]), Basel: Schwabe & Co.: 1025–43.

Labrousse, Elisabeth (1996, 11964), *Bayle II: Hétérodoxie et rigorisme*, Dordrecht: Nijhoff.

Landucci, Sergio (1986), *La teodicea nell'età cartesiana*, Naples: Bibliopolis.

Lariviére, Anthony & Lennon, Thomas M. (2001), "Bayle on the Moral Problem of Evil", in: Kremer, Elmar & Latzer, Michael John (eds.), *The Problem of Evil in Early Modern Philosophy*, Toronto: University of Toronto Press: 101–17.

Larmore, Charles (1998), "Pierre Bayle", in: Edward Craig (ed.), Routledge *Encyclopedia of Philisophy*, London-New York: Routledge, vol. 9: 672–7.

Larrimore, Mark (ed.) (2001), *The Problem of Evil. A Reader*. Oxford: Blackwell.

Latzer, Michael (1994), "Leibniz's Conception of Metaphysical Evil", in: *Journal of the History of Ideas* 55, 1: 1–15.

Lauer, Gerhard & Unger, Thorsten (eds.) (2008), *Das Erdbeben von Lissabon und der Katastrophendiskurs im 18. Jahrhundert*, Göttingen: Wallenstein.

Laursen, J.Ch. (2003), "Temporizing after Bayle: Isaac de Beausobre and the Manicheans", in: S. Pott (ed.), *The Berlin Refuge: 1680–1780. Learning and Science in European Context*, Leiden: Brill.

Laywine, Allison (1999), "Malebranche, Jansenism, and the Sixth Meditation", in: *Archiv für Geschichte der Philosophie* 81: 148–73.

Lempp, Otto (1976, 1910[1]), *Das Problem der Theodizee in der Philosophie und Literatur des 18. Jahrhunderts bis auf Kant und Schiller*, Hildesheim-New York: Georg Olms.

Lénardon, Dante (1986), *Index du Journal de Trévoux, 1701–1767*. Geneva: Slatkine Reprints.

Lennon, Thomas M. (1999), *Reading Bayle*, Toronto: University of Toronto Press.

Lennon, Thomas M. (2006), "Theology and the God of the Philosophers", in: Donald Rutherford (ed.), *The Cambridge Companion to Early Modern Philosophy*, Cambridge: Cambridge U.P.: 274–98.

Ley, Hermann (1982), *Geschichte der Aufklärung und des Atheismus*, Berlin: Deutscher Verlag der Wissenschaften, 5 volumes.

Lin, Martin & Melamed, Yitzhak (2020), "Principle of Sufficient Reason", in: Edward N. Zalta (ed.), *The Stanford Encyclopedia of Philosophy* (Spring 2020 Edition). Available at: https://plato.stanford.edu/entries/sufficient-reason/. Last view: May 2020.

Löffler, Ulrich (1999), *Lissabons Fall – Europas Schrecken: die Deutung des Erdbebens von Lissabon im deutschsprachigen Protestantismus des 18. Jahrhunderts*, Berlin: Walter de Gruyter.

Look, Brandon C. (2020), "Gottfried Wilhelm Leibniz", in: Edward N. Zalta (ed.), *The Stanford Encyclopedia of Philosophy* (Spring 2020 Edition). Available at: https://plato.stanford.edu/entries/leibniz/. Last view: May 2020.

Lorenz, Stefan (1997), *De mundo optimo. Studien zu Leibniz' Theodizee und ihrer Rezeption in Deutschland (1710–1791)*, Stuttgart: Franz Steiner.

Lovejoy, Arthur (1936), *The Great Chain of Being: A Study of the History of an Idea*, Cambridge, MA: Harvard U.P.

Lütgert, Wolfgang (1901), *Die Erschütterung des Optimismus durch das Erdbeben von Lissabon 1755*, Gütersloh: Bertelsmann.

MacDonald, Scott (1999), "Primal Sin", in: Gareth B. Matthews (ed.), *The Augustinian Tradition*, Berkeley-Los Angeles: University of California Press: 110–39.

Mackie, John L. (1955), "Evil and Omnipotence", in: *Mind* 64: 200–12. (Also in: Adams & Adams [1994]).

Mann, William E. (2001), "Augustine on Evil and Original Sin", in: Eleonore Stump & Norman Kretzmann (eds.), *The Cambridge Companion to Augustine*, New York: 40–8.

Marion, Jean-Luc (2007), *On the Ego and on God: Further Cartesian Questions* (trans. Christina M. Gschwandter), New York: Fordham U.P.

Markie, Peter (2017), "Rationalism vs. Empiricism", in: Edward N. Zalta (ed.), *The Stanford Encyclopedia of Philosophy* (Fall 2017 Edition). Available at: https://plato.stanford.edu/entries/rationalism-empiricism/. Last view: May 2020.

Marquard, Odo (1981), "Der angeklagte und der entlastete Mensch in der Philosophie des 18. Jahrhunderts", in: *Abschied vom Prinzipiellen*, Stuttgart: Reclam, 1981: 39–66.

Marquard, Odo (1986), "Entlastungen. Theodizeemotive in der neuzeitlichen Philosophie", in: *Apologie des Zufälligen*, Stuttgart: Reclam, 1986: 11–32.

Marquard, Odo (2007), "Die Krise des Optimismus und die Geburt der Geschichtsphilosophie", in: *Skepsis in der Moderne*, Stuttgart: Reclam: 93–108.

Marquardt, Anton (1885), *Kant und Crusius. Ein Beitrag zum richtigen Verständnis der Crusianischen Philosophie*, Kiel: Univ. Diss.

Mason, Haydn (2006), "Optimism, Progress, and Philosophical History", in: Mark Goldie (ed.), *The Cambridge History of Eighteenth Century Political Thought*, Cambridge: Cambridge U.P.

Matthews, Gareth B. (2001), "Post-medieval Augustinianism", in: Eleonore Stump & Norman Kretzmann (eds.), *The Cambridge Companion to Augustine*, New York: 267–79.

Matthews, Gareth B. (2005), *Augustine*, Oxford: Blackwell.

Mauthner, Fritz (1923), "Optimismus", in: *Wörterbuch der Philosophie*, Leipzig: Feliz Meiner, vol. 2: 460–508.

May, William E. (2001), "The God of Leibniz", in: Catherine Wilson (ed.), *Leibniz*, Aldershot: Ashgate/Dartmouth: 257–79.

Menn, Stephen (1997), "Descartes, Augustine, and the Status of Faith", in: Michael Alexander Stewart (ed.), *Studies in Seventeenth-Century Philosophy*, Oxford: Oxford U.P., S. 1–31.

Menn, Stephen (1998a), "The Intellectual Setting", in: Daniel Garber & Michael Ayers (eds.), *The Cambridge History of Seventeenth-Century Philosophy*, Cambridge: Cambridge U.P., vol. 1: 33–86.

Menn, Stephen (1998b), *Descartes and Augustine*, New York: Cambridge U.P.

Menzer, Paul (1912), "Einleitung ('Versuch einiger Betrachtungen über den Optimismus')", in: *Kants gesammelte Schriften* (ed. Prussian Academy of Sciences), Berlin: Reimer, vol. 2: 461–2.

Mercer, Christia (2001), *Leibniz's Metaphysics: Its Origins and Development*, Cambridge: Cambridge U.P.

Mercer, Christia & Sleigh, Robert C. (1995), "Metaphysics: The Early Period to the *Discourse on Metaphysics*", in: Nicholas Jolley (ed.), *Cambridge Companion to Leibniz*, Cambridge: Cambridge U.P.: 67–123.

Moore, Cecil A. (1917), "Did Leibniz Influence Pope's *Essay*?", in: *The Journal of English and Germanic Philology* 16, 1: 84–102.

Moreau, Denis (2000), "The Malebranche-Arnauld Debate", in Steven Nadler (ed.), *The Cambridge Companion to Malebranche*, New York: Cambridge U.P.: 87–111.

Mori, Gianluca (1999), *Bayle philosophe*, Paris: Champion.
Murray, Michael (1996), "Intellect, Will, and Freedom: Leibniz and His Precursors", in: *The Leibniz Review* 6: 25–60.
Murray, Michael (2005), "Spontaneity and Freedom in Leibniz", in: Donald Rutherford & J.A. Cover (eds.), *Leibniz: Nature and Freedom*, Oxford: Oxford U.P.: 194–217.
Murray, Michael (2016), "Leibniz on the Problem of Evil", in: Edward N. Zalta (ed.), *The Stanford Encyclopedia of Philosophy (Winter 2016 Edition)*. Available at: https://plato.stanford.edu/entries/leibniz-evil/. Last view: May 2020.
Nadler, Steven (1994), "Choosing a Theodicy: The Leibniz-Malebranche-Arnauld Connection", in: *Journal of the History of Ideas* 55, 4: 573–89.
Nadler, Steven (2000), "Introduction", in: Steven Nadler (ed.), *The Cambridge Companion to Malebranche*, New York: Cambridge U.P.: 1–7.
Nadler, Steven (2008a), "Arnauld's God", in: *Journal of the History of Philosophy* 46, 4: 517–38.
Nadler, Steven (2008b), *The Best of All Possible Worlds: A Story of Philosophers, God, and Evil*, New York: Farrar, Straus and Giroux.
Nadler, Steven (2011a), "Conceptions of God", in: Desmond Clarke & Catherine Wilson (eds.), *The Oxford Handbook of Philosophy in Early Modern Europe*, New York: Oxford U.P.: 525–47.
Nadler, Steven (2011b), "Spinoza, Leibniz, and the Gods of Philosophy", in: Carlos Fraenkel, Dario Perinetti & Justin E.H. Smith (eds.), *The Rationalists. Between Tradition and Innovation*, London-New York: Springer: 167–82.
Neiman, Susan (2002), *Evil in Modern Thought. An Alternative History of Philosophy*, Princeton-Oxford: Princeton U.P.
Nichols, Ryan (2014), "Re-evaluating the Effects of the 1755 Lisbon Earthquake on Eighteenth-Century Minds: How Cognitive Science of Religion Improves Intellectual History with Hypothesis Testing Methods", in: *Journal of the American Academy of Religion*, 82, 4: 970–1009.
O'Keefe, Cyril B. (1956), "A Jesuit Journal in the Age of the Enlightenment", in: *Canadian Catholic Historical Association* 23: 53–6.
O'Keefe, Cyril B. (1974), *Contemporary Reactions to the Enlightenment 1728–1762: A Study of 3 Critical Journals: the Jesuit 'Journal de Trévoux' the Jansenist 'Nouvelles ecclésiastiques', and the Secular 'Journal des savants'*, Geneva: Slatkine.
O'Meara, Dominic (2010), "Plotin – Woher kommt das Böse?", in: Ansgar Bekermann & Dominik Perler (eds.), *Klassiker der Philosophie heute*, Ditzingen Reclam: 100–17.
O'Meara, John (1982), "The Neoplatonism of Saint Augustine", in: Dominic O' Meara (ed.), *Neoplatonism and Christian Thought*, Albany: State University of New York Press: 34–41.
Osborne, Thomas M. (2003), "The Augustinianism of Thomas Aquinas' Moral Theory", in: *Thomist* 67: 279–305.

Paice, Edward (2008), *Wrath of God: The Great Lisbon Earthquake of 1755*, London: Quercus.

Peirce, Charles Sanders (1891), articles "Necessarian", "Necessarianism", "Necessitarian", "Necessitarianism", in: William Dwight Whitney (ed.), *The Century Dictionary and Cyclopedia*, New York: The Century Company, vol. 5: 3951.

Perler, Dominik (2001), "Cartesische Möglichkeiten", in: Thomas Buchheim, Corneille Henri Kneepkens & Kuno Lorenz (eds.), *Potentialität und Possibilität. Modalaussagen in der Geschichte der Metaphysik*, Stuttgart-Bad Cannstatt: Frommann-Holzboog: 255–72.

Perler, Dominik (2003), "Was ist ein frühneuzeitlicher philosophischer Text? Kritische Überlegungen zum Rationalismus/Empirismus-Schema", in: Helmut Puff & Christopher Wild (eds.), *Zwischen den Disziplinen? Perspektiven der Frühneuzeitforschung*, Göttingen: Wallstein: 55–80.

Perler, Dominik (2006), *René Descartes*, Munich: C.H. Beck.

Plantinga, Alvin (1974), *God, Freedom, and Evil*, New York: Harper & Row.

Poirer, Jean-Paul (2005), *Le tremblement de terre de Lisbonne*, Paris: Odile Jacob.

Popkin, Richard H. (1959), "Pierre Bayle's Place in 17th Century Scepticism", in: Paul Dibon (ed.), *Pierre Bayle. Le philosophe de Rotterdam. Etudes et documents*, Amsterdam-London-New York-Princeton: Elsevier-Vrin. 1–19.

Popkin, Richard H. (1967), "Bayle's Sincerity", in: *The New York Review of Books* 9, 6.

Popkin, Richard H. (1998), "The Religious Background of the Seventeenth Century", in: Daniel Garber & Michael Ayers (eds.), *The Cambridge History of Seventeenth-Century Philosophy*, Cambridge: Cambridge U.P.: 393–423.

Popkin, Richard H. (2003), *The History of Scepticism: From Savonarola to Bayle*, Oxford: Oxford U.P.

Pyle, Andrew (2003), *Malebranche*, London-New York: Routledge.

Rateau, Paul (2008), *La question du mal chez Leibniz. Fondements et élaboration de la Théodicée*, Paris: Honoré Champion.

Rateau, Paul (ed.) (2009), *L'idée de théodicée de Leibniz à Kant: héritage, transformations, critiques*, Stuttgart: Steiner.

Reichenbach, B. R. (1979), "Must God Create the Best Possible World?", in: *International Philosophic Quarterly* 19, 74: 203–12.

Rescher, Nicholas (1979), *Leibniz: An Introduction to His Philosophy*, Oxford: Basil Blackwell. Reprint: Hampshire: Gregg Revivals, 1993.

Rescher, Nicholas (1981), *Leibniz' Metaphysics of Nature*, Dordrecht: D. Reidel.

Rescher, Nicholas (2003), *On Leibniz*, Pittsburgh: University of Pittsburgh Press.

Rex, Walter (1965), *Essays on Pierre Bayle and Religious Controversy*, New York: Springer.

Rist, John (1972), "Augustine on Free Will and Predestination", in R.A. Markus (ed.), *Augustine: A Collection of Critical Essays*, New York: Anchor Books: 218–52.

Röd, Wofgang (1984), "Die deutsche Philosophie im Zeitalter der Aufklärung", in: Wofgang Röd (ed.), *Geschichte der Philosophie*, Munich: C.H. Beck, vol. 8: 235–96.

Rogers, Robert W. (1948), "Critiques of the *Essay on Man* in France and Germany 1736–1755", in: *ELH* 15, 3: 176–93.

Rohrer, Berthold (1933), *Das Erdbeben von Lissabon in der französischen Literatur des achtzehnten Jahrhunderts*, Heidelberg: Brausdr.

Roldán, Concha (1990), "Crusius: un jalón olvidado en la ruta hacia el criticismo", in: *Revista de Filosofía* III, 3: 123–40.

Ross, George MacDonald (1999), "Leibniz und Sophie Charlotte", in Silke Herz, Christoph Martin Vogtherr & Franziska Windt (eds.), *Sophie Charlotte und ihr Schloß*, Munich-London-New York: Prestel: 95–105.

Rothstein, Edward (2005), "Seeking Justice, of Gods or the Politicians", in: *New York Times*, September 8, 2005.

Russell, Bertrand (2005, 11900), *A Critical Exposition of the Philosophy of Leibniz*, London, Routledge.

Rutherford, Donald (1995a), *Leibniz and the Rational Order of Nature*, Cambridge: Cambridge U.P.

Rutherford, Donald (1995b), "Perfection and Happiness in the Best Possible World", in: Nicholas Jolley (ed.), *Cambridge Companion to Leibniz*, Cambridge: Cambridge U.P.: 382–410.

Rutherford, Donald (2000), "Malebranche's Theodicy", in: Steven Nadler (ed.), *The Cambridge Companion to Malebranche*, New York: Cambridge U.P.: 165–89.

Rutherford, Donald (ed.) (2006), *The Cambridge Companion to Early Modern Philosophy*, Cambridge: Cambridge U.P.

Safranski, Rüdiger (1997), *Das Böse oder das Drama der Freiheit*, Munich-Vienna: Hanser.

Schalk, Fritz (1977), "Eine neue Bayledeutung", in: Fritz Schalk, *Studien zur französischen Aufklärung*, Frankfurt am Main: Vittorio Klostermann: 292–305.

Schlüssler, Werner (1992), *Leibniz' Auffassung des menschliches Verstandes (Intellectus)*, Berlin: Walter de Gruyter.

Schmaltz, Tad M. (1999), "What Has Cartesianism to do with Jansenism?", in: *Journal of the History of Ideas* 60, 1: 37–56.

Schmid, Stephan (2011), *Finalursachen in der frühen Neuzeit: eine Untersuchung der Transformation teleologischer Erklärungen*, Berlin-New York: Walter de Gruyter.

Schmidt, Andreas (2009), *Göttliche Gedanken. Zur Metaphysik der Erkenntnis bei Descartes, Malebranche, Spinoza und Leibniz*, Frankfurt am Main: Vittorio Klostermann.

Schmidt-Biggemann, Wilhelm (1988), *Theodizee und Tatsachen. Das philosophische Profil der deutschen Aufklärung*, Frankfurt am Main: Suhrkamp.

Schmidt-Biggemann, Wilhelm (2009), "Die Rationalität des Christentums: Leibniz als Theologe", in: Reydon, Thomas; Heil, Helmut & Hoyningen-Huene, Paul (eds.), *Der universale Leibniz. Denker, Forscher, Erfinder*, Stuttgart: Franz Steiner: 51–62.

Schneewind, J.B. (1996), "Voluntarism and the Foundations of Ethics", in: *Proceedings and Addresses of the American Philosophical Association* 70, 2: 25–41.

Schneewind, J.B. (1998), *The Invention of Autonomy. A History of Modern Moral Philosophy*, New York: Cambridge U.P.

Schneiders, Werner (2006), "Concepts of Philosophy" in: Knud Haakonssen (ed.), *The Cambridge History of Eighteenth-Century Philosophy*, Cambridge: Cambridge U.P., vol. 1: 26–44.

Schönberger, Rolf (1998), "Die Existenz des Nichtigen. Zur Geschichte der Privationstheorie", in: Friedrich Hermanni & Peter Koslowski (eds.), *Die Wirklichkeit des Bösen*, München: Wilhelm Fink: 15–47.

Schröder, Winfried (1998), *Ursprünge des Atheismus*, Stuttgart-Bad Cannstatt: Frommann-Holzboog.

Scribano, Emanuela (2003), "False Enemies: Malebranche, Leibniz, and the Best of All Possible Worlds", in: Daniel Garber & Steven Nadler (eds.), *Oxford Studies in Early Modern Philosophy* 1: 165–82.

Seeskin, Kenneth E. (1994), "Moral Necessity", in: Roger S. Woolhouse (ed.), *Gottfried Wilhelm Leibniz – Critical Assessments*, vol. 4, London: Routledge: 323–33.

Seitz, Anton (1899), *Die Willensfreiheit in der Philosophie des Christian August Crusius gegenüber dem Leibniz-Wolff'schen Determinismus*, Würzburg: Andreas Göbel.

Sentis, Laurent (1992), *Saint Thomas d'Aquin et le Mal*, Paris: Beauchesne.

Sertillanges, A.D. (1948–51), *Le Problème du Mal*, 2 vols, Paris: Aubier.

Shank, J.B. (2008), *The Newton Wars and the Beginning of the French Enlightenment*, Chicago: University of Chicago Press.

Shrady, Nicholas (2008), *The Last Day: Wrath, Ruin & Reason in The Great Lisbon Earthquake of 1755*, New York: Penguin.

Sleigh, Robert C. (1996), "Leibniz's First Theodicy", in: *Noûs* 30, Supplement Philosophical Perspectives 10: 481–99.

Sommervogel, Carlos (1864–5), *Table méthodique des Mémoires de Trévoux (1701–1775)*, 3 vols, Paris: Auguste Durand. Reprint: Geneva: Slatkine Reprints, 1969.

Sparn, Walter (2006), "Einleitung", in Johann Franz Budde, *Gesammelte Schriften* (ed. Walter Sparn), Hildesheim-New York: Georg Olms, vol. 1: i–lxii.

Steinberg, Jesse R. (2007), "Leibniz, Creation and the Best of All Possible Worlds", in: *International Journal for Philosophy of Religion* 62: 123–33.

Steiner, Uwe (1998), *Poetische Theodizee. Philosophie und Poesie in der lehrhaften Dichtung im achtzehnten Jahrhundert*, Munich: Wilhelm Fink.

Stolzenburg, Arnold (1979, 11926), *Die Theologie des Jo. Franc. Buddeus und des Chr. Matth. Pfaff. Ein Beitrag zur Geschichte der Aufklärung in Deutschland*, Aalen: Scientia-Verlag.

Stricker, Nicola (2003), *Die maskierte Theologie von Pierre Bayle*, Berlin: Walter de Gruyter.

Strickland, Lloyd (2006), *Leibniz Reinterpreted*, London: Continuum.

Strickland, Lloyd (2019), "Staying Optimistic: The Trials and Tribulations of Leibnizian Optimism", in: *Journal of Modern Philosophy* 1 (1), 3: 1–21.

Stump, Eleonore (2001), "Augustine on Free Will", in: Eleonore Stump & Norman Kretzmann (eds.), *The Cambridge Companion to Augustine*, New York: 124–47.

Terral, Mary (2002), *The Man Who Flattened the Earth: Maupertuis and the Sciences in the Enlightenment*, Chicago: University of Chicago Press.

Theis, Robert (1987), "Le meilleur des mondes possibles, le mal métaphysique et le mal moral chez Leibniz", in: *Freiburger Zeitschrift für Philosophie und Theologie* 34/3: 169–84.

Theis, Robert (2001), "Gottes Spur in der Welt? Kant über den Optimismus um die Mitte der 1750er Jahre", in: Michael Oberhausen (ed.), *Vernunftkritik und Aufklärung. Studien zur Philosophie Kants und seines Jahrhundertes*, Stuttgart-Bad Canstatt: Frommann-Holzboog: 351–63.

Tonelli, Giorgio (1966), "Die Anfänge von Kant's Kritik der Kausalbeziehungen und ihre Voraussetzungen im 18. Jahrhundert", in: *Kant-Studien* 57/4, 1966, S. 417–456.

Tonelli, Giorgio (1969), "Einleitung", in: Crusius, Christian August, *Die philosophischen Hauptwerke* (ed. Giorgio Tonelli), Hildesheim-New York: Georg Olms, vol. 1: vii–lxv.

Treash, Gordon (1989), "Kant and Crusius. Epigenesis and Preformationism", in: Gerhard Funke & Thomas M. Seebohm (eds), *Proceedings of the Sixth International Kant Congress*, Washington: Pennsylvania State University, vol. 2: 95–108.

Vereker, Charles (1967), *Eighteenth Century Optimism*, Liverpool: Liverpool U.P.

Van Inwagen, Peter (ed.) (2004), *Christian Faith and the Problem of Evil*, Grand Rapids: Eerdmans.

Van Inwagen, Peter (2006), *The Problem of Evil* (The Gifford Lectures Delivered in the University of St Andrews in 2003), Oxford: Clarendon Press.

Vyverberg, Hans (1958), *Historical Pessimism in the French Enlightenment*, London: Harvard U.P.

Wachterhauser, Brice R. (1985), "The Problem of Evil and Moral Scepticism", in: *International Journal for Philosophy of Religion* 17: 167–74.

Watkins, Eric (2005), *Kant and the Metaphysics of Causation*, New York: Cambridge U.P.

Watkins, Eric (ed.) (2009), *Kant's Critique of Pure Reason: Background Source Materials*, Cambridge: Cambridge University Press.

Weinrich, Harald (1986), "Literaturgeschichte eines Weltereignisses: Das Erdbeben von Lissabon", in: *Literatur für Leser*, Munich: DTV: 74–90.

Wenzel, Uwe Justus (2005), "Lissabon und andere Katastrophen", in: *Neue Zürcher Zeitung*, October 29, 2005.

Wetzel, James (2001), "Predestination, Pelagianism, and Foreknowledge", in: Eleonore Stump & Norman Kretzmann (eds.), *The Cambridge Companion to Augustine*, New York: 48–58.

Whitney, Barry L. (1994), "An Aesthetic Solution to the Problem of Evil", in: *International Journal for Philosophy of Religion* 35, 1: 21–37.

Whitney, Barry L. (1998), *Theodicy. An Annotated Bibliography on the Problem of Evil 1960–1991*, Bowling Green: Bowling Green State University.

Williams, Bernard (2005; 11978), *Descartes: The Project of Pure Enquiry*, New York: Routledge.

Williams, Bernard (2006), "Descartes and the Historiography of Philosophy", in: *The Sense of the Past. Essays in the History of Philosophy* (ed. Myles Burnyeat), Princeton: Princeton U.P.: 257–64.

Wilson, Catherine (1983), "Leibnizian Optimism", in: *The Journal of Philosophy* 80, 11: 765–83.

Wilson, Catherine (1995), "The Reception of Leibniz in the Eighteenth Century", in: Nicholas Jolley (ed.), *Cambridge Companion to Leibniz*, Cambridge: Cambridge U.P.: 442–74.

Wilson, Catherine (2018), "Leibniz's Influence on Kant", in: Edward N. Zalta (ed.), *The Stanford Encyclopedia of Philosophy* (*Spring 2018 Edition*). Available at: http://plato.stanford.edu/archives/win2009/entries/kant-leibniz/. Last view: May 2020.

Woerle, Hans (1900), *Der Erschütterungsbezirk des großen Erdbebens zu Lissabon*, Munich: Th. Ackermann.

Woolhouse, Roger S. (1998), "Introduction", in: Richard Francks & Roger S. Woolhouse (eds.), *G. W. Leibniz – Philosophical Texts*, New York: Oxford U.P.: 5–50.

Wundt, Max (1945), *Die deutsche Schulphilosophie im Zeitalter der Aufklärung*, Tübingen: Mohr Siebeck.

Index

Antognazza, Maria Rosa 9n, 58
Arnauld, Antoine 7, 34, 36, 60, 64, 69n, 87, 114
Augustine of Hippo
   his doctrine of evil, or 'Augustinian theodicy' 15–23, 83

Bayle, Pierre
   and the problem of evil 5–7, 9, 15, 26–27, 78, 100–101, 103, 114n, 119, 184
   on divine freedom 48–49, 141
   skepticism 91–92, 99, 112
best of all possible worlds
   according to Leibniz 4, 9–10, 14–15, 20, 28–32, 39–41, 58, 113–115, 117–121, 123, 140, 172–173, 184, 194, 197, 198
   in Budde and Knoerr's criticism of Leibnizian optimism 56, 66, 75, 77, 81, 85, 88
   in Castel's criticism of Leibnizian optimism 104–105, 118
   in Crusius's criticism of Leibnizian optimism 123, 125–128, 130 141, 143, 186
   in Reinhard's criticism of Leibnizian optimism 151–152, 160, 162, 170

Carboncini, Sonia 122n, 124, 134n
Clarke, Samuel 8, 38, 49, 123, 132, 135n, 137, 178
counter-optimism
   and the debate between intellectualism and voluntarism 180, 183, 186–187
   as understood in the present work 2–4, 88, 169, 172, 194, 199–200
Crousaz, Wolff Jean Pierre de 102n, 112, 150–151, 168

Descartes, René 7, 26n, 33–34, 36, 48, 55, 60n, 64–66, 68–69, 86–87, 91, 114, 141, 143, 181, 184–185, 195
divine freedom
   according to Leibniz 1, 4, 7–9, 35–36, 46, 54, 64, 157, 172, 187, 199
   in Budde and Knoerr's criticism of Leibnizian optimism 67, 73, 86, 185
   in Castel's criticism of Leibnizian optimism 97, 105–107, 109, 111, 176
   in Crusius's criticism of Leibnizian optimism 125, 130–131, 133, 145, 176, 178, 181
   in Reinhard's criticism of Leibnizian optimism 162–163, 165–167, 169, 191–192

eternal truths
   according to Descartes 48, 60, 66, 86
   according to Leibniz 19, 36–37, 41, 47, 60–64, 172, 176–177, 188, 196, 200
   in Budde and Knoerr's criticism of Leibnizian optimism 55–57, 59, 62, 64, 66–69, 71–72, 75–76, 83–87, 107n, 180–181, 185
everything is good
   in the context of criticisms of Leibnizian optimism 100–104, 112, 116–118, 121, 146
evil
   metaphysical evil according to Leibniz 15, 19–20, 59, 61, 62n, 155, 172
   metaphysical evil in Budde and Knoerr's criticism of Leibnizian optimism 56–59, 64, 69
   metaphysical evil in Reinhard's criticism of Leibnizian optimism 154
   moral evil according to Leibniz 15–17, 20, 25–26, 57, 61, 117, 120
   moral evil in Budde and Knoerr's criticism of Leibnizian optimism 56, 82n,
   moral evil in Reinhard's criticism of Leibnizian optimism 154–155, 168
   physical evil according to Leibniz 15, 18, 20–21, 25, 57, 59, 61, 117–118
   physical evil in Budde and Knoerr's criticism of Leibnizian optimism 56, 82n
   physical evil in Reinhard's criticism of Leibnizian optimism 154, 156
   problem of 6–7, 9, 14–15, 18, 21, 56, 61, 69, 81, 100, 114n, 121, 154, 185n, 195, 199

Fonnesu, Luca 2, 81n, 92n, 107n, 110n, 194n

INDEX

God as a "divine strategian"   29–30 32, 41, 45

Harnack, Adolf von   22n, 146n, 147n, 148–149, 168
Hume, David   2, 184, 186, 195

intellectualism or intellectualist
and voluntarism or voluntarist   4, 35, 67, 68n, 87, 113, 123, 162, 165–167, 169, 181, 183, 186–187, 192, 195–196, 199, 200

Jansen Cornelius
author of Augustinus   7
Jansenism   7, 98
Journal de Trévoux   3, 90–93, 174

Kant, Immanuel   2, 122, 148, 171, 184, 198

Lessing, Gotthold Ephraim   146n, 148–149, 171, 184
Lisbon Earthquake   1–2, 4 146, 171, 175, 183, 194–195, 197–199
Lorenz, Stefan   2, 56n, 59n, 60n, 72, 81n, 83, 94n, 191, 194n
Lovejoy, Arthur   29n, 42–44, 46n, 118n, 119, 152n

Malebranche, Nicolas   7, 24, 29–30, 32, 34, 43–44, 87, 91, 181, 184, 195
Marquard, Odo   1n, 118n, 122n, 197–199
Mendelssohn, Moses   146n, 148–149, 170–171, 184
Mercer, Christa   42n, 44–45

Nadler, Steven   7n, 32–35, 60n, 64n, 65–66, 68n, 87, 113, 114n, 116n, 121, 181185n, 195–196
necessity
absolute or metaphysical necessity according to Leibniz   51–52
hypothetical or moral necessity according to Leibniz   46, 49–51, 54, 172, 188
in Castel's criticism of Leibnizian optimism   178–179
in Crusius's criticism of Leibnizian optimism   136–137, 141, 144–145
in Adolf Friedrich Reinhard's criticism of Leibnizian optimism   156, 162–164, 169

original sin or the Fall of Man
in Budde and Knoerr's criticism of Leibnizian optimism   58, 76–77, 81–82, 84, 88, 173, 186
in Castel's criticism of Leibnizian optimism   111

pessimism   2, 57, 82, 103, 119, 184–186, 195
Pope, Alexander   91, 102, 104, 112, 116, 119, 146–147, 149–152, 155–156, 175, 184, 197
Popkin, Richard   6, 199
principle of continuity
and Leibniz's optimism   39, 46
principle of determinant reason
in Crusius' criticism of Leibnizian optimism   134, 136–138, 140, 163, 169, 178–179
principle of identity
and Leibniz's optimism   38–39, 137
principle of perfection or principle of the best
and Leibniz's optimism   39–41, 44–45, 47, 50, 61, 87, 89, 106n, 128–130
in Castel's criticism of Leibnizian optimism   106–107, 110
in Crusius' criticism of Leibnizian optimism   140
principle of plenitude
and Leibniz's optimism   28–29, 42, 44–47
principle of sufficient reason
and Leibniz's optimism   4, 28–29, 38–42, 44–47, 50, 52, 61, 87, 89, 96–97, 106, 113, 172, 176, 179, 188, 196, 198, 200
in Castel's criticism of Leibnizian optimism   182
in Crusius' criticism of Leibnizian optimism   122–123, 125, 128–131, 133–135, 145, 154, 177–178, 180, 185
in Reinhard's criticism of Leibnizian optimism   163, 169, 181
problem of evil   see evil
Prussian Academy of Sciences in Berlin   3, 5, 93n, 102, 104, 112, 146–150, 168–171, 177, 195

Rescher, Nicholas   11–12, 14, 29–31, 39–41, 44, 66n, 74n, 128n, 142–143, 175–176

Rutherford, Donald   7, 12–14, 29–30, 45–46, 57n, 112n, 114–115, 117, 121, 142–143, 175–176

Schmidt-Biggemann, Wilhelm   32n, 83n, 113, 115
Schopenhauer, Arthur   2, 93n, 184, 186, 195
skepticism   34, 92, 99–100, 184
Sleigh Jr., Robert C.   7, 45, 48n
Spinoza, Baruch   32n, 34, 55, 87, 106, 108, 179, 184, 195
spinozism   91, 105–106, 182
Strickland, Lloyd   1n, 197n

Thomasius, Christian   55, 123

universal connection, doctrine or dogma of   152–154, 168, 170, 172

Voltaire   90–91, 102, 104, 147, 175, 198
   as critic of Leibnizian optimism   1, 93n, 112, 114, 117, 146, 171, 184, 186, 194–195, 197
voluntarism or voluntarist see intellectualism or intellectualist

Warburton, William   150–151, 168
whatever is, is right
   according to Alexander Pope   104, 116, 119, 146, 197
Williams, Bernard
   on 'history of ideas' and 'history of philosophy'   196–197
Wilson, Catherine   3n, 28–30, 32, 42–43, 123n, 129n, 155, 173n
Wolff, Christian   13, 55, 58n, 122–124, 134, 137, 150, 163

Printed in the United States
By Bookmasters

Printed in the United States
By Bookmasters